Advance Praise

"George Geary's *Made in California* takes you on a delightful journey down memory lane. It's a must-read guide for anyone who loves history, food, and California's culture of innovation. Fortunately, you can still visit many of these iconic locations, so plan your road trip now!"
— LINDA DISHMAN, president and CEO, Los Angeles Conservancy

"This delicious book serves up more than a feast of information—it's food for the soul of anyone who is hungry for the back stories and glories of California's classic cuisine, iconic kitchens, famous flavors, and tastiest landmarks."
— CHARLES PHOENIX, author of *Addicted to Americana* and *Holiday Jubilee*

"I gained fifteen pounds reading this book, but it was worth it because ten of those went to my brain! A smart, encyclopedic, delightful read worthy of a coffee table, a classroom syllabus, or a car seat as a road-trip companion!"
— GUSTAVO ARELLANO, author of *Taco USA: How Mexican Food Conquered America*

MADE IN CALIFORNIA

VOLUME 1

THE CALIFORNIA-BORN BURGER JOINTS, DINERS, FAST FOOD & RESTAURANTS THAT CHANGED AMERICA 1915–1966

GEORGE GEARY

PROSPECT PARK BOOKS

Copyright © 2021, 2024 by George Geary

All rights reserved. No part of this book may be reproduced or transmitted in any form or by any means, electronic or mechanical, including photocopying, recording, or by any information storage and retrieval system, without permission in writing from the publisher.

 Published by Prospect Park Books
An imprint of Turner Publishing
www.turnerpublishing.com

Distributed by Ingram Publisher Services

Library of Congress Cataloging in Publication Data is on file with the Library of Congress.
The following is for reference only:

Geary, George
Made in California: The California-Born Burger Joints, Diners, Fast Food & Restaurants that Changed America / by George Geary— 1st ed.
  p. cm.
ISBN 978-1-945551-91-8 Hardcover | 978-1-684424-20-7 Paperback | 978-1-945551-92-5 Epub
1. History: California. 2. History: Food & Restaurants. 3. Restaurants & Food: American. Title.

Editor: Colleen Dunn Bates
Assistant editors: Susan Champlin, Julianne Johnson & Katelyn Keating
Copyeditor: Leilah Bernstein
Proofreader: Margery L. Schwartz

Original photography by Keegan Dunn

Designed by Amy Inouye, Future Studio

Printed in the United States of America

*To my father, George L. Geary,
who taught me at the age of six to eat a Foster's Freeze
chocolate-dipped cone without messing my shirt.*

Table of Contents

Foreword: Lighting Up at the Intersection of Food and History, by Chris Nichols ... 10
Introduction: Out of the Kitchen and into the Drive-Thru 12

1915 Saratoga Chips (Van de Kamp's Holland Dutch Bakeries) 14
1919 Root Beer (A&W Restaurants) 20
1921 See's Candies 24
1923 Sonora Café (El Cholo) 32
1926 The Brown Derby 38
1926 Orange Julius 44
1931 Clifton's Cafeterias (Clifton's Republic) 48
1934 Hinky Dink's (Trader Vic's) 52
1936 Bob's Pantry (Big Boy Restaurants) 58
1938 Du-Pars Farm House (Du-par's) 64
1938 Lawry's the Prime Rib 68
1939 Pink's Hot Dogs 74
1940 McDonald's Barbeque (McDonald's) 80
1941 The Blimp (Carl's Jr.) 88
1945 Burt's/Snowbird Ice Cream (Baskin-Robbins) 92
1946 Foster's Old Fashion Freeze (Fosters Freeze) 98
1946 Tommy's (Original Tommy's) 102
1946 Party Puffs (Hot Dog on a Stick) 106
1946 Walsh's Hot Dogs (Cupid's Hot Dogs) 110
1947 Mr. Fatburger (Fatburger) 114
1948 In-N-Out 118
1948 Love's Wood Pit Barbeque (Love's BBQ) 126
1948 Marie Callender Pie Shop (Marie Callender's) 130
1948 Snack Shop (Coco's Restaurant and Bakery) 136

1948 Swensen's Ice Cream 140
1948 Winchell's Donuts 146
1949 Chris' & Pitt's 150
1949 McConnell's Fine Ice Creams 154
1949 NORMS Restaurants 158
1949 The Red Onion Cafe (The Original Red Onion) 162
1950 Hamburger Hamlet 166
1951 Jack in the Box 170
1952 Baker's Burgers (Baker's Drive-Thru) 174
1953 Big Do-Nut Drive-In (Randy's Donuts) 178
1953 Danny's Donuts (Denny's) 182
1954 El Torito 186
1954 Shakey's Pizza Parlor 190
1957 Sambo's Restaurants (Chad's) 194
1958 Copper Penny Family Restaurants 200
1958 Sizzler Family Steak House (Sizzler) 204
1958 The International House of Pancakes (IHOP) 208
1959 Round Table Pizza 214
1961 Der Wienerschnitzel (Wienerschnitzel) 218
1961 Pioneer Take Out (Pioneer Chicken) 224
1962 Taco Bell 228
1963 The Coffee Bean & Tea Leaf 232
1964 Casa Del Taco (Del Taco) 236
1965 Pup 'n' Taco 240
1966 House of Pies 244
1966 Peet's Coffee, Tea and Spices (Peet's Coffee) 248

Acknowledgments 252
Photo Credits 254
About the Author 256

Foreword

Lighting Up at the Intersection of Food and History

by Chris Nichols

LIKE GENERATIONS before them, Dick and Mac McDonald came west looking for new opportunities. The brothers wanted to be in the movie business, so they headed to Hollywood. After an unfulfilling stint as stagehands, they rented a movie theater and soon discovered that they made more money selling candy than admission tickets. By the 1940s, they found themselves at the helm of a drive-in restaurant in San Bernardino with an idea for a new kind of food service that would change the way the world eats. They worked with architect Stanley Clark Meston to design an extraordinary little glass box with red-and-white tiles and a slanted roof pierced by soaring golden arches. The design brought a taste of California style and innovation to cities across the country.

By the time I first encountered one in the '80s, it was a run-down relic, with a limited menu and no indoor seating. In high school, I walked past the now-boarded-up restaurant daily and was mesmerized by the melancholy of a futuristic building falling into decay. My father gave me a copy of *Googie: Fifties Coffee Shop Architecture*, and there it was—all bright and shiny and new. It had architectural cousins with names like Carolina Pines and Pioneer Chicken, and I made my parents drive me around to visit them all.

I called the author out of the phone book and he became a mentor, offering advice on how to save my forlorn McDonald's. It turned out that America's largest preservation group, the Los Angeles Conservancy, had recently formed a task force charged with protecting midcentury-modern architecture. I immediately joined in as the group launched successful efforts to landmark historic restaurants like Bob's Big Boy in Burbank, alongside sleek hillside homes by architects like Richard Neutra. We helped get neon signs into museums and led thousands of Angelenos on tours of glamorous homes and glamorous coffee shops alike.

Working on advocacy issues and educational programs with the Conservancy led me to writing about old restaurants and forgotten architecture, and I've been exploring hidden corners of Los Angeles for twenty years at *Los Angeles* magazine. I met George Geary while he was volunteering at the Conservancy and was instantly struck by the way he lights up with excitement when discussing the intersection of food and history. I was mesmerized by his own place in California food history as the inventor of iconic dishes, from the corn dogs at Disneyland to the endless cheesecakes on *The Golden Girls*.

In *Made in California*, George cranks back the time machine to reveal the local origins of foods known around the world, like the McDonald's cheeseburger or the all-night menu at Denny's, as well as classics like the Double Cream Lemon Pie at Marie Callender's, which have remained only-in-California favorites. We find out how the International House of Pancakes went from one modest

coffee shop in Burbank to serving up flapjacks from Guatemala to Kuwait.

Get out on the road and savor this gastronomical guide to the Golden State. Pull up under the neon at Bob's on cruise night or wait in line with the stars at Pink's Hot Dogs and experience living history in full color and three dimensions. A burger always tastes better under an exuberant roof or in the glow of a neon sign. "We don't just need buildings with good taste," Alan Hess said in *Googie*. "We need buildings that taste good."

CHRIS NICHOLS is senior editor at *Los Angeles* magazine, where he pens the "Ask Chris" column, and is the author of *The Leisure Architecture of Wayne McAllister* and *Walt Disney's Disneyland*.

Foreword

Introduction

Out of the Kitchen and into the Drive-Thru

ONE EVENING, I was watching a local newscast here in Los Angeles and saw a story about the first Taco Bell building. It was being moved in the middle of the night from Downey through city streets toward corporate headquarters in Orange County so it could be restored. I was thrilled. I started wondering how many other food companies began in California and if their original locations were still operating. I started making a list. Right off the top of my head, I knew that McDonald's, In-N-Out Burger, Denny's, See's Candies, and a few others were on the list. I started researching, and before long, the list had grown to more than one humdred businesses.

A little while later, while teaching in Lafayette, Indiana, near Purdue University, I noticed a large sign on the side of the interstate listing twenty-four places to eat at the next off-ramp. I quickly counted in my head—twenty-two of them had their start in the Golden State, many close to where I grew up. That's when the idea for this book hit me.

When you walk into a See's store, you'll often see historical photos hanging on the pristine white walls. Besides Mary See's famous picture, you'll typically see a photo of the first See's location, but no mention of where it is. I had to find out if the building was still standing, so I got busy researching. While combing through old *Los Angeles Times* stories, I learned that ten years earlier, the Los Angeles Conservancy had tried to save the building from becoming a mini-mall. The address was a few miles from downtown, on Western Avenue, so off I went to see it. The turn-of-the-twentieth-century building was still intact, repurposed as a coffeehouse. When I travel to Europe, I stop and read every historical plaque I see, so of course I looked for a plaque marking the auspicious history of this location. I looked in vain. Sadly, we here in America dispose of buildings and history after a mere fifty years.

A little later, I went to the grand opening of a See's store and met Pat Egan, the then-new CEO of See's. I told him about my trip to that first location. Soon after, he went to see it himself, emailing me a report on his visit afterward. When he asked one of the sales staff at the coffeehouse if she knew that the building had once housed See's Candies, she said she'd never heard of it. Her colleague piped up and said, "Oh, I think that's the place with the old lady on the box of candy, right?" Pat promised to get a plaque for the building by the candy company's 100th anniversary in 2021.

Across the country and the decades, Americans and visitors have enjoyed many an A&W root beer, a Pink's hot dog, a Shakey's pizza, and a Peet's coffee. But what are their origin stories? Who started the very first branch? Where were the original buildings? What made them famous? And for the few that are no longer around, or that have a smaller footprint than they had in their glory days, what happened? I wanted to capture the stories of these essential businesses and structures before they are gone forever. And so I did.

In my earlier years as a food writer and professional, I would never have admitted to anyone that I actually eat at these establishments. But after seeing Julia Child eat McDonald's french fries in person and say that they were her favorite, and after hearing Anthony Bourdain claim that In-N-Out Burger was the best burger around, I knew that I, too, could come out of my kitchen and into the drive-thru. Now I get to celebrate these places in this book.

— GEORGE GEARY

Saratoga Chips

NAME BECAME: Van de Kamp's Holland Dutch Bakeries
ORIGINAL LOCATION: 236½ Spring Street, Los Angeles
ORIGINAL FACTORY & OFFICES: 2960 Fletcher Drive, Los Angeles

OPENED: January 6, 1915
COFOUNDERS: Theodore Van de Kamp & Lawrence L. Frank
CURRENTLY AT THE FIRST LOCATION: Parking lot (Saratoga Chips); Los Angeles City College, Van de Kamp Campus (Van de Kamp's factory)

At one point, there were more than 320 bakeries/cafés dotting the west coast. Today, none remain.

vandekamps.com

YOU CAN TELL someone's age or when they arrived in Southern California by how they remember Van de Kamp's brands: as bakery products sold in freestanding stores, with the bakery girls wearing traditional Holland-style blue dresses, white hats, and aprons; as restaurant/coffee shops; as packages of cookies in the local market; or as fish sticks in the frozen food section of the market.

For those of us lucky enough to have lived in Southern California for some decades, the Dutch-themed blue bakeries—and later, coffee shops—marked by huge fake windmills were beloved destinations. Their roots were in a partnership that began in 1915. Theodore Van de Kamp, his sisters, Marian and Henrietta, and Henrietta's husband, Lawrence L. Frank, began selling their potato chips, which they called Saratoga Chips. Marian and Henrietta served as the saleswomen, dressing in Dutch costumes and selling out of the chips after just two hours each day. Their potato chip factory had no seating, just a window that looked like a theater ticket booth.

A potato shortage forced them to diversify their product line, so they moved into baked goods. In 1916, they renamed the business Van de Kamp's Holland Dutch Bakery, and they opened their first full store in 1921 at Beverly Boulevard and Western Avenue. There they sold cakes, pies, and danishes, building a roster that eventually included 140 products. The women designed the logos and the traditional dress of the salesgirls.

In 1923, they opened their first coffee shop, at Fifth and Spring streets, where the twelve-story Alexandria Hotel annex now sits. Many of the locations were famed for their windmill designs; Academy Award–nominated art director Harry Olive created these windmill buildings, along with many other notable buildings around the Southland. Later, the family opened a central production facility on Fletcher Drive, which eventually included a coffee shop. By 1929, the original store had grown into a chain with more than 95 locations in the Los Angeles area. The company would eventually become a chain of more than 200 locations around Southern California and 120 outside of the area; along with baked goods and general coffee-shop fare, Van de Kamp's became known for its fried halibut.

Dutching it up at Van de Kamp's

Original location of Saratoga Chips

The Van de Kamp family also founded Atwater's Tam O'Shanter Inn (in 1922) and, in 1938, Lawry's the Prime Rib in Beverly Hills (page 69). In 1956, when Theodore Van de Kamp passed away, the family split the company in two: the bakeries and the frozen foods division, which had grown because of the popularity of the fried halibut (which led to frozen fish). The family sold the bakeries to General Baking Company, which also controlled Lawry's Brands and a number of other food ventures. Pinnacle Foods bought the frozen division in 2001 and continues to this day to sell Van de Kamp's frozen seafood products. As a result of the company split, partner Lawrence Frank devoted more time to the Lawry's at the California Center and Lawry's Prime Rib on La Cienega Boulevard. He sold the Lawry's Brand spices (including the famous seasoned salt) to private investors in 1979.

I have a personal fondness for Van de Kamp's. When the holidays came, Mom would slice its date nut loaf and display it in a spiral on a fancy glass plate for the family to enjoy. But Van de Kamp's goes even further back in my family: My grandmother worked as a Van de Kamp's salesgirl in the Vons Market on Wilshire in Santa Monica, where my mother worked at the snack bar. My father came into the market to visit his mother while he was on military leave, and he met my mom; they married a few years later. In addition, my aunt worked as an area supervisor for Van de Kamp's. The company's influence continued into my life as well. In 1980, while I was in culinary school, Mr. Perkowski, one of our instructors, was the lead cake decorator at the Glassell Park plant, and he took all of us on a

Left: Lawrence L. Frank
Right: Walter Van de Kamp

Corner location in Santa Monica

tour of the three-story building. I was finally able to see how butter sprinkle cookies, my favorite as a kid, were made.

September of 1990 saw a sad development: Van de Kamp's Holland Dutch Bakeries filed for Chapter 11 bankruptcy protection. The original 1929 manufacturing plant in Glassell Park closed its doors, and 500 bakers, plant workers, and office staff lost their jobs. In 1992, the building was designated a Historic-Cultural Monument by the city of Los Angeles and sat empty for many years. Finally it was renovated by the Los Angeles Community College District and is now the Van de Kamp satellite campus of Los Angeles City College. Tiny Naylor's bought the remaining coffee shops, and those were later taken over by Denny's (page 183). In Arcadia, California, a Denny's now occupies the only fully intact Van de Kamp's windmill restaurant/coffee shop left in Southern California. The earliest partially intact Van de Kamp's building can be found at 4157 Figueroa at 41st, near the USC campus—at this writing, it's a Bestway Liquors store.

Five Most Popular Products
Butter Crunch Cookies
Chocolate Cupcakes
Date Nut Loaf Cake
Milk Chocolate Bells
Powdered Sugar Donuts

Below: Saleswomen in uniform
Opposite top: Early saleswomen · Opposite bottom: Bread manufacturing at the plant

Root Beer

SLOGAN: "All American Food"
NAME TODAY: A&W Restaurants
ORIGINAL LOCATION: 13 Pine Street, Lodi

OPENED: June 20, 1919
FOUNDER: Roy W. Allen
PARTNER: Frank Wright
CURRENT OWNER: A Great American Brand LLC
CURRENTLY AT THE FIRST LOCATION: Beauty of the Beast ~ Animal Groomers

There are 969 locations in 6 countries.

awrestaurants.com

BACK IN THE DAY, pharmacists created drinks, tonics, and remedies to cure and satisfy. While visiting the new state of Arizona, Roy W. Allen purchased the formula for a unique drink blend of juices from sixteen flavor profiles of spices, herbs, berries, and barks. Allen took this formula back to the central California city of Lodi. Setting up a simple outdoor counter on a hot June day in 1919, he began selling cold mugs of what he called "root beer" for just 5¢. He soon opened a second stand in Sacramento, the state capital, and the business was called, simply, Root Beer. The stand began implementing a unique drive-in service featuring "tray-boys" to deliver sodas and food. After opening three concession stands in Sacramento in under three years, Allen knew the work was getting out of hand, so he brought in one of his Lodi employees, Frank Wright, as a partner. They proceeded to open locations in Northern California, Texas, and Utah, changing the name of the stands to A&W Root Beer (using the first letters of their last names), and a soda legend was born.

By 1933, 170 franchise locations were operating from the Midwest to the Pacific Ocean. To make sure that the root beers tasted the same everywhere, Allen and Wright turned to chemist J. Hungerford Smith to make their A&W Root Beer concentrate exclusively, and each franchise operator got the formula.

With sugar rationings and employee shortages, times were tough during World War II, but A&W hung in there. After the war, many servicemen returning home went looking for businesses to open, and GI loans helped grease the entrepreneurial wheels. The number of A&W franchised restaurants soon tripled.

By 1950, Allen had more than 450 units in business, and he decided to retire, selling the business to a fellow named Gene Hurtz from Nebraska, who then formed the A&W Root Beer Company. In 1956, Manitoba, Canada, became the first location outside the United States to get a branch, and A&W was now international. Thanks to the increase of the car culture and drive-ins, A&W had opened up more than 2,000 locations by 1960.

Roy Allen & Frank Wright

Lodi A&W in the 1960s

In 1963, Dale Mulder, a franchisee from Lansing, Michigan, added a bacon cheeseburger to his menu after repeated requests from a customer to add bacon on top of a burger. Newspaper ads featured Mulder boasting that he was the first to create and serve a bacon cheeseburger. A&W introduced four sizes of burgers: Papa Burger, Mama Burger, Teen Burger, and Baby Burger. Each burger's wrapper featured its own cartoon character.

In 1970, United Brands Company took over ownership, changed the name to A&W International, and soon grew A&W into a franchised chain of full-fledged restaurants. Systems changed to meet franchisees' needs, including the expansion of a distribution network of everything from glass mugs to paper products. The McDonald's clown mascot, Ronald McDonald, inspired A&W to roll out Rooty the Root Bear, who first appeared in Canada in 1974 and arrived in the US markets two years later.

In 1971, United Brands formed a spin-off, A&W Beverages, to get A&W Root Beer onto grocery store shelves. After successful testing in California and Arizona supermarkets, retailers nationwide soon carried the soda. A few years later, A&W Sugar-Free and Cream Soda hit the market.

By the mid '70s, A&W had more locations than McDonald's (page 81), but then things went south. The systems weren't consistent, and some franchisee grew unhappy; branches started closing. A&W changed its operations and agreements, but nothing seemed to work, and many more locations closed. To address the problem, A&W created a more upscale concept that included fresh 100 percent beef burgers, ice cream bars, salad bars, and

Timeline
1919: 1 unit
1920: 2 units
1922: 4 units
1933: 170 units
1950: 450 units
1953: First Canadian location opened
1960: 2,000 units
1963: First American overseas location opened in Malaysia, Guam, and the Philippines
1966: First American quick-service restaurant in Singapore
1974: 2,400 units
1985: 500 units
1986: 560 units
2019: 969 units

mugs of root beer. Later, it expanded into food courts, airports, shopping centers, college campuses, and other pedestrian-friendly locations.

In 1989, as part of a joint agreement with Carousel Snack Bars, A&W converted its 200 stores into A&W Hot Dogs & More. These were mainly small-footprint fast-food locations in shopping malls and pedestrian areas. The company sold a couple of more times, and the parent company paired A&W with Long John Silver's to form Yorkshire Global Restaurants. This led to experiments of combining brands into their own mini–food courts, starting with marriages of:

- 83 Kentucky Fried Chickens and A&Ws
- 6 Kentucky Fried Chickens and Long John Silver's
- 3 Taco Bells and Long John Silver's

This was a very successful move.

Between the 1970s and 1990s, Rooty the Root Bear, fitted with an orange turtleneck sweater and cap to match, was the face of both A&W Restaurants and A&W Beverages. In 2011, Rooty came out of retirement, and as I write this, he's back on the A&W website and in print ads and social media videos. The classic comic book characters Blondie and Dagwood also appeared in marketing campaigns.

In the late 2000s, looking back at A&W's roots, the company started creating locations with a retro look and modern technology, outfitted with drive-thru and carhop service, perfect for car clubs and parking lot events. What started with a root beer stand turned into a huge international beverage and fast-food company that's gone through many ups and downs. Now that it's gone back to its roots and cranked up the nostalgia, A&W is growing again.

Three generations of Hundertmarks

The oldest A&W in continuous operation at the same location is in Clintonville, Wisconsin, open since 1939. Three generations have kept it going:
1939–1975: Howard and Rella Hundertmark
1975–1990: Bruce (son) and Jean Hundertmark
1990–present: Erica Kelley and Kristin Nelson

See's Candies

SLOGAN: "Quality Without Compromise"
ORIGINAL LOCATION: 135 North Western Avenue, Los Angeles
OPENED: 1921
CURRENT OWNERSHIP: Part of the Berkshire Hathaway Portfolio
CURRENTLY AT THE FIRST LOCATION: Tom N Toms Coffee, a Korean coffeehouse

There are currently more than 200 in 20 states and 4 countries.
There are 3 factories: two in San Francisco and one in Los Angeles.

sees.com

MARY SEE is not just a face on See's Candies' iconic white and black boxes of chocolates. She was born Mary Wiseman in Ontario, Canada, in 1854. For years, she and her husband, Alexander, ran a hotel together on Tremont Park Island. Raising her three children—Charles, May, and Bertha—left her little spare time. With what little time Mary did have, she enjoyed working on candy recipes in her kitchen at the hotel.

Mary's son, Charles See, left their Canadian home for the sunny skies of Southern California in his twenties with his new bride, and he fell in love with the climate in his new home. When his father died in 1919, Charles talked his mother into moving to Pasadena, just outside of Los Angeles.

Mary adapted quickly to life in beautiful Pasadena, and set about making candies in the small kitchen of the post-Victorian bungalow where she resided on tree-lined Marengo Avenue. That kitchen was done up in black-and-white checkered tile.

One of the first jobs Charles had when he moved to Los Angeles was as a chocolate salesman for Merckens Chocolate, and since then, he'd dreamed of opening his own candy company. He also knew that his mother's confections were the best he'd ever tasted. But at the time, Los Angeles had more than a dozen candy factories, so competition was aggressive. Nevertheless, he moved forward. He found a building on Western Avenue and opened the first See's Candy Kitchen and Shop in 1921. He installed black-and-white tiled flooring with a Victorian look, just like his mother's kitchen in Pasadena. Glass display cases were never empty of beautiful dishes filled with chocolates for customers to admire. To this day, every See's store retains this original look, from the 1920s-style light fixtures to the black-and-white trim.

When Charles founded See's Candies, he envisioned an environment in which employees were treated like family and customers were greeted warmly with a free sample. He established a policy of "Three Ss" (Smiles, Samples, and Service) on day one. Inspired by his mother, Charles insisted on only the finest and freshest ingredients, and his suppliers began to refer to "See's quality," which was

Boxing up the chocolates

higher than "top quality." Many of the candies first developed by Mary are still in production today, using the same recipes.

In the early 1920s, Charles offered a bold new program for that time, "Quality Candy by Mail." Chocolates were packaged with cotton padding and enclosed in a strong corrugated shipping carton. Prospective customers were told that rates included postal insurance in case the package was damaged or lost. This created tremendous growth and international recognition, from Cairo to London, South America to Asia. The program also helped expand the company's range of flavors, because it led to access to such ingredients as maple sugar from Canada, pineapple from Hawaii, nuts from the Southern states, and chocolate from South America and Africa.

By 1925, the Los Angeles area had a dozen See's shops, including one at Grauman's Chinese Theatre on Hollywood Boulevard. At the time, all chocolates cost 60¢ a pound. Three years later, Hugh Fry, a shipping clerk, started a motorcycle delivery service. He dressed in a chauffeur's uniform and rode around L.A. on a customized black-and-white Harley Davidson, delivering boxes of candy.

After a strong start in the 1920s, times got tough, as was true for so many American businesses. In 1929, just after the stock market crash, Charles's competitors were selling candy at 80¢ a pound, and many were closing their doors. In November 1932, he created a bulk-rate program in which companies could buy larger quantities throughout the year to qualify for discounts. This allowed him to charge just 42.5¢ per pound for prepaid orders of over fifty pounds. A version of that program continues today. And when sugar supplies were short, he reduced the output instead of compromising on quality, which led to long lines at his shops.

On November 24, 1931, Charles debuted See's Sunlit Candy Studio (519 Washington Boulevard., Los Angeles), a new concept. It had an open-air feel, and customers could view the candy-making process. He threw a gala opening, with searchlights and live music, to tie into the upcoming 1932 Los Angeles Summer Olympics.

That same year, Eddie G. Peck came on board as sales manager. While traveling and studying candy/chocolate trends, Charles would send back candies from other companies, like Fannie Mae's chocolates in Chicago, for Eddie to try and compare. The company also hired Dorothy Gray Forbes

Left: Mary See with young children • Right: Charles See

First location, on Western Avenue

to create artwork, and she stayed on as the company's artist for more than sixty years. Her advertising and shop displays, with the image of See's Famous Old Time Candies, became one of the keys to the brand's success.

Great Depression or not, Charles knew that expansion was the only way to go. He focused on the San Francisco area and sent Eddie to open new shops. Within four years, the Bay Area had eighteen locations. This expansion came just in time for the 1939 Golden Gate International Exposition on Treasure Island. The See's exhibition included a small factory, so fairgoers could look through the floor-to-ceiling plate-glass windows to watch candy dippers create confections by hand. This was the first time for so many to taste the beautiful sweets. The See's exhibit was second only in popularity to the display of the Liberty Bell from Philadelphia.

In 1940, increasing demand led Charles to open a 15,000-square-foot production kitchen in San Francisco, on Market Street not far from Valencia. More than 8,000 people attended the opening to watch the assembly line, taste the candy, and experience the ultra-modern factory, which had such bold new amenities as air-conditioning (unheard of in the City by the Bay). A few years later, in 1947, back in L.A., Charles left the original Western Avenue location for a new 15,000-square-foot factory on La Cienega Boulevard, which to this day remains the production headquarters in Southern California.

CEOs

Charles See	1919–1949
Laurence See	1949–1969
Harry See	1969–1972
Charles Huggins	1972–2006
Brad Kinstler	2006–2019
Pat Egan	2019–present

See's Candies

The See's team at the 1943 employee Christmas party

In 1942, during the war, rationing meant butter, sugar, and cream were in extremely short supply. See's took a risk and did what it had done during the sugar shortages of the Depression: use the best ingredients even if it meant producing less candy. When the candy sold out, the store closed for the day. The plan worked—customers were willing to wait in long lines for the promise of quality.

From 1919 to 1949, Charles grew the company from one store on Western Avenue in L.A. to seventy-eight shops statewide, never compromising quality. When Charles passed away, Laurence Alexander See—Charles's son and Mary's grandson—succeeded him as president, a post he held until 1969. Laurence had graduated from Stanford University in 1946 and completed three years of military service overseas before becoming president, and he brought a younger perspective to the business. When television reached into American homes, he decided to bring See's into every home, too. He set his sights on the Rose Parade. Pasadena was where his grandmother had honed the See's recipes, so it was a natural fit. See's first-ever float in the parade was a giant Easter Bunny pulling a cart with rotating Easter-egg wheels, and millions of Ameicans saw it on their TVs on New Year's Day.

One of the most beloved episodes of *I Love Lucy* is the 1952 one called "Job Switching," when Fred and Ricky take over the housework and Lucy and Ethel get a job at a candy factory.

> **Four Originals Still in Production 100 Years Later**
> Peanut Brittle
> Victoria Toffee
> Maple Walnut Creams
> Chocolate Walnut Fudge

Made in California

Lucille Ball and Vivian Vance went to the See's kitchen on La Cienega to learn how to properly dip and package chocolates (which, as you'll certainly remember, got pretty intense in the episode), and the woman making chocolates with Lucy on the show was an actual See's candy maker.

Another key player in the See's story was Charles Huggins, who started in the packing department in San Francisco in the early 1950s and worked his way up the ladder. In 1972, he helped broker the sale of the company to Warren Buffett and Charles Munger of Berkshire Hathaway. Buffett named Huggins president and CEO, a position he held until 2006. Huggins grew the company to more than 5,000 employees and more than 200 stores around the world. He was instrumental in the development of such favorites as the Awesome Bars and saved several candies from extinction, including Marshmints, marzipan, and chocolate-covered ginger.

A few years after the acquisition, Charles Munger said that buying See's was a pivotal moment for him and Buffett. Before that, they were only interested in buying undervalued assets on the cheap. See's represented a shift—it had trusted relationships with suppliers and a quality product that customers were willing to pay for. It was the first high-quality business they had ever bought. To this

Delivery vehicles

day, Buffett remains a huge See's fan, even though it's only a tiny part of the Berkshire empire. He's always munching on See's chocolates during the annual stockholders' meetings and has even auctioned personal tours of the factories for fundraising efforts.

In 1996, See's celebrated its seventy-fifth anniversary with vintage delivery vehicles in iconic black and white, such as a 1930 Ford Model A roadster and a motorcycle with a sidecar filled with See's candies. Their chocolate, butterscotch, and cinnamon "Lollypops" had become staples in the lineup and a favorite of school fundraisers, so they opened a new factory in Burlingame devoted to making Lollypops and Little Pops. On July 18, 2012, Guinness World Records declared a See's chocolate Lollypop the world's largest, weighing more than 7,000 pounds, the equivalent of 145,000 regular-size Lollypops.

February 28, 2009, was a sad day for the company: The first San Francisco location, which opened in 1936 at

Right: Karla Marin, manager of the Corona, California, store; **below:** Mary See's grandson Harry (not the same Harry as the CEO) was an early model for See's ads

Warren Buffett learns how it's done

1519 Polk, closed. Not wanting to see another landmark disappear, Charlene Nichols, a Los Angeles preservationist and inventive author, intervened when the original factory location on Western was in disrepair and threatened with being torn down to build a strip mall. She went to the Los Angeles Cultural Heritage Commission to save the landmark, bringing a five-pound box of See's chocolates along with her proposal. She also brought smaller boxes of candies for the commissioners, but they turned them down on ethical grounds. I still wonder how they resisted. The building was saved from the wrecking ball, and the strip mall was built behind the former See's candy factory and store. Today, Tom N Toms, a Korean coffeehouse, occupies the location.

First Stores
135 North Western Avenue, Los Angeles
396 East Colorado Street, Pasadena
2030 West 7th Street, Los Angeles
333 West 6th Street, Los Angeles

Continuously Operating Stores
1949: Los Angeles ~ La Cienega Boulevard
1953: Sacramento ~ Country Club
1956: Corona del Mar
1958: Long Beach ~ Lakewood Boulevard
1950: El Cerrito Plaza

Fortunately, however, See's itself continues to thrive. Nowadays, it uses a special blend of chocolate from Guittard in Burlingame. It is delivered already melted in a tanker truck—similar to a gasoline truck—each holding 52,000 pounds of rich chocolate. At this writing, See's has more than 200 store locations in twenty US states and five countries. During the holidays, it also has pop-ups at most of the nation's airports for those last-minute gifts. *Fortune* named See's Candies one of thirteen Greatest American Brands, it's been called one of the top twenty-five places to work; and Mary See's creations are every bit as delicious today as they were in 1921.

See's Candies

SPANISH FOOD

1121 ORDERS TO TAKE OUT

CATON - WESTERN AVENUE

Sonora Café

NAME BECAME: El Cholo Spanish Café
NAME TODAY: El Cholo
ORIGINAL LOCATION: 4012 Moneta Avenue (Broadway Place), Los Angeles

OPENED: 1923
COFOUNDERS: Alejandro & Rosa Borquez
CURRENTLY AT THE FIRST LOCATION: California Modern Woodworks

Currently, 6 El Cholo restaurants and 3 upscale restaurants make up the family portfolio. Privately family owned.

elcholo.com

ALEJANDRO BORQUEZ loved his wife Rosa's cooking so much that in 1923, they decided to open a small restaurant not far from the recently completed Los Angeles Memorial Coliseum in Exposition Park. They named it Sonora Café. It sat on Moneta Avenue, which today is named Broadway Place. They called their fare "Spanish-American," and it was very simple.

The entrees offered on their opening menu were:
- Beef Tamales
- Green Corn Tamales
- Sonoma-Style Enchiladas (Beef or Chicken)
- Chili Relleno
- Tostada Compuesta
- Chili Con Carne

Other offerings included Joe's Albondigas, which was explained on the menu as Spanish meatball soup or vegetable soup, and salads of sliced fresh tomatoes, hearts of romaine, and "Mexican pickled peppers." All dishes were served with handmade flour tortillas (which they still make today), fried beans with cheese, and "Spanish" rice. Probably the first Mexican American combination plate ever served was Sonora Café's offering: an enchilada, a chili relleno, a tamale, chili con carne, fried beans, and rice. Handmade tortillas

Rosa & Alejandro Borquez

in a basket with butter and hot sauce were the staple that welcomed guests, unlike today's basket of tortilla chips and salsa.

Sonora's clientele was eclectic. It was not unusual to have Anglo businessmen from downtown

The Western Avenue location

and immigrants from Mexico sitting a few tables apart. Perhaps what drew them in were the large portions and great drinks, all at a fair price. With the Coliseum nearby, it was difficult to find a table after sporting events, and it became a hangout for USC students, athletes, and faculty.

Early Spanish settlers in California called Mexican field workers "cholos." While waiting for a table at the Sonora Café in 1925, a guest drew a figure on a menu while waiting for his table. He named his drawing EL CHOLO. Rosa and Alejandro's daughter, Aurelia, loved the drawing and took it to her father; together, they decided to change the name of their café to El Cholo Spanish Café. This original location stayed open until 1950.

Not long thereafter, Aurelia met a man named George Salisbury at El Cholo, and in 1927, the couple opened an El Cholo on Western Avenue, about a mile from the original location. Soon after its opening, they got married and moved the restaurant to a former house across the street, where it remains to this day. What was originally a small house has expanded many times over the years, adding dining rooms, kitchens, parking, and patio areas. Today you can see only a few elements of the original 1919 house.

Only a handful of L.A. restaurants from that time remain open as I write this—El Cholo, Musso & Frank Grill, Lawry's for prime rib, Philippe the Original and Cole's for french dips, and Greenblatt's and Canter's for deli fare—but the COVID-19 pandemic was threatening their survival.

Ron Salisbury, son of George and Aurelia, was born into the business, and he started officially working at the Western Avenue location in 1954. At this writing, he is still at the helm of nine restaurants. Ron remembers how, when he was a kid, lines would stretch down Western with businessmen

When Was It First Served?

1923	Handmade Flour Tortillas	1985	Blue Corn Chicken Enchiladas
	Sonora-Style Enchiladas	1989	Plato de Carnitas
	Joe's Traditional Albondigas	1990	Tres Tacos Al Carbon
	Tostada Compuesta	1991	Tortilla Soup
	Green Corn Tamales		Felix's Caesar Salad
	Chile Con Carne	1992	Annie's Early California Enchilada
1938	Combinaciones	1995	Fiesta Platter
1955	House Guacamole		Taquitos
1959	Carman's Original Nachos		Santa Barbara Enchiladas
1967	Chimichanga Appetizer	1996	A Taste of History Platter
	Chicken Chimichangas	1999	Enchiladas Mariscos
	El Cholo Margarita	2001	Fish Tacos
1969	Aged Cheese Quesadilla		Tres Cantina Tacos
1971	Crabmeat Enchilada	2006	Spicy Ceviche Tostadas
1976	Enchilada Suiza	2007	Guacamole Molcajete Style
1977	Burrito Dorado	2008	Southwest Chicken Tostada
1983	Sonora-Style Nachos	2009	Filet Mignon Tacos
1984	Carne Asada Fajitas	2019	Spicy Shrimp & Avocado Ceviche

Preparing to open on Western Avenue

from downtown high-rises and workers from nearby farmlands, waiting to be seated. When people driving by saw the lines, they'd get out of their cars and get in line, figuring that any place that had such waits must have great food.

Success led, of course, to competition. Ron's aunt and uncle opened El Coyote on La Brea, later moving it to Beverly Boulevard, where it resides today. In 1961, actor and dancer Rudy del Campo and his family opened a Mexican restaurant on Hyperion Avenue, also in a small house, later expanding it to the large restaurant and stage venue that it is today.

In 1966, George Salisbury sold the company to his son Ron. George had only served beer and wine, never hard liquor, and one of Ron's first big moves was to add a full bar, especially for margaritas. In 1967, he formed a partnership with Jose Cuervo that still exists today, and El Cholo's margaritas became a huge hit. Only Ron, his sons, and a few managers know the recipe, and as of this writing, El Cholo is the largest consumer of Cuervo 1800 tequila in the world. Three decades or so after he took over, Ron also expanded into Orange County, partnering with John Creed (of Chart House fame) to open El Cholo cafés.

Given its location in what is now Koreatown, between USC and wealthy Hancock Park, El Cholo became one of *the* places to be seen in L.A. Each costumed waitress had her area of the dining room, and she treated her guests as if they were in her home. Because of this, many of the stars who

Sonora Café (El Cholo)

visited got to know the waitresses like family. Regulars included Jack Nicholson and author Ray Bradbury, who lived only a few streets away.

Many staff members have had long tenures at El Cholo, but none have been quite so beloved as Carmen Rocha. She arrived from San Antonio in 1959 and started working as a waitress, also teaching the chefs about nachos, which quickly became a favorite with customers. They were simple, served only with melted cheese and jalapeño peppers on the side. Rocha worked at the Western Avenue location for close to forty years, retiring in the 1990s and passing away in 2008. Nicholson, a longtime regular in Rocha's station, said her death was "a community loss," and the restaurant renamed its lounge "Carmen's Cantina" in her honor. Every year during her birthday week, servers bring every table a small plate of nachos with the peppers on the side, just how she liked them.

> **Generations**
> 1st: Alejandro and Rosa Borquez
> 2nd: George Salisbury and Aurelia Borquez-Salisbury
> 3rd: Ron Salisbury (son of George and Aurelia)
> 4th: Brendon Salisbury (son of Ron)
> 5th & 6th: Many work in the various locations

El Cholo has received countless awards over the years. In 2010, Rachael Ray declared its filet mignon tacos as the best tacos in town. And while new dishes are added every decade or so to the menu, the classics always remain, with the year they joined the roster noted on the menu. The flavors of early SoCal Mexican American cooking take diners back to a simpler time, when Los Angeles was becoming its own.

Bienvendos a El Cholo

Openings

1923: Sonora Café
1925: El Cholo Spanish Café ♦ 4012 Moneta Avenue (Broadway Place), Los Angeles
1927: El Cholo ♦ 1107 South Western Avenue, Los Angeles
1931: El Cholo (moved across the street) ♦ 1121 South Western Avenue, Los Angeles
1962: El Cholo ♦ 840 East Whittier Boulevard, La Habra
1994: El Cholo Spanish Café ♦ 958 South Fair Oaks, Pasadena
1997: El Cholo ♦ 1025 Wilshire Boulevard, Santa Monica
1999: El Cholo ♦ 5465 Alton Parkway, Irvine
2001: El Cholo Cantina ♦ 5465 Alton Parkway, Irvine
2002: Sonora Café ♦ 180 South La Brea Avenue, Los Angeles
2010: El Cholo ♦ 1037 South Flower Street, Los Angeles
2013: El Cholo ♦ 8200 East Santa Ana Canyon, Anaheim Hills
2015: El Cholo ♦ 3520 East Pacific Coast Highway, Corona del Mar

Ready for business on opening day

The Brown Derby

SLOGAN: "Eat in the Hat"
ORIGINAL LOCATION: 3427 Wilshire Boulevard, Los Angeles
OPENED: November 17, 1926
RELOCATED TO: 3377 Wilshire Boulevard in 1937
MANAGER AND CO-OWNERS: Herbert Somborn & Bob Cobb
INVESTOR/CO-OWNER: Jack L. Warner, head of Warner Brothers Studio
CO-OWNER: Actress Gloria Swanson, who was married to Somborn for a while
CURRENTLY AT THE FIRST LOCATION: The Equitable Life Building, built in 1969
SECOND LOCATION: The Brown Derby Plaza strip mall; part of the building was incorporated into the back corner of the mall

THE LOS ANGELES of the 1920s and 1930s was rich with programmatic architecture—hot dog–shaped buildings, for example, that sold hot dogs. When a huge stucco derby sprang up across the street from the famed Ambassador Hotel in 1926, many thought, understandably, that it was a haberdashery.

The Brown Derby opened to fanfare in the fall of 1926, the first of what would be four locations around the Southland. It was designed by Carl Jules Weyl, an art director for Warner Brothers, who also designed Rick's Café in the movie *Casablanca*. Every booth had a light fixture with a derby-shaped shade. On top of the neon sign, it said, "Eat in the Hat." The food was simple, just a notch above that of a coffee shop—liver and onions, burgers, omelets—and it was open until 4 a.m.

Studio chief Jack L. Warner provided the financial backing for that first Derby, and it had a celebrity buzz from day one, but it was the second branch, opened by Bob Cobb on Vine Street in Hollywood in 1929 (without the derby exterior) that became world-famous for its showbiz vibe. Booths were low sided for maximum visibility, and the north wall was reserved for the A-list, which included Jean Harlow, Charlie Chaplin, Joan Crawford, Katharine Hepburn, William Powell, Rita Hayworth, and Eve Arden. The awning-covered entry was packed daily with fans three deep, much like a Hollywood premiere. It was the only way to see a star from the big screen in person, unlike today with so many news and media outlets. Everyone ate at the Derby.

Gossip columnists Louella Parsons and Hedda Hopper were regulars, taking advantage of the half-price deals the savvy owners gave to the press. They named themselves the Hollywood Women's Press Club, invited more women reporters and magazine writers, and convened at the Derby each Wednesday at noon.

A 1932 article in *Star Gazer* magazine reported, "The Brown Derby is more than a Hollywood institution. It is not only a place to meet and talk over contracts and plan divorces and further romance under the bronze derby-hatted lights, it is also a place to eat. It is famous, both as the spot

Yes, it's a giant hat!

where Jim Tully battled Jack Gilbert and the spot where you can get Special Hamburgers brought sizzling to the table in copper frying pans. It is a place where the stars gather at lunch and after premieres to be seen—and to relish some caviar."

In the early 1930s, the story goes that Sid Grauman of movie-house fame came into the Hollywood Derby late one night requesting something to eat. Bob Cobb gathered leftovers from the refrigerator and put them together in a salad of diced turkey, bacon, blue cheese, a hard-boiled egg, sliced tomato, avocado, and mixed greens of lettuce, watercress, chicory, and romaine, drenched in French dressing. The Cobb salad was born. Back then, Bob tossed everything in one bowl. Today, many establishments place the ingredients in rows as a more elegant presentation and then mix tableside. This salad put the Brown Derby on the culinary map.

By the 1940s, the Derby had locations in Hollywood at Sunset and Vine, in Los Feliz at Los Feliz and Hillhurst, and in Beverly Hills at Wilshire and Rodeo, along with the original, the only one with the derby-shaped building. The menu changed with specials of the day. Sunday was paprika chicken, Tuesday was declared meatless on account of the war effort, and Wednesday was beef Wellington. Cobb salad was always on the menu, with lobster thermidor and filet mignon becoming menu regulars as well. Tableside tossing of salads was the style of the day, and Derby waiters did that for a variety of salads. Everything was made fresh. In California, most fruits and vegetables were only a county away, so the flavors were clean and close to homemade. Even the breads and cakes were made on-site.

The Derby was Clark Gable's favorite restaurant; he reportedly proposed to Carole Lombard in booth #5 at the Hollywood location. In 1941, Lombard threw him a surprise 40th birthday party at their ranch. It was catered by the Brown Derby and featured his favorite dishes: corned beef hash,

Working lunches at the Brown Derby

pot roast, baked beans, and orange chiffon cake. A few years later, the Derby appeared in the film *Mildred Pierce*. Crawford tended the bar, famously claiming, "People have to drink somewhere. Why not here?" Like Sardi's in New York's theater district, the walls were lined with 8x10 caricatures of the stars of the day. A young man named Vitch allegedly made the first drawings in exchange for hot coffee and soup. Later, from 1947 to 1985, Jack Lane drew them all, and it was an honor for an actor to be caricatured. Many of the stars autographed their black-and-white art. A 1955 episode of *I Love Lucy*, titled "Hollywood at Last," featured Lucy, Ethel, and Fred deciding to rub elbows with the stars at the famous eatery. Lucy pointed out Eve Arden's sketch as well as Jimmy Durante's double-framed sketch—one for his face and the other for his nose—to much laughter. Jeff Earles, owner of the Original Red Onion (page 163) in Rolling Hills Estates, bought many of the drawings in an auction some years ago and has them displayed today in his dining room.

Most Famous Dishes
Cobb Salad
Grapefruit Cake
Paprika Chicken
Spaghetti and Meatballs

Because the Hollywood Derby was so close to many studios, it was a convenient place for a celebrity to enjoy a hearty meal instead of at the studio commissary or craft services. At lunchtime, it was not surprising to see Tyrone Power eating boiled brisket of beef, Janet Gaynor devouring her favorite Turkey Derby, Claudette Colbert savoring chicken hash, Eddie Cantor finishing off a

The Brown Derby

hamburger steak, or Al Jolson eating chicken chow mein. Jack Benny and Mary Livingston broadcasted their radio show close by, at Sunset Las Palmas Studios, and they'd stop in to enjoy some ham for lunch, collecting gags while they were there. They even wrote radio scripts at their booth. And in those pre–cell phone days, getting a call at the Derby was a major status symbol. The maître d' would announce that so-and-so had a phone call, and everyone heard it.

Gloria Somborn Daly, daughter of Gloria Swanson and restaurateur Herbert Somborn, had inherited majority ownership of the Brown Derby in a trust, which gave her control at age thirty. At age thirty-two, in 1952, she gave up her interest in the other restaurants to acquire sole ownership of the original Brown Derby on Wilshire. Although it was no longer a showbiz haunt, it still thrived as a tourist attraction. Sadly, by the 1970s, the tourists had also stopped coming. Finally, in September of 1980, she had her managers lay off the staff; they were told that the domed hat would be razed to make way for a high-rise building. Moving trucks quickly took away everything that was not nailed down, and all of the remaining food was sent to the Los Angeles Rescue Mission. Two days later, on Sunday, the bulldozers arrived, but protesters from the Hollywood Heritage Museum and the Los Angeles Conservancy stopped the demolition. Daly agreed to sell the dome to a preservation group, and the property was sold to developers. Years later, the dome was hoisted into the center of the new Brown Derby Plaza.

The Walt Disney Company had been looking for a higher-end restaurant to replicate for its new studio park, the Walt Disney/MGM Studios (later rebranded as Disney's Hollywood Studios),

Clark Gable & Carole Lombard at the Derby

scheduled to open in 1989. A few years before that, the Derby had begun a licensing program, which had been unsuccessful, but the Disney project worked. The park's main street, Hollywood Boulevard, houses a replica of the former Vine Street location, outfitted with the iconic derby neon lighting. Walls are adorned with replicas of the framed caricatures, the waitstaff is outfitted with uniforms from the 1940s, and the menu showcases favorites of the time, including the Cobb Salad and the Grapefruit Cake.

In 2008, the auction house Bonhams & Butterfields sold many lots of Brown Derby history, including dishes, décor, napkins, coasters, ashtrays, matchbooks, and other items. Thus ended the eighty-five-year history of one of Hollywood's most celebrated restaurants.

Brown Derby Locations
1926–1980: 3427 Wilshire Boulevard, Mid-Wilshire
1929–1989: 1628 North Vine Street, Hollywood
1931–1981: 9537 Wilshire Boulevard, Beverly Hills
1940–1990s: 4500 Los Feliz Boulevard, Los Feliz
1987–present: Disney Studios Florida, Orlando, Florida

More soup for Wallace Beery

Orange Julius

SLOGAN: "Frothy & Refreshing"
ORIGINAL LOCATION: 820 South Broadway, Los Angeles
OPENED: 1926
FOUNDER: Julius Freed & Willard Hamlin
CURRENTLY OWNED BY: Berkshire Hathaway
PARENT COMPANY: International Dairy Queen, Inc. Orange Julius of America, based in Minneapolis
CURRENTLY AT THE FIRST LOCATION: 5-story apparel building

There are currently 56 exclusive Orange Julius locations in the United States and Canada. More than 5,000 locations either sell or are certified to sell Orange Julius products.

orangejulius.com

IN 1926, a few steps from the 2,000-seat Los Angeles Orpheum Theatre, which had debuted three years earlier, Julius Freed opened an orange juice stand. Even though the orange was the symbol of the sunshine, possibilities, and growth of Southern California in the early part of the twentieth century, fresh orange juice was not available in L.A. markets, and this inspired Freed to sell cups of juice—along with medicinal tonics and Bible tracts for good measure.

The early days of his operation were modestly successful, with daily sales averaging twenty dollars. The real estate agent who'd helped him find that first stand, Willard (Bill) Hamlin, became interested in Freed's operation and approached him with the idea of creating a more delicious drink that might sell better and that might be less acidic—orange juice upset Hamlin's stomach. Hamlin used his chemistry background to devise a secret compound of ingredients (all food-based, no chemicals) that gave the drink a smooth, creamy, yet airy texture. Within three weeks of trial and error, Hamlin had developed the taste he wanted, and Freed tested it on his customers with exceptional success—sales skyrocketed to $100 a day. People were continually asking Freed, "Give me an orange, Julius," and so the Orange Julius name was conceived. In short order, Freed, Hamlin, and contractor William Larkin created the General Citrus Corporation. Freed wasn't the dynamo in this story, though. It was Hamlin, the real estate guy, who traveled the country, leasing locations for stands adorned with the motto he'd thought up: "A Devilish Good Drink," while Larkin built the stands.

Once the new drink was perfected, success came fast. By 1929, Hamlin had franchised 100 stores across the United States.

Left: The first stand • **Right:** Behind the counter in the 1960s

Orange Julius

> **Location Types**
> 56 Orange Julius locations (exclusively)
> 425 Dairy Queen Treat locations (both Dairy Queen and Orange Julius)
> 4,929 Dairy Queen Grill and Chill locations (all have Orange Julius drinks at their locations)
> 5,410 Total locations worldwide serving Orange Julius

Sales were colossal with just one item, which at that time cost 10¢. Orange Julius had become the Coca-Cola of the 10¢ drink field. For an added energy boost, customers could have a raw egg cracked into the drink while it was blending. The partners soon expanded with pineapple and strawberry drinks as well.

Legend has it that the slogan had its roots in the 1930s when customers would say, "That's a hell of a drink!" It was too risqué to use the word "hell" back then, so they switched it to "A Devilish Good Drink," which is how the devil logo came into play. In the 1970s, wanting to avoid any brand association with the occult or Satanism, Orange Julius switched from the original, more menacing-looking devil logo to a more cartoonish one. But that devil didn't last forever. It turns out it resembled Sparky, the mascot for Arizona State University, and when the ASU Alumni Association threatened a lawsuit, Orange Julius gave up on the devil.

In the late 1940s, Hamlin bought out Freed (who passed away in 1952 at the relatively young age of sixty-four). Hamlin expanded the menu, adding hot dogs in 1949 and hamburgers in 1955. He retired in 1967 and sold the company to International Industries (part of the IHOP Group); by that time, Orange Julius had stands in every state and eight other countries. He passed away twenty years later, in 1987.

Many of the stands around the Los Angeles area in the 1950s were designed by the famed Santa Monica architectural firm of Armet

> **Julius Originals**
> Orange
> Strawberry Banana
> Piña Colada
> Strawberry
> Mango Pineapple
> Tripleberry
> Berry Pomegranate
> OrangeBerry

A new stand in the 1970s

Celebrating the opening of a new branch

> **Slogans in Years Past**
> A Devilish Good Drink
> The Magic Is in the Drink
> Celebrating 75 Years of Freshness
> "Nutrified" Smoothies by Design
> Juice Is Food
> The Experts in Specialty Blended Drinks
> The Famously Refreshing Fruit Drink
> The Thicker, Richer, Creamy Smooth Drink

& Davis and were fine examples of Googie design. Each had a zigzag roof; some were built for walk-up only, while others had some seating outside under umbrellas, and almost none survive today. One cherished location, at 6001 West Pico Boulevard, came close to getting landmark status, but that effort failed, although the condo building under construction at this writing incorporated the zigzag roof, orange touches, and Googie details.

In 1964, the New York World's Fair named Orange Julius its official drink, thus catapulting the brand to worldwide recognition. Openings in London and Amsterdam followed in the early 1970s. Publicity stunts included giving Johnny Carson and astronaut Alan Shepard lifetime passes. In 1985, the company jumped on the developing smoothie wagon to introduce the Julius Creme Supreme Premium Fruit Smoothie. Today, an Orange Julius might be a 150-square-foot kiosk in a mall, selling only drinks and hot dogs, or a 750-square-foot fast-food operation with a larger menu.

When International Dairy Queen acquired Orange Julius in 1987, it became Orange Julius of America. Although Dairy Queen and Orange Julius stores are franchised locations in malls, Orange Julius single units are no longer franchised locations. The last Orange Julius single unit location to open in the United States was in Happy Valley, Oregon, in 2008, and the last one in Canada was in Kingston, Ontario, in 2014. Until 2012, you could only get an Orange Julius at an actual Orange Julius location, or at a Dairy Queen/Orange Julius mall stand. Now, however, all Dairy Queen Grill and Chill restaurants and Dairy Queen/Brazier locations (excluding Texas) are required to carry Orange Julius drinks and smoothies.

The original Orange Julius formula does contain some real orange juice, along with the ingredients first added by Hamlin, including milk, powdered egg white, vanilla, sugar, and ice—similar to an orange Creamsicle. For many, one sip still connotes the promise of California sunshine.

> **Milestones**
> 1926: 1 location
> 1929: 100 locations
> 1932: Locations coast to coast
> 1962: First Canadian location
> 1967: More than 700 locations
> Early 1970s: London and Amsterdam openings
> 1977: Hong Kong opening
> 1982: 40 locations in Asia
> Today: More than 5,400 locations sell Orange Julius products

Clifton's Cafeterias

NAME TODAY: Clifton's Republic
ORIGINAL LOCATION: "Pacific Seas," 618 South Olive Street, Los Angeles
OPENED: September 17, 1931
COFOUNDERS: Clifford E. Clinton & Nelda Clinton
CLIFTON'S REPUBLIC, AT 648 SOUTH BROADWAY (THE CHAIN'S SECOND LOCATION), IS CURRENTLY OWNED BY: Andrew Meieran, the Kinetescape Inc.
CURRENTLY AT THE FIRST LOCATION: Parking lot

At one time, there were 13 locations around Southern California.

cliftonsla.com

IN THE 1920S AND '30S, you could find more than thirty-six cafeterias in the downtown Los Angeles area—they were the fast-food establishments of the time—and in the 1930s, two of the best known were part of the Clifton's chain, which eventually grew to many branches around Southern California. Today, the only Clifton's remaining, on Broadway, is technically the oldest surviving cafeteria-style restaurant in L.A., although at this writing it was functioning only as a nightclub (which was on hold due to COVID-19).

Founder Clifford E. Clinton combined Clifford and Clinton to produce the name Clifton's. Each location had its own theme and look. The first location, on Olive, had a South Pacific look, with waterfalls, plants, and geysers, and was named Pacific Seas.

The Broadway location, called Clifton's Brookdale, opened in 1935, where Boos Brothers Cafeteria had been, and remained open for seventy-six years. It was decorated to look like the Brookdale Lodge in the Santa Cruz mountains, where Clinton had spent time as a young man. François Scotti, a rock sculptor, built a twenty-foot waterfall that cascaded into a stream past faux-redwood trees. Einar Petersen painted a huge forest on one wall, populated by a raccoon, a fishing bear, and a stuffed moose head. I would have called the style Early Disney or Theatrical Kitsch.

The restaurants held to what was known as Clifton's Golden Rule: "Dine Free Unless Delighted." And they never turned anyone away hungry. During one ninety-day period in the Depression, Clinton served 10,000 free meals and then decided to open up an emergency "Penny Cafeteria" a few blocks away. Thanks to the help of vendors and generous suppliers, he was successful. In Charles Bukowski's novel *Ham on Rye*, he writes, "Clifton's Cafeteria was nice. If you didn't have much money, they let you pay what you could. And if you didn't have any money, you didn't have to pay.... It was owned by some very nice rich old man, a very unusual person." During the war years, the restaurants served upward of 10,000 customers a day, with lines wrapping down Broadway and along 7th Street. (By 2009, the numbers had diminished to about 2,000 daily.) Every customer was greeted and

Clifton's Brookdale in the 1940s

Locations and Opening Dates

1931–1960   Clifton's Cafeteria "Pacific Seas," 618 South Olive Street, Los Angeles
1935–2011 & 2015–2018:   Clifton's "Brookdale," 1935 South Broadway, Los Angeles
1956–2001   Clifton's, Lakewood Center Mall, 5006 Pepperwood Avenue, Lakewood
1958–1960   Clifton's, 510 North Euclid Street, Anaheim
1958–1978   Clifton's, Eastland Shopping Center, 2753 West Garvey Avenue, West Covina
1960–1975   Clifton's Midtown Cafeteria "Convaline," 685 South Hoover Street, Los Angeles
1966–1986   Clifton's, 10250 Santa Monica Boulevard, Century City
1974–1984   Clifton's, Inland Center Mall, 500 Inland Center Drive, San Bernardino
1975–1997   Clifton's "Silver Spoon," 515 West 7th Street, Los Angeles
1978–2003   Clifton's "The Greenery," West Covina Fashion Plaza, I-10 at West Covina Parkway
1981–1988   Clifton's, Whittier Quad, 8704 Quad Way, Whittier
1987–1999   Clifton's, 24165 Paseo de Valencia, Laguna Hills

referred to as a "guest," and every employee was called an "associate."

Ninety percent of all the food produced in the mass kitchen was homemade, prepared without mixes or packaged products, and diners paid per item, cafeteria-style, and it was served in a line that was almost the length of a football field. The line started with an array of salads, including the ever-popular carrot raisin with pineapple, cottage cheese with fruit topping, and tossed greens with homemade dressings. Green Jell-O was cubed and stacked as high as possible in small, round dishes—you were sure to have a few of the little squares land on your tray. Three soups were always featured, and Friday was, of course, clam chowder day. The choice of main dishes was endless, with an array of potatoes and vegetables to accompany them. From the beginning, the desserts were winners, from meringue-topped pies to squares of light cake with buttercream frosting to summertime fresh berries with a dollop of whipped cream. The focus on sweets never waned—in 2001, L.A.'s *Downtown News* voted Clifton's as having downtown's best desserts.

By 1940, the cafeterias were serving up to 25,000 meals daily. With the help of Caltech, Clinton implemented a plan to serve a single nutritious meal, termed "Multi-Purpose Food," at a nickel per serving. The Clintons created a restaurant-training school, providing thirteen weeks of restaurant-management training and concluding with placement service upon graduation.

Clifford Clinton

Souvenir photo

Clifford and his wife, Nelda, sold their cafeteria interest to their three youngest children (they had five kids) in 1946 and retired to devote their attention to the charitable organization Meals for Millions, which they'd founded in the middle of World War II. The organization distributed food to millions of hungry people throughout the world.

Clifford Clinton died in his Los Angeles home in 1969 and was buried at Forest Lawn in Glendale. His cafeterias closed one by one—until finally, only the original Clifton's on Olive Street remained.

With 600 seats on three floors, the Broadway Clifton's was considered the largest public cafeteria in operation in America. One famous regular was Ray Bradbury, who routinely walked the few blocks from the Los Angeles Central Library, where he did his writing, to have lunch at Clifton's, sometimes taking advantage of the pay-what-you-can-afford policy. In the 1930s, he also attended meetings of the Los Angeles Science Fiction Society, which used to meet on the third floor. Bradbury celebrated his eighty-ninth birthday at Clifton's in 2009.

In 2006, son Robert Clinton bought the Broadway building that the family had been leasing for seventy-one years. He then sold it to Andrew Meieran of Kinetescape Inc., owner of the Edison nightclub, in 2010. Meieran said at the time that he'd restore it to preserve the food and history, including reintroducing some of the 1950s recipes. The renovations were completed in a variety of phases, from closing a few days a week, to closing and only having a bakery window open, and to complete closure. In February 2012, the remodeling process removed the building's 1963 aluminum louvered exterior cladding to reveal the original façade. During these renovations, a partition wall was removed that revealed a neon light still lit, apparently running for seventy-seven years.

Meieran planned elaborate eating, drinking, and exhibition spaces throughout the building and executed some of them to stunning effect (re-creating, for example, the Brookdale-inspired nature interior), but it was more challenging than he'd hoped to bring the restaurant back. The cafeteria closed for good in 2018, and today, it's a bar and event space called Clifton's Republic. It's been closed throughout the pandemic but hopefully will survive and keep Clifton's spirit alive.

Eastland Shopping Mall Center, West Covina, 1958

Hinky Dink's

NAME TODAY: Trader Vic's
ORIGINAL LOCATION: 6500 San Pablo Avenue, Oakland
OPENED: November 17, 1934
FOUNDER: Victor J. Bergeron
CURRENTLY AT THE FIRST LOCATION: A vacant lot

Currently, there are 20 locations in 12 countries, three of those in the United States.

tradervics.com

VICTOR J. BERGERON, a young entrepreneur, opened a thirty-seat saloon called Hinky Dink's in Oakland in 1934. The menu was typical of the time—steaks and roasted chicken—but soon he started experimenting with breakfast and what he called Ham and Eggs Hawaiian, made with fried bananas and pineapple. Then Bergeron took a vacation to Havana by way of New Orleans and came back with new ideas and recipes for drinks. The tropical flavors of daiquiris and planter's punch that Bergeron added to the Hinky Dink's menus set the stage for the next shift in his business.

In 1937, Bergeron traveled to Hollywood and dined at both Don the Beachcomber and Seven Seas, which were within a block of each other. He then decided to turn Hinky Dink's into a Polynesian restaurant with tropical drinks and a Chinese-influenced menu. His wife suggested that he change the name as well, and she came up with "Trader Vic's," because he loved to barter and make deals. Soon after he returned to Oakland, Hinky Dink's became Trader Vic's.

Although his rival and friend Donn (Don the Beachcomber) Beach disputed the claim, Bergeron said he invented the mai tai in 1944; Beach had come up with a similar cocktail, called the Q.B. Cooler, a decade earlier. Regardless of the inspiration, the mai tai came to define Trader Vic's. The next decade saw a flood of movies and music focused on islands of the South Seas, Polynesia, and Hawaii. *South Pacific* was running on Broadway to great acclaim. Hawaii became our fiftieth state. Tiki bars and restaurants were the rage, with rum drinks galore. Trader Vic's was right there with the trend, and Bergeron's bartenders whipped up many an elaborate rum cocktail, sometimes set aflame. (The Fog Cutter and the Scorpion Bowl were also Vic creations.) Signs around the restaurants proclaimed "Rum: the Inspiration of Great Deeds" and "A practiced hand, plus understanding, make rum drinks the inspiration that leaves only joy following reasonable inhibition."

Left: Welcome to the Trader Vic's in the Beverly Hilton • Above: A Trader Vic's matchbook

After his success in the East Bay, Bergeron worked with Western Hotels to franchise new locations in their hotels, including in Seattle. A Trader Vic's arrived in Hawaii in 1950, and then in 1951, he opened a branch at 60 Cosmo Place in San Francisco. The location was in a dimly lit alleyway, which not only meant lower rent but a more faux–South Pacific sense of mystery. A few years later, Bergeron partnered with Conrad Hilton, who was opening opulent hotels around the world. More than sixteen of them eventually housed a Trader Vic's. The first was in the Beverly Hilton, which opened in 1955. The only one left in a Hilton today is in downtown Atlanta.

The Beverly Hills location became, not surprisingly, a favorite watering hole for countless celebrities. Politicians were also regulars: John F. Kennedy and his administration stayed at the hotel when in Los Angeles, and then-governor Ronald Reagan and his kitchen cabinet frequented Trader Vic's.

Next came New York. After a Trader Vic's opened in 1958 at the Savoy-Plaza Hotel, Bergeron moved to the basement of the Plaza in 1965 along with most of his employees when the Savoy-Plaza Hotel was torn down to build the General Motors Building. When Donald Trump bought the Plaza, he immediately closed Trader Vic's, even though it was highly profitable—he felt it was tacky and not up to his standards for the Plaza (which he'd owned for four years, trying to recover debts by selling rooms as condominiums). Former president Richard Nixon was very upset with the closure; he used to take his daughters to Trader Vic's for special occasions.

In the 1960s, about twenty-five Trader Vic's were in operation worldwide. In the 1980s and '90s, the chain shrank as a result of poor locations and the fading of the tiki craze.

The food at Trader Vic's was largely fantasy, with no basis in actual Chinese or South Pacific traditions. A good example was the crab rangoons: wontons filled with crab meat and cream cheese and deep fried. Appetizers of oysters were also abundant, including Oysters San Juan, Oysters Casino, and Oysters Florentine. The menu had twenty seafood dishes, most cooked in a specially built Chinese oven. Bergeron would also cook an entire suckling pig to feed fifteen when given a week's notice. He introduced green peppercorns, morel mushrooms, and kiwi to

Locations Around the World
- 1963 London, UK (Park Lane Hilton)
- 1971 Munich, Germany (Hotel Bayerischer Hof)
- 1972 Emeryville (Stand-alone)
- 1974 Tokyo, Japan (Hotel New Otani)
- 1976 Atlanta, GA (Hilton)
- 1992 Bangkok, Thailand (Stand-alone)
- 1994 Emirate of Abu Dhabi, UAE (Rotana Hotel and Towers) Dubai, UAE (Crown Plaza Hotel)
- 1999 Abu Dhabi, UAE (Al Ain Rotana Hotel)
- 2000 Manama, Bahrain (Ritz Carlton) Muscat, Oman (Inter-Continental Hotel)
- 2004 Dubai, UAE (Souk Madinat Jumeirah)
- 2007 Amman, Jordan (Regency Palace Hotel)
- 2009 Riyagh, Saudi Arabia (Panorama Mall)
- 2012 Doha, Qatar (Hilton Doha)
- 2014 Ras Al Khaimah, UAE (Hilton Al Hamra)
- 2017 Mahe Island, Seychelles (H Resort)
- 2018 Dubai, UAE (Hilton Dubai Jemeirah)

Top right: The original Oakland location
Bottom right: At the Beverly Hilton

California diners; he helped popularize snow peas and salmon caviar nationally; and he pioneered the use of wood-burning ovens in restaurants.

But the dining experience wasn't really about the food. It was about the cocktails and the show—from the tiki god glasses to the flaming drinks, from the tribal masks on the walls to the flat-bottom boats hanging upside down from the ceilings.

In 1960, Bergeron hired Claudette Lum as a hat-check girl for the newly opened San Francisco location, and she ended up becoming one of the longest-employed Trader Vic's workers, retiring in 2017 at the age of eighty as a maître d'. She spent thirty-five of those years at the San Francisco location, and when it closed, she worked another twenty-two years at the Emeryville Wharf branch. Back in the '60s, a tie and coat were mandatory, and she famously turned away the Bee Gees for not adhering to the dress code. The celebrities who did dress properly whom she greeted over the years ranged from Bing Crosby to Jackie Gleason to John McEnroe (whom she did make wear a tie). Her most famous guests, arriving with just a few hours' notice on March 2, 1983, were Queen Elizabeth and First Lady Nancy Reagan. In an interview with the *San Francisco Chronicle* after her retirement, Lum remembered, "I did curtsey, and did well. In a Chinese dress. Good thing those slits were so high."

Bergeron may have been the first celebrity chef hired to consult with United Airlines. In 1972, United hired Vic to design and implement the food and beverage service aboard its new Boeing 747s and McDonald Douglas DC-10s. He got pay equal to that of a bank president, as well as publicity and free travel passes. One month later he delivered, coming up with fruity dressings for salads and hand-shaken cocktails.

In his later years, he took up sculpting and painting and had many gallery shows. Bergeron also wrote several books on food and drink, including *Trader Vic's Bartender's Guide*, *Trader Vic's Book of Mexican Cooking*, and *Trader Vic's Island Cooking*. All of his books are still popular today. He died in 1984, survived by his wife and four children, all of whom were working in the company at the time.

Today, tiki culture is cool again, and although at this writing only three Trader Vic's are open in the United States (the flagship in Emeryville, California, the one in the Atlanta Hilton, and a new outpost at the San Jose International Airport), it's easy to see the potential for mai tais and pupu platters to come back.

Polynesian kitsch inside Trader Vic's

Former Hilton Properties with Trader Vic's

1955–2007	The Beverly Hilton, Beverly Hills, CA
1957–2005	Palmer House Hilton, Chicago, IL
1958–1960	Haban Hilton, Havana, Cuba
1961–1995	Capital Hilton, Washington, DC
1963–1975	Detroit Satler Hilton, Detroit, MI
1965–1976	Satler Hilton, Boston, MA
1965–1986	Shamrock Hilton, Houston, TX
1967–1989	Hilton Inn Dallas, Dallas, TX
1975–1991	Hilton Toronto, Toronto, Canada
1978–1985	Denver Hilton, Denver, CO
2003–2009	Hilton Berlin, Berlin, Germany

Bob's Pantry

NAME TODAY: Big Boy Restaurants
ORIGINAL LOCATION: 900 East Colorado Boulevard, Glendale

OPENED: August 6, 1936
FOUNDER: Robert C. Wian
CURRENT OWNER: Big Boy Restaurant Group, LLC
CURRENTLY AT THE FIRST LOCATION: Soo Good Lutong Pinoy Filipino Restaurant

There are 77 locations in 4 US states, and 279 locations in Japan.

bigboy.com

ROBERT C. WIAN migrated to California from Philadelphia as a teen with his parents in the late 1920s. His father, the owner of a furniture craftsman business, went bankrupt during the start of the Great Depression in 1929. To pay for his lunch, Wian started washing dishes in the school cafeteria. In 1933, when he graduated from Glendale High School, his classmates voted him as most likely not to succeed. After graduation, he found work in many different coffee shops, which piqued his interest in how a restaurant works. While working at Glendale's White Log Tavern, which was built to look like a log cabin, he was promoted to fry cook and then manager. After learning the "White Log System" of pricing and merchandising, plus some of the recipes, he wanted to gain more experience, so he started working at Sternberger's Rite Spot Café. Here he learned how Rite Spot created its chili, hamburgers, and a special red relish sauce. The Rite Spot also offered curbside service in your car, which intrigued him.

In 1936, with $300 earned from the sale of his car, Wian purchased a ten-stool stand on Colorado Boulevard in Glendale and opened Bob's Pantry to great fanfare. One evening, while he was busy making hamburgers, a group of musicians came in wanting something more than just a burger. Because of this request, as a joke, he started making a burger. He took a sesame bun and cut it into thirds instead of half. He placed double patties on the bread with cheese, resulting in a double-decker burger. He named it The Big Boy after a local kid, Rick Woodruff, who was a regular. Another aspect that set Wian's apart from the other burger joints at the time was that he used steer beef and ground it in front of the customers. This was especially effective because people of the day were skeptical as to what patties were made from.

A vintage Bob's menu; see photo credits, page 254

> **Ownership**
> **Bob's Pantry**
> 1936: Robert C. Wian Enterprises
> 1967: Marriott Corporation
> 1988: Elias Brothers Restaurants, Inc.
> 2000: Big Boy Restaurants International ~ Robert Liggett Jr.

Woodruff was also the vision for the Big Boy character: a chubby little boy with bright red-and-white overalls, a slingshot in his back pocket, and a swooped head of hair. Over the years, the character has evolved. The first drawing had him barefoot, holding a burger with a bite missing, his cheeks full of food. The East Coast versions now are a bit different, with the Big Boy running and not quite as hefty. Wian rechristened Bob's Pantry as Bob's Big Boy in 1938.

The February 1940 *LIFE* magazine cover story on carhops made some interesting notes about the standards for drive-in carhops at the time. Only girls between eighteen and twenty-five could be carhops. Not only did they have to have high school educations and health cards, but they also needed good figures and flirtatious personalities. Once hired, they were required to smile, stand erect, memorize the menu, and make an effort to sell large orders of food. These young women worked seven-and-a-half-hour shifts, six days a week, for no pay—although they typically earned five dollars a day in tips. Rules forbade them from touching a customer or his car; they were, however, allowed to visit with a favorite caller for up to ten minutes, but then had to get back to work. The girls were coached in diction, deportment, and how to laugh at customers' jokes. Guests were urged to "come back and see us and ask for me." Change was to be placed on the tray and not in the customers' hands. The rules at one drive-in said that if the carhop held her tray too low, she'd have to fold 1,000 napkins after her shift. The standards described in the article may not have been explicitly for Bob's Big Boy, but Wian's rules were still strict. Despite this, he had hundreds of applicants for the carhop jobs.

Besides owning the restaurant, Wian was elected to the Glendale City Council and then became mayor in 1948 after the previous mayor was recalled. He gave up his mayoral position after less than a year, however, as he felt owning a restaurant in the city was a conflict of interest.

Wian quickly went national. He co-branded his Big Boy restaurants with at least thirty-four different names representing various franchises over the years, thus resulting in hundreds of Big Boy models coast to coast. Frisch's Big Boy in the central part of the country (Indiana, Ohio, Kentucky, Tennessee, and a few in Florida) began appearing in 1948. Due to the popularity of drive-ins, Alex Schoenbaum opened the Parkette Drive location in West Virginia after meeting Wian in 1951. He became a Big Boy franchisee, calling several of his locations Parkette Big Boy Shoppes. In June 1954, he renamed and branded his locations as Shoney's, a name that remains even today. At one point, Shoney's was the largest Big Boy franchise in the country, with 392 locations. (In 1984, Shoney's dropped the Big Boy name and menu items to focus on its own line of food.)

The country's oldest surviving Bob's Big Boy is on Riverside Drive in Burbank, where it has thrived since 1949. It was designed by Googie pioneer Wayne McAllister (who also designed the Sands Hotel in Las Vegas); he merged a sense of

> **Iconic Menu Items**
> The "Big Boy": double-patty cheeseburger
> Fudge Cake
> Strawberry Pie
> Chocolate Milkshake
> Large Onion Rings
> Blue Cheese Dressing

Car hops ready for duty

streamline moderne with swoopy 1950s coffee-shop style, with huge plate-glass windows facing the street and a carhop lot in the rear. The seventy-foot sign can be seen illuminating the sky from miles around. In 1965, during the Beatles tour stop at the Hollywood Bowl, the group dined at the Big Boy. The booth they dined in is still the most requested by customers: the last booth on the right, where the windows face Riverside Drive. The plaque at the booth describing the event has been stolen many times by fans, but it's always replaced by management. The 1995 film *Heat*, starring Robert De Niro and Al Pacino, was filmed at the Big Boy. In 1992, the restaurant was designated a Point of Historical Interest (#779) by the state of California, and it hosts weekly car rallies in the large parking lot, often attended by former talk-show host and car enthusiast Jay Leno. This Burbank Big Boy also sits across the street from the very first International House of Pancakes (page 209).

The '50s brought car clubs, and Bob's became a place for high schoolers to congregate after football games. Wian hired security. At a 1950s restaurant convention held at the Biltmore Hotel in downtown L.A., he told the crowd that the teens were better mannered and more appreciative than adults; the security was to control the traffic more than the teens.

The Adventures of Big Boy was a free comic that kids could pick up at the cash register. Many issues, including the first, were created by famed animator Stan Lee, and it ran from 1956 to 1996 with

Bob's Pantry (Big Boy Restaurants)

466 issues. It was the longest-running promotional comic distributed for free on record.

According to a full-page story in the *Los Angeles Times*, Wian tore down his first Bob's Pantry in Glendale in 1956 to make way for "California's fanciest hamburger joint," the newest Bob's Big Boy. He hired Wayne McAllister to design a diner that would accommodate ninety customers in booths and at the counter, along with a drive-in outside that had room for fifty-five cars. Pastel shades of pink, brown, ivory, and green were used throughout the interior and exterior with extensive use of ceramic and mosaic tile. At the time, there were nine Bob's Big Boys in the Los Angeles area, and a Phoenix branch had been opened the year prior by four former employees. In 1955, the various Bob's restaurants sold more than 4 million burgers yearly. Many of the Bob's locations were designed by Armet & Davis, an architectural firm noted for its contributions to Googie architecture.

> **Bob's: A Trailblazer**
> - Employee relations: Bob's was an early adopter of profit sharing and employer-sponsored health insurance
> - Created the Big Boy, a double-patty cheeseburger
> - Produced free comic books featuring Big Boy
> - First to use a sesame seed bun
> - First to use freshly cracked black pepper

The general offices and commissary (Bob's Kitchens) serving the Bob's California locations were housed only a few blocks from the original site of Bob's Pantry. They conducted tours so visitors could get a firsthand look at the finest steer beef being freshly ground, at highly skilled women cleaning large conquistador shrimp, and at other kitchen staff slicing and battering onion rings, cooking "greaseless" chili in huge stockpots, and making Yummy Boy cake doughnuts. When the Marriott Corp. bought Bob's Big Boy in 1967, it also took over the kitchen production facility. In 1989, Kathy Taggares approached Marriott with an offer to purchase Bob's Kitchens, which was making the salad dressings for the restaurants. Taggares changed the name to KT Kitchens and produced more than 1.8 million bottles of dressing a year for over thirty-two years, as well as eight varieties of sauces for grocery stores and the Big Boy locations. In 2019, Taggares sold the rights to make Bob's dressings and sauces to Flavor of California, which produces the versions you find in local markets today.

Wian had always believed that success or failure of any company, large or small, depended on the people who served the public, and he insisted on courteousness and excellent customer relations. This was one of the reasons he supported a pension plan, which was unique for the restaurant industry at the time, to help attract a higher caliber of employee. He was also a nut about cleanliness—health and sanitation inspections always resulted in 100 percent approval and commendation. Bob's won many national awards for excellence for its

> **Bob's Dressings & Sauces Sold in Stores**
> Blue Cheese
> Caesar
> Lite Blue Cheese
> Ranch
> Roquefort
> Seafood Sauce
> Tartar Sauce
> Thousand Island

> **The Big Boy Is Big in Japan**
> Big Boy Japan owns and operates more then 216 locations under four different names: Big Boy, Victoria Station, Grill Dan, and Milky Way.

operations and facilities.

In the 1960s and '70s, the Big Boy statues became a part of the memories of many high schoolers. When the Norco, California, location opened, Big Boy made a statue to reflect the "Horsetown USA" motto, with Bob dressed in a cowboy hat. Many of the statues were stolen as high school pranks and placed on top of gymnasiums or in other places. Owners started cementing them down or placing heavy sand into them to make them too heavy for a group of football players to lift.

Johnie's Broiler in Downey, California, a Bob's-style diner and drive-thru dating to 1958, was demolished by fire in 2007. Bob's took it over, renamed it Bob's Big Boy Broiler, and rebuilt it based on the initial floor plan, and today it features carhop service, a drive-thru, and an original neon sign. The historical landmark is a perfect example of Googie architecture and is a regular spot for filming TV shows, music videos, and movies.

After opening twenty-two Big Boy restaurants and franchising hundreds of others, Wian sold the business to Marriott, which in turn, over the years, turned the restaurants into other brands. In his later years, he moved his family to an 800-acre ranch in Valyermo, about thirty miles southeast of Palmdale, California. An avid hunter, rancher, and yachtsman, Wian passed away in 1992.

The Big Boy lives on in Toluca Lake!

Bob's Pantry (Big Boy Restaurants)

CAPITOL RECORDS

Du-par's
RESTAURANT

Breakfast ALL HOURS

BURGER

Du-par's

1718

Du-par's Farm House

NAME BECAME: Du-par's Pies
NAME TODAY: Du-par's
ORIGINAL LOCATION: 6333 West 3rd Street, Los Angeles

OPENED: 1938
COFOUNDERS: James Dunn & Edward Parsons
CURRENT OWNERS: Pacific Southwest Restaurants, LLC

Only the original, plus a franchisee in the Suncoast Casino in Las Vegas, remain in operation.

dupars.net

FOUR YEARS AFTER the Original Farmers Market in Los Angeles opened with stalls that sold fresh produce, James Dunn and Edward Parsons put together the first few letters of their last names and opened a restaurant: Du-par's Farm House. With only seven employees, including the cooks and bakers, Du-par's soon became known for first-rate food, including such comforting dishes as split-pea soup, pancakes, french toast, fruit pies, and—especially in those early days—meat pies. Regulars adored the Chicken Pie, "Old English" Beef Steak Pie, and Beef Steak and Kidney Pie, each made with fresh peas, carrots, celery, and potatoes. You could eat them in the restaurant or take them home frozen and bake them later.

Breakfast was also a big draw, just as it is today. The buttermilk hotcakes, served with boysenberry or maple syrup, have been the house staple since opening day in 1938. The recipe has always been locked up—to this day, only four people know it. As for the acclaimed boysenberry syrup, it has its own origin story: The kitchen used to make so many boysenberry pies that it had a huge amount of leftover berry juice that the cooks felt bad about wasting. So they thickened it with cornstarch, added a little sugar, and turned it into pancake syrup.

During the war years, manufacturing of pie tins ceased because the metal was needed for making military supplies. To retrieve the 408 tins that had gone home with takeout customers,

Farmers Market Capacity
1938: 12 stools; 12 customers
1939: 22 stools; 22 customers
1940: 22 stools; 9 booths; 58 customers
1958: 22 stools; 22 booths; 110 customers

Left: Hollywood location • Right: At Farmers Market

Du-par's told its customers to bring them back in and they'd get a small payment. To make light of the situation, it jokingly said that Los Angeles councilman Dave Stannard was holding out four pie tins. He was coming up for reelection, and Du-par's needed his tins back. Sadly, Stannard lost his reelection bid and never returned his tins.

The partners opened a Hollywood location in the early 1940s and another in Studio City in 1948. They did not approve of the common commissary system of running chain restaurants, in which the basic preparation is done in one place and shipped out to locations. They believed that each restaurant gained strength and pride from accomplishing the entire cooking process for itself. Instead of maintaining quality by making dishes in one location, they mandated particular ingredients and standardized the recipes, which is why a Du-par's chicken pot pie tastes the same today as it did decades ago.

> **Du-Par's Locations Through the Years**
> Farmers Market, 3rd and Fairfax, Los Angeles (still in operation)
> 214 South Lake Street, Pasadena
> 5601 Wilshire Boulevard, Los Angeles
> 1718 Vine Street, Hollywood
> Imperial Boulevard and Crenshaw Avenue, Inglewood
> 12036 Ventura Boulevard, Studio City
> 16650 Ventura Boulevard, Encino
> 55 Freeway and 17th Street, Tustin
> 401 Brand Avenue, Glendale
> 6411 Sepulveda Boulevard, Van Nuys
> 33 West Thousand Oaks Boulevard, Thousand Oaks
> 400 J Street, San Diego

In 1968, Dunn and Parsons sold the nine Southern California restaurants—a few of which had cocktail lounges and a few of which were open twenty-four hours—to the Hyatt Corporation, but they continued to run them; when they retired in the mid-1970s, their general manager, Herb Oberst, stepped up. After a while, Hyatt decided to focus on its hotels and sold the remaining Du-par's restaurants to the Oberst family. When Herb died in 1994, his daughter, Shirley Kauffman, took the helm.

For a short-lived venture, Du-par's expanded into the San Diego and Oxnard areas by purchasing four bankrupt Bakers Square locations. Converting them into Du-par's didn't improve business,

The staff at a Du-Par's

> **Las Vegas Locations**
> + Golden Gate Casino, Las Vegas
> + Suncoast Hotel and Casino, Las Vegas (still in operation)

When air-conditioning was a big deal—a San Fernando Valley location

so eventually they all closed. In 2010, Du-par's ventured into Las Vegas by opening branches inside two casinos. After seven years, they closed one, and the other licensed the name and recipes.

With business gradually dwindling, the Oberst family finally sold the remaining three locations—Farmers Market, Studio City, and Pasadena—to Biff Naylor, who had been in the restaurant business for years and whose father had founded Tiny Naylor's. Naylor closed all three locations for a month to remodel and hire new staff. All employees had to reapply for their positions. The Original Farmers Market location stayed closed for even longer, to much dismay. Rumors circulated that it was going to close permanently, but the remodel just took longer than expected, and Biff's daughter, Jennifer, an accomplished chef, brought it back to new life. The Studio City location, alas, closed when its lease expired in 2017 (it's now a Sephora), and in 2018, the Naylor family sold the remaining two restaurants. The COVID-19 pandemic killed the Pasadena location in 2020, but at this writing, the original remains the cornerstone of Farmers Market, still making the best buttermilk pancakes with boysenberry syrup in Los Angeles.

Behind the counter and ready to cook

> **Former Bakers Square Locations**
> + Granada Hills
> + Oxnard
> + San Diego (Midway District)
> + San Diego (Gaslamp Quarter)

Lawry's the Prime Rib

ORIGINAL LOCATION: 150 North La Cienega Boulevard, Beverly Hills

OPENED: June 15, 1938
Still on the same property, although the address is now 100 North La Cienega Boulevard

COFOUNDERS: Lawrence L. Frank, aka "Mr. Lawry," and Walter Van de Kamp

OWNED BY: Lawry's Restaurants Inc.

There are a total of 10 Lawry's locations in 6 countries.

lawrysonline.com

Lawrence L. Frank (left) and Walter Van de Kamp

AFTER THEIR MANY SUCCESSES with the Van de Kamp's bakeries and coffee shops (page 15) and the stand-alone Tam O'Shanter restaurant, Lawrence Frank and Walter Van de Kamp (brother of Van de Kamp's cofounder Ted Van de Kamp, page 15) turned their attention in the late 1930s to a new restaurant concept. Frank wanted to open an establishment that was elegant yet appealing to all, built around a menu that showcased the amazing standing ribs of beef served on Sundays in his boyhood home. The partners chose La Cienega Boulevard to locate their restaurant, as it was between the westside and downtown. (La Cienega soon became the first "Restaurant Row" in the country, and today Lawry's is sometimes called the King of Restaurant Row, since it was one of the first on the street and has been operating there the longest.)

For three months, Frank tested various seasoning combinations with his prime rib, settling on a mix of seventeen herbs and spices. This concoction became Lawry's Seasoned Salt, still a staple in American supermarkets. He started with seven-rib roasts, aging them and then cooking them according to a 200-year-old English method—by encasing them in rock salt to distribute the heat evenly and retain the juices. This was the only main course offered, and to give his meat its due attention, he decided to have it carved tableside with flair.

Using the English Sheffield roast beef cart (a metal tray and folding lid on a four-legged walnut-wood base) as his inspiration, Frank designed a majestic 900-pound domed stainless steel cart with room for several standing ribs, au jus, and side dishes. Unquestionably the largest of its kind ever built, the Blimp (its nickname in the early days) had sleek lines that exemplified the art deco style of the 1930s. One Blimp

Left: Nurse or waitress?
Right: The Tam O'Shanter on Los Feliz Boulevard

Lawry's the Prime Rib

Ready to carve

required 740 person-hours to assemble and cost as much as a new Cadillac—and that's still true today. Today's carts are exactly the same as the originals, except the small drawer that once housed charcoal to heat the water beneath the warming pan now holds a canned heat product. They're so heavy that the floors at most locations have to be reinforced to be able to handle the weight.

In 1992, after fifty-four years of service, the carts in Beverly Hills were rebuilt, but many still have their original handles, casters, and domes. All locations have their own carts, the newer of which are made in Las Vegas using modern fabrication techniques: Single stainless steel pieces are cut, bent to shape, welded, ground, and polished, while the aluminum wheels and handles are cast in proprietary molds.

One to two hours before the restaurant doors open, the cart's water bath is filled and electrically heated to close to boiling. Fifteen or twenty minutes before service, the heater is unplugged and the cooking fuel is put in place. Only then does each carver, adorned in a starched white chef's jacket with a toque and white apron, stock the cart with prime rib roasts, au jus, gravy, mashed potatoes, creamed spinach, and creamed corn, all of which are resupplied throughout the night. Finally, the carvers sharpen their knives, and it's show time.

It takes six months of training to become a carver for Lawry's. A new carver is inducted into the Royal Order of Carvers and given a medallion worn proudly around his or her neck. Today both

---

Frank/Van de Kamp Restaurants

Tam O'Shanter ♦ 1922–present: Los Angeles
Stears for Steaks ♦ Early 1950s–early 1970s: Beverly Hills
Richlor's (later became Mediterrania) ♦ 1942–early 1960s: Beverly Hills
Lawry's California Center ♦ 1953–1992: Los Angeles
Mediterrania (formerly Richlor's) ♦ Early 1960s–mid-1970s: Beverly Hills
Five Crowns ♦ 1965–present: Corona del Mar
The Ben Jonson ♦ Late 1960s–late 1970s: San Francisco
Tonio's (three locations) ♦ Late 1960s–late 1970s: Pasadena and Newport Beach
Casey's (still in operation; sold in 1978) ♦ Late 1960s–present: Los Angeles

men and women work as carvers, but in the early days, men were the carvers and women were the servers. (Lawry's was one of the first fine-dining restaurants to hire women as servers.) The server uniform was similar to that used by the former Harvey House chain: a brown dress with a white collar, a starched white apron, and a hat.

Lawry's was one of the first establishments to offer valet service. After your car is whisked away, you enter the reception area and are greeted by a smiling host or hostess, and then a uniformed server leads you to your leather booth. The aisles are unusually wide—not just because of the Blimps, but also so your server can pull your table out for you to get into the booth without having to awkwardly scuttle over. Today's meals start the same way they did in 1930, with the famous spinning salad bowl. Your server brings out a bowl filled with iceberg,

Showtime with the salad spinner

romaine, endive, watercress, shoestring beets, and chopped hard-cooked eggs, sets it in a larger bowl filled with crushed ice, adds Lawry's sherry dressing, and spins the bowl on the ice to mix it. You're then offered a chilled fork. To be served a green salad instead of a Jell-O type was unheard of back in the '30s. If you order a baked potato, your server will also prepare it tableside, adding whatever combination of butter, chives, sour cream, and freshly crumbled bacon bits that you desire.

When World War II came, rationing impacted meat supplies. In early April of 1943, Lawry's took out a half-page ad in the *Los Angeles Times* announcing a temporary closure: "We regret our inability to continue serving prime rib of beef, for which this establishment has become so widely and favorably known." They were getting enough beef to be open only three weekdays per month. Two weeks later, Lawry's reopened to serve "prime" turkey with all the trimmings, featuring grand birds that were the finest raised in the country. Prime rib returned to the menu in the latter part of 1945, and turkey made a return engagement every Thanksgiving.

Two years after the war ended, Lawry's moved across the street, to 55 North La Cienega, into a new building designed by Wayne McAllister. It was a bold, modern building made of brick and stone, complete with a porte cochere under which patrons could wait while the valet retrieved their cars. Eleven years later, in 1958, architect Savo M. Stoshitch and contractor Donald Shaw redesigned the building by extending the porte cochere into

Lawry's Prime Rib Cuts
+ California Cut ~ for lighter appetites
+ English Cut ~ Three thin slices
+ Lawry's Cut ~ Traditional and most popular
+ Diamond Jim Brady Cut ~ Extra-thick portion, rib bone-in
+ Beef Bowl Cut ~ Rib bone-in

a cantilevered roof and enclosing the windows that faced the street. In 1993, Lawry's headed back across La Cienega, into a completely new building on the land that had housed the original 1938 space. With a press event like no other, the entire staff, all dressed in their uniforms and looking very sharp, stopped traffic on the boulevard as they rolled their Blimps back home for good.

By then, a new company had evolved: Lawry's Foods, Inc., makers of specialty food products that were sold at grocery stores in the United States and overseas, including the famous Seasoned Salt. (In 1959, world-famous graphic designer Saul Bass created the "Fanciful L" logo that is still used on the salt bottles today.) Guests often asked for the recipes for the dressings and dips, so Lawry's spent two years perfecting a dip mix for home cooks, and that was a hit at grocery stores. Frank sold this division to Lipton/Unilever in 1979, which sold it a second time, in 2008, to spice company McCormick & Company, which still owns it. The restaurants keep the Seasoned Salt on their tables to this day, even though McCormick owns the brand now.

The original location in 1938

A yearly tradition began in 1956, just before the 1957 Rose Bowl game between the Oregon State and Iowa State football teams. Lawry's served the Oregon players at the Beverly Hills restaurant and the Iowa players in Pasadena after they'd practiced at Pasadena City College. It has become known as the Lawry's Beef Bowl; today, the Dallas location feeds the Cotton Bowl players.

Other than during the war years, prime rib was the only main course for decades. Finally, in 1994, Lawry's added poultry and seafood (including lobster tails) to the menu. You could now order a lobster tail and make your dinner surf and turf. As the international markets opened up in the mid-'90s, Lawry's created menu items to reflect the tastes in their new regions. Some of the dishes that are not served in the US locations include garlic rice, clam chowder, pork ribs, lamb, and various appetizers that appeal to local tastes.

Essential to any meal is the only dessert that is finished tableside: a C.C. Brown's hot fudge sundae. Early in the twentieth century, a downtown L.A. candy merchant named Clarence Clifton Brown created a hot fudge sauce that would not harden when poured onto cold ice cream, thereby inventing the hot fudge sundae. In 1924,

Lawry's Locations and Dates of Operation:

1938–present:	Beverly Hills
1974–2020:	Chicago
1983–present:	Dallas
1996–2005	Jakarta
1997–present:	Las Vegas
1999–present:	Singapore
2001–present:	Tokyo
2002–present:	Taipei
2006–present:	Hong Kong
2008–2011:	Shanghai
2008–present:	Osaka
2013–present:	Seoul

Lawry's Carvery
2002–present:	Costa Mesa
2007–2019:	Los Angeles

Lawry's goes modern in 1947

the Browns moved the business from downtown to Hollywood Boulevard. It became the famous ice cream parlor that stars knew and loved. The Browns sold it to the Schumacher family in 1963, who closed the business in 1993 to the great anguish of many Angelenos. Thankfully, however, Lawry's purchased the rights and recipes for the historic fudge sauce, and today the C.C. Brown's hot fudge sundae is the top-selling dessert at Lawry's in Beverly Hills. Made with vanilla ice cream from acclaimed local creamery Fosselman's, the sundae is prepared tableside with a pitcher of hot fudge, toasted almonds, and freshly whipped cream. You can also purchase jars at the hostess desk in the Southern California locations. In 2015 alone, they served more than sixty-three sundaes per day.

Not long ago, Lawry's spent six months on a complete makeover of the La Cienega location, lightening and modernizing the interior. Kit Scarbo, a costume designer for actors and musicians, replaced the iconic "brown gowns" worn by the female servers with new uniforms that look more like something a midcentury dinner party hostess might wear instead of a Colonial maid. To further keep with the times, the chef added lighter, seasonal side dishes and more vegetarian options, including grilled broccoli rabe and cauliflower steaks. Prime rib, however, remains the star.

Today, new generations of the Frank and Van de Kamp families are continuing down the path the company began nearly a century ago. Representing the third generation are Richard Frank, CEO; Susan Frank, director of design and archival images; and Nick Ward, staff accountant. The fourth generation includes Ryan O'Melveny Wilson, chief marketing and strategy officer and great-grandson of founder Lawrence Frank. Who says Los Angeles has no history?

A full crew outside today's La Cienega location

Pink's Hot Dogs

ORIGINAL LOCATION: 709 North La Brea Avenue (at Melrose), Los Angeles

OPENED: November 8, 1939
FOUNDERS: Paul & Betty Pink
CURRENT OWNERS: Pink's Hot Dogs, Inc.

There are 15 locations in 5 states throughout the United States and in the Philippines, all licensed.

pinkshollywood.com

IT STARTED WITH a modest food cart. While Paul and Betty Pink were looking through the *Hollywood Citizen News* classifieds in 1939, Betty came across an advertisement for a hot dog cart for sale for $50. With a loan from her mother, Betty bought the cart on La Cienega Boulevard and walked it all the way to a vacant dirt lot at La Brea and Melrose, next to an Atlantic Richfield gas station. She knew that the cars filling up would be able to see the stand from there. For the next two

Opposite: Pink's in the pandemic • Above: The original stand in 1939

Pink's Hot Dogs

years, Betty rented the lot for $15 a month, but in 1941 the landlord doubled the rent. So with a loan from Bank of America for $4,000, she and Paul purchased the lot—a major step forward in growing their business, especially since it was large enough for the stand to provide curbside service. Preparing a hot dog was fast: They were steamed and ready to serve, so Betty or Paul just had to dress the dog the way the customer wanted.

Top 3 Dogs
Chili Cheese Dog (aka the Brando Dog) ▲
Philly Cheesesteak Dog
Giada De Laurentiis Dog

Hoffy has supplied the dogs with the "snap" casing since the very first day. When Pink's opened, the hot dogs sold for 10¢ and a Coke was 5¢. The site did not have electricity, so Paul and Betty plugged into a nearby hardware store, which allowed it as long as the couple purchased the necessary 200-foot-long extension cord from their store. Once they owned the lot, expansion was in order. They put a canvas awning over the cart and added a shed for storage. In 1946, they constructed a complete building with a dining room and patio to seat eighty—the same building you see today. Not one day of business was lost during construction.

Paul and Betty were raising two children, Richard and Beverly, so they had to look for other sources of income besides the stand. Betty had learned the art of flower arranging from her florist brother, so she decided to build a flower shop on the north side of the property in 1958 so she could be close to the stand, and her business thrived for ten years. The building remains on the property today and is rented out to an antiques dealer. Many weekend nights, the line for Pink's wraps past the antiques shop.

Both Paul and Betty were active in the oversight of the business until their passing: Betty at the age of eighty-three in 1993, and Paul in 1996 at age eighty-eight.

After Richard Pink completed his undergraduate education at UCLA, followed by an MBA at USC and a law degree from Loyola, it was time for the next generation to take over Pink's. The older generation of Pink's had turned down many opportunities to franchise, and Richard also felt that they'd lose control of the quality and pricing if they franchised. Instead, he set up a plan for licensees rather than franchisees, with a strict agreement regarding the use of products and cooking proce-

After the 1946 remodel

Betty & Paul Pink

dures. To this day, all US licensees must purchase the products listed on the spec sheets from the same L.A.-area suppliers that the original Pink's buys from; locations in the Philippines receive supplies manufactured in that country according to rigid guidelines. Pink's also controls its licensees' quality through annual training, by using mystery shoppers (customers who are actually management spies), and by following social media reviews. Furthermore, its succession plan ensures that future management will have extensive restaurant experience and a passion for excellence.

Perhaps the most notable Pink's creation is its chili, a secret recipe. Of course, so many L.A.-founded stands are known for their chili, including Der Wienerschnitzel (page 219), Tommy's (page 103), and Cupid's (page 111), but Pink's chili doesn't taste like anyone else's. Richard says it's all about the balance of sweetness and spice, as well as making it smooth yet sturdy enough to be ladled atop a hot dog.

In 1998, Richard, his wife, Gloria, and his sister, Beverly, wanted to make a big splash for the sixtieth anniversary of Pink's, so they marketed the occasion like the launch of a feature film. Pink's sits at the epicenter of Hollywood, with Paramount, CBS Television City, and many production facilities surrounding it. They invited celebrities to work behind the counter, encouraged them to hang their 8x10 glossies in the dining room, named some dogs and burgers for stars, and gave all profits from the celebration to charity. The lines started early, and people waited many hours to get in. The stunt paid off big-time, making Pink's a top tourist destination in L.A. and growing its reputation internationally.

Many TV shows started to film scenes at the little stand, from *California's Gold* to *The Martha Stewart Show*. When Rosie O'Donnell was filming close by, she ordered hot dogs for the cast and crew. When Jay Leno filmed a skit at Pink's for *The Tonight Show*, he had the band members of Aerosmith play the cooks. Bruce Willis reportedly proposed to Demi Moore at Pink's. First Lady Michelle Obama, her daughters, and her mom stopped by for a tasty lunch on a warm June day in 2010. Some of the other movies and TV shows filmed there include *Glee*, *L.A. Law*, *Mulholland Drive*, *The Boost*, *The Golden Child*, *Luther*, *Ray Donovan*, and *My Dinner with Hervé*.

Orson Welles consumed eighteen chili dogs in one sitting in 1970. Since Welles dined at the stand at least twice a week, Pink's never wanted anyone to challenge his record, so they've never held a hot dog–eating contest.

Retired Dogs
Hulk Dog
Robin and Batman Dog
Wendy Williams Dog
David Hasselhoff Dog

Pink's Hot Dogs

A typical line of hot dog lovers wraps past Betty's former flower shop

Special Dogs:
- **Three Dog Night:** Three dogs wrapped in a tortilla with cheese, bacon, and chili
- **Rosie O'Donnell Long Island Dog:** Stretch dog, mustard, onions, chili, and sauerkraut
- **Martha Stewart Dog:** Nine-inch stretch dog, relish, onions, bacon, tomatoes, sauerkraut, and sour cream
- **Ozzy Spicy Dog:** Spicy Polish dog, nacho cheese, American cheese, grilled onions, guacamole, and tomatoes
- **Emeril Legasse Bam Dog:** Nine-inch stretch dog, mustard, onions, cheese, jalapeño, bacon, and coleslaw
- **Giada De Laurentiis Dog:** Nine-inch stretch dog, sautéed peppers, onions, mushrooms, tomatoes, and mozzarella cheese
- **The Brando Dog:** Nine-inch stretch dog, mustard, onions, chili, and shredded cheddar cheese
- **Lord of the Rings Dog:** Nine-inch stretch dog, BBQ sauce, topped with onion rings
- **Carl Reiner Dog:** Nine-inch stretch dog, topped with mustard and sauerkraut
- **Patt Morrison Baja Vegan Dog:** Guacamole, chopped tomatoes, and onions
- **Huell Howser Dog:** Two hot dogs in one bun, mustard, chili, cheese, and onions

At this writing, Pink's sells twenty-nine types of hot dogs and twelve varieties of hamburgers, along with french fries, chips, sausages, onion rings, two types of cakes, and an array of beverages. The hot dog is all beef with a natural casing, and the popular stretch varieties feature nine-inch-long weiners. The secret to the success of Pink's is threefold: 1. A consistent quality product; customers want to taste the same dog they remember from the first time they ate one, which is why the chili recipe and the hot dog supplier never change. 2. Value; if customers walk away feeling that they got what they paid for, they'll be back. 3. Good service and atmosphere; most of the thirty employees have been with Pink's for twenty-five to thirty years.

> **That's a Lot of Hot Dogs!**
> **Hot Dogs Served**
> Weekdays: 1,200
> Weekend days: 2,000
> Per year for the past 15 years: 547,000
> Since opening 70 years ago: Approximately 16 million
> Hamburgers sold per day: 200 to 300
>
> **Sold Per Year**
> 152,880 pounds of french fries
> 65,520 pounds of chili
> 146,000 Polish dogs
> 312,000 pounds of bacon
> 10,092 pounds of sauerkraut

Waiting in a line that extends down the street is part of the Pink's experience. The anticipation is half the fun, as is the camaraderie of the crowd waiting. And if your visit happens to coincide with a Dodgers home game, plenty of customers will be dressed in Dodger blue.

In September 2018, the city of Los Angeles dedicated the intersection of La Brea and Melrose as Pink's Square, installing special light poles, signs, and a historical plaque. City Council members and the Pink family were on hand to cut the (of course) pink ribbon. Pink's may have been in L.A. since 1938, but it has only just begun.

Current owners Gloria & Richard Pink & Beverly (Pink) Wolfe

McDonald's Barbeque

ORIGINAL SLOGANS: "Speedee Service"; "Buy 'em by the Bag"
NAME TODAY: McDonald's
ORIGINAL LOCATION: 1398 North E Street (at 14th Street), San Bernardino

OPENED: May 15, 1940
COFOUNDERS: Richard "Dick" McDonald & Maurice "Mac" McDonald
CURRENTLY AT THE FIRST LOCATION: McDonald's unofficial museum and offices of Juan Pollo Restaurants

The oldest operating McDonald's is in Downey; it opened in 1953 and was the third one opened and the second franchised by the McDonald brothers. Today there are more than 34,000 outlets in 188 countries around the globe, serving 145 menu items.

mcdonalds.com

THE MCDONALD BROTHERS, Richard (Dick) and Maurice (Mac), grew up in Manchester, New Hampshire, at a time when jobs were scarce everywhere, but particularly in New Hampshire. They worked hard at a shoe factory until Mac lost his job at the age of thirty-one. The only other type of work to be found was in the lumber mills. Through the help of a friend who was a Hollywood police officer, the brothers decided to come out west and work in the up-and-coming movie industry. The year was 1931, and the brothers were like twins, working together as a crew in Hollywood, doing everything from driving trucks to building sets.

The McDonald brothers

After a few years, the pair purchased the Mission Theater, a movie theater in Glendale, and soon changed the name to the Beacon. It thrived for only a handful of years. When it began losing money and the bank wanted to be paid, the brothers decided to take a leap into the food business. In 1937, they opened a food stand, the Wigwam, on Foothill Boulevard in Arcadia, selling hot dogs, potato chips, and orange juice. Citrus was abundant in the San Gabriel Valley, and the brothers had become friends with the owners of Sunkist Citrus Packers. Many of the oranges that had blemishes and imperfections could not be sold as the perfect Sunkist orange, so the brothers made a deal to take the oranges off their hands—low-cost oranges meant high profits.

First Locations
- San Bernardino ~ Owned by the McDonald brothers
- Phoenix ~ Owned by Neil Fox
- Downey ~ Owned by Roger Williams and Burdette Candon

Top left: The first location • **Bottom left:** An early branch

McDonald's

> **These "Big Five" Account for 25 Percent of All Sales**
> Big Mac
> Quarter Pounder
> Chicken McNuggets
> French Fries
> Egg McMuffin

Date night in 1949

Also in 1937, their father, Patrick, opened the Airdrome, a hexagon-shaped food stand near the Monrovia airport. In 1940, the brothers moved their father's building east, to E Street in San Bernardino, and opened a drive-in featuring an exposed kitchen and outdoor-only seating. The area was booming with the citrus industry and high school kids. The drive-in menu had twenty-five items, including hamburgers, hot dogs, and pulled-pork sandwiches with a list of options. A shake, fries, and a burger were a favorite of the car crowd. Keeping the prices down by selling large quantities was the focus of the brothers's strategy. They also found another use for their usherette uniforms from the Beacon Theater, repurposing them as uniforms for the carhops. It became obvious to the brothers that the carhops were distracted with attention from the fry cooks and the guys in the cars. When young women applied for a carhop job, the McDonalds would inform them not to fill out the application if they weren't willing to work weekend evenings. Many left on the spot.

The parking lot was often packed with teens staying in their cars and cruising for hours on end. Many customers left because the service was so slow. After realizing that their best-selling items were burgers and shakes, the McDonald brothers closed for three months in 1948 to focus on retooling. They put up a sign that proclaimed, "Drive-in Hamburger Bar. The First One in America. Reopening Soon!"

The first thing they did was stop using carhops. To get your food, the carhop had to bring you a menu, leave, come back, and take your order. If you weren't ready, they had to leave again, return for the order, take it to the fry cook, pick it up, deliver it, then return again to take away the dirty dishes. It was a lot of work for a small tab, and each car would take up a spot for over an hour. The new system made people get out of their cars and order at a walk-up window. For the first couple of months, customers would sit outside and honk, thinking that a carhop would appear. After the third month, Dick said to Mac, "I think we've made a mistake." Just as they were about to bring back the carhops, people started getting it.

The brothers also reinvented everything around the food.

> **Famous People Who Once Worked at a McDonald's**
> James Franco
> Mark Hamill
> Sharon Stone
> Jeff Bezos
> Macy Gray
> Pink
> Seal
> Shania Twain
> Jay Leno
> Willard Scott

Product Launches and Dates

1968: Fried Apple Pie
1973: Quarter Pounder
1975: Egg McMuffin
1977: Full Breakfast
1978: Ice Cream Sundae (Hot Fudge, Strawberry, Caramel)
1979: Happy Meal
1980: McChicken Sandwich
1981: McRib
1982: Deluxe Breakfast
1983: Chicken McNuggets
1986: McPizza
1987: Fresh Salads
1988: Cheddar Melt
1989: McSpaghetti
1992: Baked Apple Pie
1993: McCafé
       McValue Menu Launch
1995: McFlurry Dessert
1997: The Big 'N Tasty
2000: Fruit 'N Yogurt Parfait

First, they shortened the menu to nine of the most popular items, aiming to sell mass quantities of just a few things. They stopped using ceramic dishes and silverware and started wrapping burgers in little paper bags and putting each meal into a larger bag—an innovation at the time. Now they could eliminate the dishwashers, too. All this brought down the operating costs, so they could price hamburgers at just 15¢. The malts (three flavors) were the high-cost item, at 20¢.

One day, Dick went to L.A. to check out a candy factory, claiming to be writing a story on candy-making practices. He wanted to see how one of his favorite candies, the mint patty, was made. The candy maker demonstrated how the creamy mint filling was put in a funnel with a wooden plunger that dispensed the exact amount needed. That's what he was really looking for: a machine to deposit equal amounts of mustard and ketchup in a single action. He called on another set of brothers, Florian and Edward Toman of Toman's Machine Shop, who filed patent number 2,599,955 in 1950 for a mustard and ketchup dispenser. To turn out burgers even faster, the McDonalds skipped lettuce and tomatoes and used only a small amount of chopped onions. To promote these made-in-minutes burgers, they created a mascot, "Speedee," showcased in neon signs to advertise the "Speedee Service System." You could not get a faster meal anywhere.

In the early 1950s, Dick knew he needed to create an iconic building if they were going to franchise. In 1953, he took his ideas to architects Stanley Clark Meston and Charles Fish to help him come up with a prototype that focused on seeing the action, like a fishbowl. They came up with a roof that slanted upward, inviting you to the take-out windows underneath and to the large yellow arches illuminating the night sky and to the rows of red and white tiles around the building. Windows gave views of the cooks, dressed in clean white uniforms, grilling and dressing the burgers in a tightly orchestrated assembly line. Dick also had a sign created with changeable numbers to boast how many burgers had been sold. It didn't take too long for the number to be in the millions; later it was stated in billions. Finally, it just became "billions and billions served."

"Speedee"

The McDonald brothers landed on the cover of the September 1952 issue of *American Restaurant Magazine*. This brought people out from all over to see for themselves what their "Speedee Service" motto actually meant. They started franchising their system and iconic building design, expanding to six locations in less than two years. The cost: a one-time fee of $2,500. This included the plans for a building, the detailed "Speedee Service" method, training at the San Bernardino location, a list of equipment needs, and permission to use the name. The brothers soon saw competitors trying to copy their system and likeness, so they speeded up the franchise effort, hiring Bill Tansey to lead it. Within a few years, he'd sold about twenty-five franchises before retiring due to health issues.

Ray Kroc and his wife, Ethel, lived on a quiet, tree-lined street in Oak Park, Illinois. Kroc sold the Multimixer, which could blend four malts or shakes directly into a paper cup at the same time, reducing the prep time for four shakes to less than a minute. Kroc went from soda fountains to burger joints, showing the owners how his mixer could change their business. Little did he think that a trip to San Bernardino in 1954 would change his life—and the fast-food industry.

The McDonalds had bought several Multimixers, and Kroc wanted to see their operation for

Running a tight ship in the early days

Iconic Menu Items and Who Created Them
1962: Filet-O-Fish Sandwich   Lou Groen ~ Cincinnati, OH
1967: Big Mac Sandwich   Jim Delligatti ~ Uniontown, PA
1968: Fried Apple Pie   Litton Cochran ~ Knoxville, TN
1972: McMuffin Sandwich   Herb Peterson ~ Santa Barbara, CA
1977: Happy Meal   Robert Bernstein ~ Corporate Headquarters
1983: Chicken McNuggets   Chef Rene Arend ~ Corporate Headquarters
1995: McFlurry Dessert   Ron McLennan ~ Bathhurst, New Brunswick, Canada

himself. In San Bernardino, he watched more than 100 patrons order burgers and fries that were prepared faster than he'd ever seen. When he got home, he called the brothers and said he'd heard their sales manager and franchising agent had left, and he wanted the job. He saw that his biggest customers, drug store ice cream/soda fountains, were closing and his sales would suffer. They hired him as the new franchise agent, mandating that all products had to stay the same price—only the brothers could change pricing—and all nine products had to be offered at all locations. Kroc came up with fees for the franchisees:

> • According to the Big Mac index in *The Economist*, at this writing the most expensive Big Mac is in Switzerland, at $7.29, and the cheapest is in Lebanon, at $1.77, with the US at $5.66.
> • One in 8 Americans has worked at a McDonald's.

$1,900 for the franchise, plus 1.9 percent of gross sales, with the McDonalds getting .5 percent of that and Kroc getting the rest as his compensation.

Though Kroc felt that the brothers had too much control of the company, he sold a lot of franchises. When the McDonald brothers began to think about selling their business, they realized that Kroc had been telling the media and franchisees that he was the founder of the company, and the relationship grew tense. They told him he could buy them out for $3 million cash, and he ended up buying it for $2.7 million. To raise the money, he asked for help from Princeton, Swarthmore College, Howard University, and the Ford Foundation. Dick McDonald felt that the company would expand in the future, so he bought corporate stock as soon as it became available. That became his nest egg.

In later years, the locations would have a plaque installed that reads:

In 1955, Ray A. Kroc established the McDonald's System with the highest standards of quality, service, cleanliness, and value. His vision persisted and leadership has guided McDonald's from one location in Des Plaines, Illinois to the World's Community restaurant.

It's easy to see why people would think that Kroc started the company. He renamed his first restaurant McDonald's #1, some 2,000 miles away from the first location opened by the McDonald brothers. Over the next five years, Kroc created a chain of 228 restaurants. The company honored him yearly on their Founder's Day and did not include the McDonald brothers until after Mac passed away in 1991. Kroc, in his 1992 autobiography, *Grinding It Out: The Making of McDonald's*, claimed the first McDonald's restaurant was located in Des Plaines, Illinois.

One problem the brothers encountered after selling was that their original location in San Bernardino (not part of the sale to Kroc) was not allowed to be called McDonald's anymore. They changed the restaurant's name to the Big D. Soon afterward, Kroc placed a McDonald's down the street from the Big D, a competitive move that the McDonald brothers did not appreciate.

There's been a lot of confusion over which McDonald's building was "the first." One of the contenders was actually the third location, opened by a franchisee in Downey in August 1953. In 1990, McDonald's bought the building from the original franchisees but closed it after it was damaged in the Northridge earthquake in 1994; later, a new drive-thru-only location opened half a mile down the street. They sold the land under that original location to Pep Boys, which was next door and hoped to expand. Both the Downey Conservancy and the Los Angeles Conservancy put up a fight to save the little burger joint, trying to get McDonald's to reopen it, but the company said it had been losing more than $50,000 a year just trying to keep it open—probably in part because it only served the original nine menu items instead of the 145 on today's rosters. After huge efforts and protests, a

The golden arches in Downey—the last location to use this architectural design

deal was struck to save the building, which still operates to this day. A discreet drive-thru was added to the rear of the building, but from the front, it looks just like it did in 1953.

Kroc started a major advertising campaign in the early 1960s with the slogan, "Look for the Golden Arches." Keeping prices down throughout the 1960s also brought the "Real Good and Still Only 15¢" campaign. In 1969, "Change from Your Dollar" was popular when the United States was going through a recession, and two regular burgers, french fries, and a drink were offered for under a dollar. From 1971 to 1975, the whole world saw the "You Deserve a Break Today" ad campaign.

Ronald McDonald first appeared in 1963 as the mascot. Trying to appeal to kids, the company developed him as a friendly clown to appear at store openings, in TV ads, and at children's hospitals. Ronald lived in McDonaldland where he had adventures with his pals, Mayor McCheese, Grimace, Captain Crook, the Professor, the Fry Kids, Officer BigMac, the Hamburglar, and Birdie the Early Bird. The characters inspired equipment in the "PlayPlaces" attached to some McDonald's.

On April 21, 1965, Kroc took the McDonald's corporation public, and since then, the stock has split twelve times. In 1980, McDonald's became one of the thirty companies that make up the Dow Jones Industrial Average.

A major change for the franchises came in 1969 with the launch of the new mansard roof design, which eventually included drive-thrus, PlayPlaces for kids, and dining rooms to sit down. The original franchises sold by the McDonald brothers were exempt from having to remodel. The drive-thru's story began in 1975 in Sierra Vista, Arizona, where a McDonald's was located close to Fort Huachuca. Military members were not permitted to get out of their vehicles off-post while wearing fatigues, so that location created a drive-thru to accommodate the soldiers. Today, 70 percent of all sales take place at a drive-thru. They have different names in different countries: McAuto in Spain and Russia; AutoMAC in Mexico, Chile, and Argentina; and McDrive in northern European countries.

In the late '70s, the former Burger Chef chain created the "Funmeal" for kids. Not to be outdone, McDonald's tasked Bob Bernstein with developing a kids' product, and he invented the Happy Meal. (Although before that, Yolanda Fernández de Cofiño, who worked with her husband operating McDonald's in Guatemala, came up with her own "Menu Ronald," offering kids a hamburger, small fries, small drink, and a small sundae.) Bernstein test-marketed his Happy Meal in Kansas City in 1977, served in a paper box with handles shaped like the Golden Arches and holding a small burger, fries, drink, cookies, and surprise gift. The Happy Meal rolled out nationwide in 1979. In 1987, Disney paired with McDonald's to provide the toy; in later years, Disney and other companies would co-brand their children's movies with McDonald's. In the mid-'90s, with the Beanie Baby craze in full force, McDonald's paired with Ty, Inc. to put miniature Beanie Babies in their Happy Meals, and they gave out more than 60 million units. McDonald's started selling the children's toys separately when they found that many people were buying the meals for the Beanie Babies and throwing away the food.

As for the food, it was all about consistency from day one. The standard hamburger/cheeseburger was called a "ten to one." This meant ten burger patties were made from one pound of meat. Making the fries—which in the early days were more like thick steak fries—consistent was challenging, but they started making suppliers prepare the potatoes to precise specifications. They had to be aged up to a week before cutting—fresh potatoes are high in water and sugar, which left fries too brown or soggy.

In primarily Catholic neighborhoods, burger sales dropped dramatically on Fridays and during Lent. Frozen fish sticks were popular in those days, so in 1962, Lou Groen, a franchise owner in Cincinnati, Ohio, created a sandwich with a wide fish stick between a bun, with cheese and a tangy tartar sauce. The Filet-O-Fish was born. A few years later, franchisee Litton Cochran in Knoxville, Tennessee, created the first dessert, the Fried Apple Pie, which went companywide in 1968. McDonald's switched to baking the pies in 1992 when it felt consumers wanted more healthful foods. That historic Downey location, however, still offers the Fried Apple Pie.

Two all-beef patties, special sauce, lettuce, cheese, pickles, and onions on a sesame seed bun were the biggest things to change the burger landscape at McDonald's. In 1967, Jim Delligatti created the larger burger that customers at his Uniontown, Pennsylvania, franchise were asking for. He owned forty-seven locations and started selling the burger at each within a few months. The next year, the entire chain rolled out the Big Mac. The company claims that roughly every seventeen seconds a Big Mac is sold somewhere in the world. (And no, Delligatti did not get paid for creating the Big Mac.)

In its first couple of decades, McDonald's was a lunch and dinner spot. Seeing potential, it tested the New York City locations to see if people would eat breakfast outside the home. Indeed they would, and the Egg McMuffin was born in 1975, created by Herb Peterson. By 1987, 25 percent of all breakfasts outside the home in America were purchased at a McDonald's. In 2015, in response to customer demand, McDonald's rolled out "Breakfast All Day."

With an array of coffee products and pastries, McCafé launched first in Australia in 1993, inspired by the coffee craze that was spreading around the world. Some global locations have placed a McCafé in the front of their restaurants, and some have opened as stand-alones.

Today, there are McDonald's in 118 countries, with menu items to accommodate many religious practices and regional tastes, from McRamadan Meals in the Middle East to McAloo Tikki Burgers made with potatoes and green peas in India. In Hong Kong, you can even celebrate your wedding with a "Happiness Party," complete with a pair of McDonald's balloon wedding rings, character gifts for the guests, and an apple pie wedding cake. What started as a burger stand in San Bernardino is now an inescapable global phenomenon.

Apple Pies ~ 6 Varieties in Each Pie
Fuji
Gala
Golden Delicious
Ida Red
Jonagold
Rome

Pie Flavors
Apple
Blueberries and Crème
Cherries and Crème
Cherry
Guava and Crème
Lemon
Mixed Berry
Peach
Peaches and Crème
Pumpkin
Pumpkin and Crème
S'More
Strawberry
Strawberry and Crème
Sweet Potato
Sweet Potato and Crème

CARL'S DRIVE IN BARBEQUE

CAR SERVICE
DINNERS

Excelsior
ICE CREAM

The Blimp

NAME BECAME: Carls Drive In Barbeque
NAME TODAY: Carl's Jr.
ORIGINAL LOCATION: Florence and Central avenues, Los Angeles
OPENED: July 17, 1941
COFOUNDERS: Carl & Margaret Karcher
CURRENT OWNER: CKE Restaurant Holdings, Inc.
CURRENTLY AT THE FIRST LOCATION: United States Postal Center

There are 3,036 locations in 43 states and 13 countries, including 1,121 Carl's Jr. brands and 1,915 Hardee's brands.

carlsjr.com

CARL KARCHER WAS BORN in Upper Sandusky, Ohio, in 1917. He had to work on his family farm, so his formal school years lasted only until he was thirteen. A few years of hard farm work during the Depression inspired Carl to pack his bags and move to Anaheim to work in his uncle Benjamin's feed and seed store, where he spent twelve-hour days. He met Margaret Heinz while working at the feed shop, and they married in 1939. By this point, he was working at Armstrong Bakery in Los Angeles, where he started as a bread wrapper and was later promoted to delivery person. While delivering breads and buns around South L.A., Carl noticed a number of hot dog carts doing great business.

His dream was to own a business, so the Karchers borrowed $311 on their 1941 Plymouth Super Deluxe and used the $15 Margaret had stashed in her purse to purchase a hot dog cart. They placed the cart in South L.A. and sold chili dogs, hot dogs, and tamales for 10¢, and sodas for 5¢. Business was good from day one—sales on the first day were $14.75—and over the next few years they opened four additional carts.

Yearning to get back to Anaheim, which was more rural and bucolic in those days, Carl and Margaret looked for property close to his uncle's feed store. On January 16, 1945, they opened Carls Drive In Barbecue at 1108 North Palm Street (now Harbor Boulevard). The restaurant had carhop service and inside full-service dining and was a favorite of high school kids and soldiers returning from the war. It was the place to be seen on the weekends. When it came time to consider expanding, the Karchers decided on a place with a limited menu and faster service. They opened Carl's Jr. in 1956, a year after Disneyland opened its gates, next to St. Boniface Catholic Church, their parish. (Today the original building is the church's Bethany Hall.) They opened a second Carl's Jr. north of Anaheim in Brea.

The original Carls Drive In

> **Firsts in the Industry**
> Salad bars
> Grilled chicken sandwiches
> Natural turkey burgers
> Angus beef burgers
> Self-service sodas
> Credit cards accepted

Left: An early employee at Carl's hot dog cart • Right: Carl (holding daughter Anne Marie) and a helper at his new stand

While other restaurants used a flat grill to cook hamburgers, Carl's Jr.'s burgers were broiled over an open flame. Customers paid at the counter and sat in the carpeted dining room, with their meals delivered "restaurant style" to their table, which featured salt and pepper shakers. Even though this was fast food, Karcher wanted the feeling to be homey.

Orange County had four Carl's by the end of the 1950s, each sporting signs with a vibrant yellow star character holding a burger on one of its star points and a soda on another. They were run by Carl's younger brother, Donald, who later became the company's president.

In 1968, Carl's Jr. (now incorporated as Carl Karcher Enterprises) started expanding. Soon came stand-alone restaurants with used-brick interiors, tiled roofs, carpeted dining rooms, and cushioned seats—all innovations in the fast-food industry. There was even music and partial dining-room service for guests. But it was still burger-joint fare: hamburgers, hot dogs, fries, and malts.

In 1975, the Karchers opened their 100th location to great fanfare, with giveaways of safety reflector kits and raffle tickets for new bicycles. Carl was always present at the various openings to cut the ribbon with local dignitaries. Carl's Jr. was one of the first burger places to open in a mall—the newly constructed, three-level Fox Hills Mall in L.A. in 1975—and in the late '70s, it launched in other western states. Las Vegas opened, and then in 1980, Arizona expansion was nonstop with four locations opening within two years.

In seven short years the California landscape was dotted with more than 100 Carl's Jr. locations. In 1976, the Karchers celebrated by breaking ground on corporate administrative headquarters only a few blocks from the first Carl's Jr. The following year, they built a new 149,000-square-foot distribution facility next to the corporate headquarters. Carl lobbied for Romneya Drive, where the headquarters sat, to be renamed Karcher Way in recognition of the contributions he and his company had made to the city. A showdown in the city council started, as the offices of Alex Foods, which made tamales, tortillas, burritos, and other Mexican foods, were on the other end of the same block. A year later,

Best-selling Burgers
The Western Bacon Cheeseburger
Famous Star (Carl Karcher's favorite)
Super Star

Made in California

Alex Foods sold, and the single block of Romneya Drive in front of Carl Karcher Enterprises was renamed West Carl Karcher Way. The only business that had to change its street name was Carl Karcher Enterprises. Today, only a Carl's Jr. is located on the street—the headquarters moved to Tennessee

Carl's Jr. was innovative. Many full-service restaurants, such as Marie Callender's (page 131) and Sizzler (page 205), had incorporated self-service salad bars into their floor plans. Carl's Jr. placed fresh salad bars in all 200 of its locations in 1977, a first in fast food. All of the locations were in California at the time, where it was easier to get year-round fresh produce.

Carl's hired its 10,000th employee in 1980, having doubled its staff in just three years. In 1981, with 300 restaurants in operation, Carl Karcher Enterprises went public, and in 1984, Carl's Jr. started franchises for the first time.

As consumer tastes changed, Carl's Jr. introduced such new high-end fast-food items as the Thickburger, made from a full half-pound of Angus beef, also known as the "Six Dollar Burger." Opening stores earlier in the day with breakfast items also boosted sales.

Don Karcher died too young, in 1992, so a new management team came in, and Carl Karcher Enterprises became a wholly owned subsidiary of CKE Restaurants, Inc. (CKE). They revitalized with a major remodeling and an image-enhancement program, and they began a dual branding campaign with Green Burrito. This was kicked off by Anne Wiles, Carl's daughter and the franchisee of a Carl's Jr. in Dana Point, California, who first opened the dual restaurant.

CKE started growing more by acquiring. The biggest was Hardee's, a huge chain with almost 2,500 locations, mostly in the Southeast and Midwest. It was the perfect fit for western-focused Carl's, and the chains borrowed from each other's strengths—Hardee's added the Angus-beef Thickburgers that had launched Carl's Jr. into the high-end burger realm, for example, and Carl's Jr. started making fresh biscuits for breakfast like Hardee's had done for years. CKE also purchased the Santa Barbara Restaurant Group, which owned the Green Burrito brand that Carl's had already been partnering with. The company moved its headquarters from Anaheim to Carpinteria, just south of Santa Barbara.

Columbia Lake Acquisition Holdings bought CKE Restaurants in 2010, and the new ownership helped keep up the innovations at both Carl's Jr. and Hardee's. They rolled out hand-breaded chicken tenders, made fresh throughout the day in each restaurant, and in 2011 began offering charbroiled turkey burgers, a first in the fast-food world.

In 2016, CKE Restaurant holdings moved its corporate headquarters out of California to Franklin, Tennessee, to consolidate the Hardee's and Carl's Jr. brands. Besides selling fast food, the company does strong community outreach, offering scholarships and charitable-giving programs.

The Carl's Jr. character was named Happy Star

Burt's / Snowbird Ice Cream

NAME BECAME: 31 Flavors
NAME TODAY: Baskin-Robbins
SNOWBIRD ICE CREAM ORIGINAL LOCATION: 1130 South Adams Boulevard, Glendale
BURT'S ICE CREAM ORIGINAL LOCATION: 561 South Lake Avenue, Pasadena
OPENED: December 7, 1945
COFOUNDERS: Burton Baskin & Irving Robbins
CURRENTLY AT BURT'S ICE CREAM ORIGINAL LOCATION: Baskin-Robbins
CURRENTLY AT SNOWBIRD ICE CREAM ORIGINAL LOCATION: Adams Kabob House
CURRENT OWNERS: Dunkin' Brands

There are 8,000 locations in 52 countries, including 2,500 in the United States.

baskinrobbins.com

IRVING (IRV) ROBBINS grew up working in his Russian-immigrant family's Tacoma, Washington, ice cream store called Olympic Dairy. Irv noticed that the customers always seemed happy, and he wanted to have the same sort of good feeling with his own business. In 1945, after serving in the army, Irv cashed in an insurance policy his father had given him for his bar mitzvah and, with a small loan, opened Snowbird Ice Cream in Glendale, offering twenty-one flavors. This much variety was unheard of at the time; later, in the mid-1950s, the east coast coffee shop Howard Johnson's announced twenty-eight flavors.

Burton (Burt) Baskin owned a men's store in the famous Palmer House Hotel in Chicago (now the Palmer Hilton). In 1942, he married Shirley Robbins, Irv's sister. After serving in the South Pacific as a lieutenant commander in the Naval Reserve for four years, he moved to California, where his brother-in-law convinced him that selling ice cream was more fun and exciting than selling men's clothing. A few months later, Baskin opened his first store, Burt's Ice Cream, on Lake Street in Pasadena, which is still in operation as a Baskin-Robbins.

By 1949, brothers-in-law Irv and Burt had more than forty shops in Southern California between them. They merged in 1953, and with a toss of a coin, they decided whose name would be first: Baskin won the toss. They came up with the 31 Flavors concept, featuring a flavor for every day of the month. And they launched a flavor of the month, a tradition that continues today. The first franchise location was Irv's former Snowbird Ice Cream on South Adams in Glendale, named store #1 on May 20, 1948. A year later, they opened a production facility in Burbank and created the thirty-first flavor, Mint Chocolate Chip. In 1949, the brothers-in-law renamed the corporation Huntington Ice Cream Company before finally changing it back to Baskin-Robbins in 1962.

Keeping up with store openings and management got out of hand, so in the early '50s, the brothers-in-law started selling their

> Every Baskin-Robbins ice cream flavor is kosher, except for Pink Bubblegum and Rocky Road, because they are made with gelatin.

Top: Snowbird in Glendale • Bottom: Inside the first Burt's on South Lake Avenue

Burt's/Snowbird Ice Cream (Baskin-Robbins)

stores to the managers. Without realizing it, they were turning their company into a franchising business, among the first food companies to make franchise deals.

With the number of store openings rapidly increasing, advertising was the next item of business. They hired Carson/Roberts, the largest advertising firm in Los Angeles at the time. In the 1953 meeting, Ralph Carson and Jack Roberts wanted to play on the number 31 and the thirty-one flavors. They suggested using a circus theme for the paper products, adding polka dots in pink and brown over a white background—pink representing a cherry, brown for hot fudge, and white for whipped cream. Many of the stores had an A-frame look with pink and brown round abstract balloons, and the "31" logo in a stylized circus font.

Baskin-Robbins first competed in the Dairy Ice Cream division of the Los Angeles County Fair in the summer of 1954, winning a gold medal. It has competed and won every year since.

Founders Irving Robbins & Burton Baskin

Irv and Burt were constantly inventing new flavors in their Burbank plant; it's said that for every flavor that made it into production, another twenty or thirty were rejected. (Later, in the 1970s, a man named Less Moffitt ran the flavor-developing operation and was just as picky.) Among the rejects were Lox & Bagels, Grape Britain, Ketchup, Sophia Lemon, Nudie Frutti, Berry Goldwater, Can't Elope Tonight, and even Turkey Dinner, a turkey-flavored ice cream with a gravy ribbon and bits of stuffing.

When the Dodgers moved to Los Angeles from Brooklyn in 1958, Baskin-Robbins honored the occasion by creating Baseball Nut, vanilla ice cream with cashews and a black raspberry ribbon—the raspberries to "heckle" the umpires. The creation returned in 2010 as June's Flavor of the Month. In the fall of 1959, Hazelnut Toffee became one of the 150 flavors in the company's flavor library. In 1964, at the height of Beatlemania, a reporter asked Irv what flavor would honor the Fab Four's visits to the United States. He replied, of course, Beatle Nut, and so they had to invent the flavor quickly; the pistachio ice cream with a chocolate ribbon and walnuts was in stores for just five days and was a top seller. A favorite story of Irv's involved the creation of Plum Nuts—a young man came into a store in the early days, when both Baskin and Robbins were behind the counter, and said that anyone who could dream up all these flavors must be "plumb nuts." Burt replied, "Congratulations, you just invented a new flavor!" (It ended up as vanilla with plums and walnuts.)

By 1960, there were 100 stores open, mainly in California and Arizona. In late 1961, they introduced the small pink tasting spoons, with a matching larger one for full servings. A character named Pinky the Spoon was born, alongside another mascot, Coney the ice cream cone.

In 1967, only a few months before Burt's death, the partners sold the company to United Brands Company (United Fruit); Irv stayed involved until 1978. At the time it was sold, it had 476 outlets in thirty-one states, with fifty-seven more stores in the works. New ownership brought investment and innovation; it introduced ice cream cakes, the first in the industry, in the early 1970s, and branches started opening around the world in that decade.

The partners had fun with the lifestyle. Burt had a personalized car license plate, "31 BR," and people often stopped him to pitch ideas for flavors. At the Robbins family home in Encino, California, there was a soda fountain and a swimming pool shaped like an ice cream cone. After the company's sale in 1967, the Robbinses rented an apartment on Balboa Island in Newport Beach, not far from where he moored his boat, *32nd Flavor*. In a 1976 *New York Times* interview, Irv said he ate three to four scoops of ice cream per day, sometimes on his morning cereal. In later years, he lectured on entrepreneurship at both USC and UCLA before passing away in 2006 at the age of ninety in Rancho Mirage.

Luckily for consumers, the flavors did not stop with thirty-one varieties—today there are more than 1,000 flavors, and everyone has their favorite. Some memorable ones include:

- Jamoca Almond Fudge, a 1959 invention that was Robbins's favorite and the first that Baskin-Robbins trademarked: coffee ice cream with toasted almonds and a fudge ribbon.
- Pink Bubblegum, which kids went wild for in 1970: a hot-pink ice cream with enough bubblegum in each scoop to make bubbles for hours after the ice cream was gone.
- Here Comes the Fudge, a 1971 invention inspired by Sammy Davis Jr.'s "Here Comes the Judge" comedy sketch on the hit TV show *Laugh-In*.
- Pralines 'n Cream, originally a 1979 flavor of the month after Robbins and his wife, Irma, visited New Orleans and tasted the hometown confection, but it became a huge hit and is still a top seller worldwide: vanilla with pralines and caramel ribbons.
- Gold Medal Ribbon, created for the 1980 Lake Placid, New York, Winter Olympics, and still a big hit today: chocolate and vanilla ice creams swirled with a caramel ribbon throughout.
- Cookies 'n Cream, a 1985 creation that remains massively popular: vanilla ice cream studded with Oreo pieces.

Top 5 Flavors Today Worldwide
Chocolate
Chocolate Chip
Mint Chocolate Chip
Pralines 'n Cream
Vanilla

A classic Baskin-Robbins store

- Love Potion #31, a play on words from the Searchers '60s hit "Love Potion No. 9," introduced for Valentine's Day in 1995: white chocolate and raspberry ice cream with a raspberry ribbon, chocolate chips, and raspberry-filled chocolate hearts.
- Red Bean, Mango Tango, Green Tea, Tiramisu, Dulce de Leche, and Hokey Pokey: just some of the flavors developed for ice cream lovers outside of the United States.

When coffeehouses began introducing cold coffee drinks in the early '90s, Baskin-Robbins responded by creating the Cappuccino Blast, one of the first coffee-ice-cream–based beverages in the industry. Later, it became the only national chain to offer hand-scooped ice cream and soft serve in the same place. And when trends started moving toward healthier desserts, it created a line of lighter, lower-fat, and/or no-sugar frozen yogurt and ice cream options called Bright Choices. In 2014, Baskin-Robbins began selling some of its most popular flavors in grocery store freezer cases. Today, its parent company owns Dunkin' Donuts, and the two brands are partnering.

Baskin-Robbins has broken and maintained many Guinness World Records. In 2000, a store on Maui made the world's largest ice cream scoop pyramid with 3,100 scoops. Sweden broke this record in 2017 with 5,435 scoops. New York franchise owner Mitch Cohen scooped nineteen cones in one minute in 2008, setting the world record; he'd set a previous record of sixteen on a Food Network show one year earlier. Another record was set in 2005 to honor the company's sixtieth birthday in Canton, Massachusetts: a giant cup holding 8,865 pounds of vanilla ice cream. During that same sixtieth-anniversary year, South Korea launched Café 31, the first "supreme and exquisite" dessert shop.

A bronze plaque outside of the Hyde Park Baskin-Robbins in Chicago memorializes where Barack Obama and Michelle Robinson shared their first kiss after ending a date with an ice cream cone. Around the world, a Baskin-Robbins cup or cone continues to be a beloved treat for first-daters, families, kids' sports teams, and pretty much everyone else.

Milestones
1945: 1 store
1949: 40 stores
1960: First branch outside of California opens in Arizona
1967: 476 stores in 31 states
1971: First international location opens in Toronto
1973: First Asian stores open in Tokyo and Osaka
1974: First European store opens in Brussels
1978: First Middle East store opens in United Arab Emirates
 2,000 stores around the globe
2019: 8,000 stores in 52 countries

Flavor Timeline
1945: French Vanilla
1948: Mint Chocolate Chip
1958: Baseball Nut
1959: Hazelnut Toffee
 Jamoca Almond Fudge
1964: Beatle Nut
1969: Lunar Cheesecake
1970: Pink Bubblegum
1971: Here Comes the Fudge
1975: Campfire S'mores
1979: Pralines 'n Cream
1980: Gold Medal Ribbon
1985: Cookies 'n Cream
2007: Superfudge Truffle
 Caramel Praline Cheesecake

Top: The A-frame phase
Left: The old logo
Bottom: The new logo

Burt's/Snowbird Ice Cream (Baskin-Robbins)

Foster's Old Fashion Freeze

ORIGINAL SLOGAN: "California's Original Soft Serve"
NAME TODAY: Fosters Freeze
ORIGINAL LOCATION: 999 South La Brea Avenue, Inglewood

OPENED: November 18, 1946
FOUNDER: George Foster
CURRENT OWNERS: Fosters Freeze LLC

There are 67 locations in California today. The first location is still in operation.

fostersfreeze.com

WHEN WORLD WAR II ENDED, George Foster went looking for a good business opportunity and settled on buying development rights from Dairy Queen for the entire state of California. His plan was to open a number of franchises in the state. But when he arrived in California, he was unhappy to learn that the dairy industry had passed strict regulations regarding the use of the word *dairy*. These rules decreed that Foster's product was ice milk that lacked a high enough percentage of butterfat to be called dairy. So he named his business Foster's Old Fashion Freeze. The first location, in Inglewood, sold soft-serve ice milk, sundaes, and milkshakes.

Foster was extremely quick to open new stores, which were run as franchises. Many of the locations added hamburgers, fries, hot dogs, and other fast-food items, but the staple was always soft-serve, whether in cones, dishes, sundaes, or shakes. By 1951, the state had more than 360 Foster's Freezes, most of them notable for their clean-lined architecture, sky-blue roofs, and walk-up windows. That year, Foster sold control of his franchises for $1 million to the Meyenberg Milk Products Company, which switched to its own dairy goods instead of the soft-serve mix that had been made by Compton Dairy.

"Favorite Dessert of Famous Families" was a popular print-ad campaign that Foster's ran in small-town newspapers around California in the fall of 1951. Movie star Harpo Marx, radio star Andy Devine, and sports and TV host Tom Harmon, as well as their families, were just a few of those featured in the promotion. All the ads mentioned driving to the "clean blue and white stores" and included photos of the famous families enjoying Foster's soft-serve.

With its locations in car-crazed California, many near high school and college campuses, Fos-

Milestones
1946: 1 location
1949: 135 locations
1951: 360 locations
Mid-1960s: 264 locations
1985: 206 locations
1991: 163 locations
2020: 67 locations

The Eagle Rock Foster's Freeze today

Top: A midcentury-modern dream in Morro Bay
Right: Early soft-serve truck

ter's became popular places for teens to show off their cars on the weekends. The Hawthorne location was very close to the childhood home of Brian, Dennis, and Carl Wilson of the Beach Boys; in the 1963 song "Fun, Fun, Fun," Brian's lyric "She cruised through the hamburger stand now" was a reference to Foster's. Hollywood got into the act by using the former Atwater Village location as a backdrop in Quentin Tarantino's 1994 film *Pulp Fiction*. It was used again in Ryan Murphy's Netflix series *Hollywood*. In 2008, before leaving for the Olympics in Beijing, the US women's softball team feasted on Fosters Freeze in Salinas.

After selling Foster's, George Foster ran the restaurants at Marineland of the Pacific in Palos Verdes and then moved to the up-and-coming area of Lake Havasu on the Colorado River in Arizona. On the eighty-five acres he owned along the river, he ran a boat rental, a bait and tackle shop, and a repair shop/fueling station. He and his wife split their time between Arizona and their Bel Air mansion.

By the mid '80s, Foster's was called Fosters Freeze and was owned by an investment group named SLOBAK, with Cliff Hiatt as CEO. He moved the headquarters from Sacramento to Arroyo Grande to be more centrally located. At that time, the locations sold 60 percent food products and 40 percent sweets. He began focusing on new savory menu items and started phasing out old restaurants to update Fosters' new look and menu. He felt it was easier to revoke a franchise than to make it remodel, and he wanted more consistency across the chain. In 1990, twenty-eight new outlets had opened and thirty-five old ones had closed. That same year, *Success Magazine* rated the Fosters Freeze chain as the second-best deal for franchise shoppers in the nation.

Oldest Locations Still in Operation
1946: Inglewood
1947: Torrance
1947: Burbank
1948: Los Angeles (Whittier Boulevard)
1949: Santa Rosa
       Berkeley
       San Jose
1950: Gilroy
1952: Brawley
1959: Carson
1962: Los Angeles (Eagle Rock)
1964: Bell Gardens

In 1994, El Pollo Loco signed a franchise contract to sell Fosters Freeze soft-serve in 163 locations, and this boosted sales significantly. By 2002, there were 122 Fosters Freeze branches, not including the 163 El Pollo Locos offering the soft-serve.

In September of 2015, Sung Lee, owner of the Menlo Park/Palo Alto location, closed his business after thirty years. Rent had skyrocketed, and he and his wife were forced to close. For years the iconic building stood vacant, and although the community tried to save it, today it is a condo complex. That branch was the last of its kind on the peninsula, leaving the Highway 101 corridor from San Jose to Santa Rosa without a Fosters. Preservation efforts also failed for the Redondo Beach branch, which is now a strip mall. The San Jose location still has the old-fashioned look, fortunately, as do some of the Southern California early branches, including in Eagle Rock, Torrance (which serves only ice cream, no hot food), Wilmington, and Carson. All are well worth a drive to visit for both the midcentury design and the soft-serve.

Many franchisees in the mid '80s hosted community events, like Folsom, California's very popular Pow Wow Parade and banana split–eating contest. Today, many sponsor local sports teams, and some branches are meeting spots for classic-car collectors. It's common to see three generations getting soft-serve together. Moving forward, the company is updating store designs and playing up the California ethos with a new motto: "Sunshine & Happiness." The future looks bright for this iconic California brand.

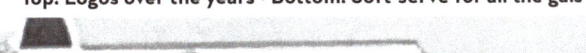

Top: Logos over the years • Bottom: Soft-serve for all the gals

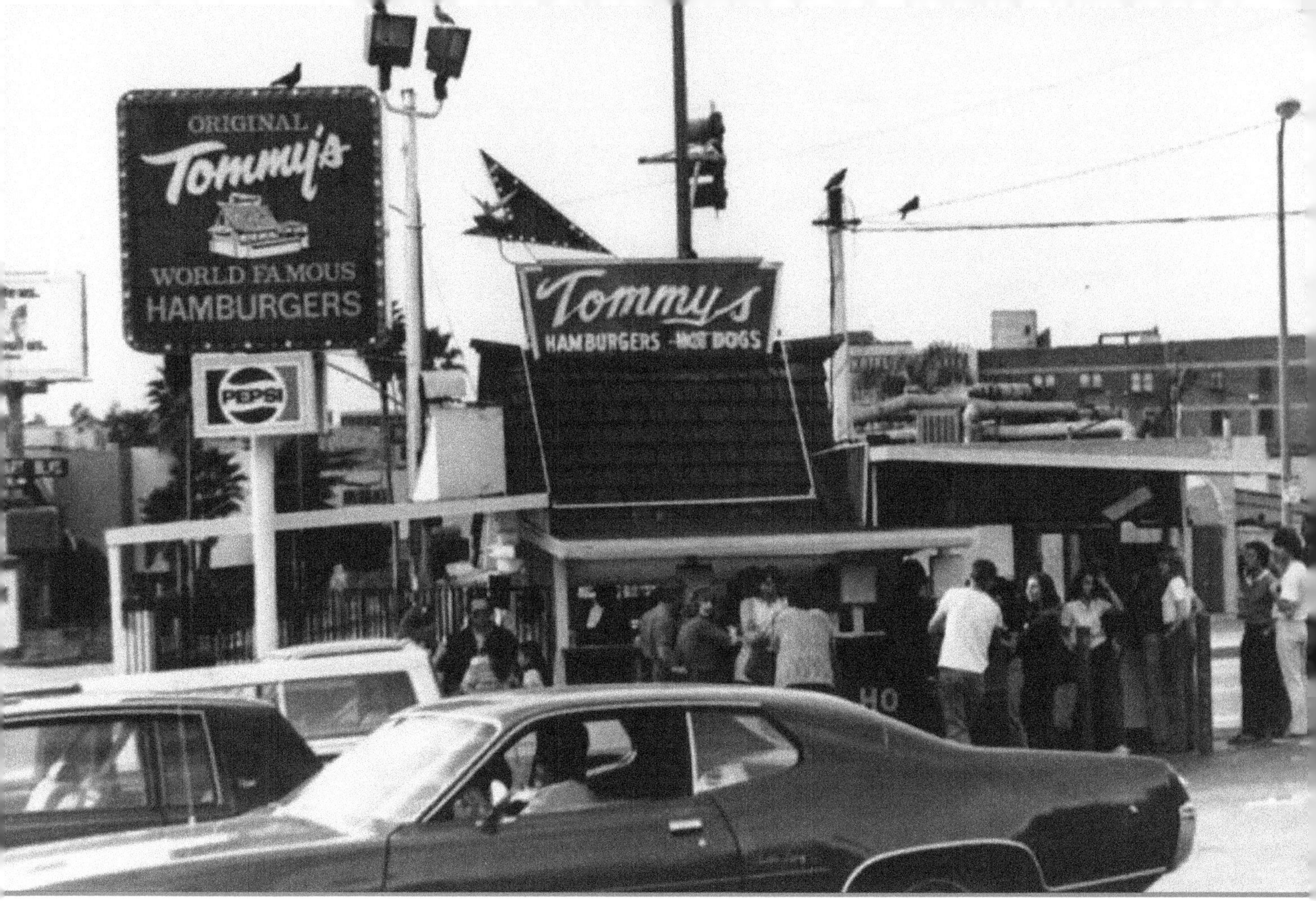

Tommy's

SLOGAN: "World Famous"
NAME TODAY: Original Tommy's
ORIGINAL LOCATION: 2575 West Beverly Boulevard (at Rampart), Los Angeles

OPENED: May 15, 1946
FOUNDER: Tom Koulax
PARENT COMPANY: Tomdan Enterprises, Inc.

There are 34 locations in 2 states, and the original location is still operating.

originaltommys.com

JUST SIX DAYS after he got his certificate of occupancy, Tom Koulax opened Tommy's on the busy corner of Beverly and Rampart. Koulax, formerly a ship welder, gas station attendant, and newspaper salesman, bought the spot with a partner for $800. Together, they built an eight-by-fifteen-foot wood and cinder-block hamburger stand with an order counter, no space for stools in the front, and just enough room inside for the cooks. For opening day, Koulax purchased five pounds of beef. At the time, he didn't weigh or portion out the patties; he just knew what looked good. Sales on the first day were $8—quite good.

The lines are just as long today at the original location, a little red and white hut where the patrons order at the window, the cashier yells out to the cook how many burgers, and the line keeps moving. It sits on a corner a few blocks from the Rampart Division police station depicted in the popular 1960s–'70s show *Adam-12*. If you watch the reruns, you'll often see Jim Reed and Pete Malloy driving past Tommy's.

Looking across the busy grill, you'll notice a huge pot of chili, because chili comes on everything, even though the burgers are not called chili burgers. All patties are seven ounces and dressed with cheese, chili, mustard, pickles, and onions. These are adult burgers!

For more than forty years, fountain drinks were unheard of at Tommy's. After you received your burger in a cardboard box, you'd pick your small glass bottle of soda out of an old-timey cooler and you'd get bagged potato chips instead of fries. In the 1990s, they replaced the coolers to create more standing room, and they installed a fountain-drink area across the parking lot. You won't find a single chair or napkin at the original location—if you try to sit to eat your burger, you'll get a lap full of chili, so you stand. And because napkins are "wimpy," Tommy's has industrial paper towel holders strategically placed every six feet so you can clean yourself up.

Top: Fans lined up at the original location in the 1970s • Bottom: 50¢ burgers brought the crowds for the fortieth anniversary celebration in 1986

The Original Tommy Burger

For its first three years, Koulax operated his stand during normal business hours. On October 1, 1949, popular singer Buddy Clark was killed only a block from Tommy's when his chartered plane crashed into the nearby intersection. For weeks after the crash, it was utter chaos in the neighborhood, with utility linemen working nonstop to replace the downed power lines, and Tommy's stayed open twenty-four hours to feed the workers and the curious onlookers. From then on, Koulax decided to keep the place open around the clock, and that's still the case. These days, the slowest time at the stand is between 5 and 6 a.m.

> **Milestones**
> 1946:   1 location
> 1970s: 6 locations
> 1992:   17 locations
> 1998:   20 locations
> 2021:   34 locations

In 1969, Tommy's employed thirty-three men full-time, each of whom benefited from profit-sharing, pensions, paid vacations, and holiday bonuses. Each day, they prepared 1,050 gallons of chili and 385 gallons of pickles. They cut 6,800 pounds of ripe tomatoes into thick slices, chopped 2,000 pounds of lettuce, and made 2.5 tons of prime beef into patties. Business was booming, and the need for additional parking and storage was obvious. Koulax purchased a former florist and café space across the southwest corner of Rampart, and he used it for storage and parking. The footprint of the little shack was now greatly expanded! Today, there's room for dozens of cars.

A story ran in newspapers coast to coast in the fall of 1970 that introduced the country to Tommy's. "Hamburger Stand Makes 1 Million" proclaimed one headline in a business story on Koulax and how he grossed $1 million a year from one little hut in Los Angeles. After that publicity, a trip to the Southland didn't just include Hollywood, but Tommy's, too.

Oscar Wilde once said, "Imitation is the sincerest form of flattery." Wilde probably should have added, "Unless it means a former employee steals your recipes and your name and opens a burger stand." In the 1970s, more than twenty imitators sprang up. Koulax went to court to defend the likeness and name of his business as well as the recipe for his chili. Confusion set in for lovers of the stand. In 1978, after many court battles, Koulax was able to trademark the logo and the words "The Original" and "World Famous," but not the name Tommy's, because many men have that name. After the lawsuit, many of the phony proprietors made slight changes to their signs.

On June 15, 1971, Koulax opened his first branch across the street from the once-popular Anheuser-Busch Gardens and Brewery in Van Nuys. It was a hit from the first day, and Koulax and his son Nick cooked burgers late into the night to serve the crowds—tourists of the famous gardens by day and brewery workers after their shifts by night.

In 1980, with seven L.A. locations open, Tommy's expanded southward to great fanfare into the Orange County city of Fountain Valley. Nick Koulax served as the manager.

Tommy's almost never advertised, because word of mouth was so significant and because it benefited from regular stories in newspapers and magazines. Even the foreign press covered it; the Swedish magazine *Chic* declared Tommy's to be L.A.'s quintessential fast food. Tourist groups show up regularly, and when the

> **Copycat Names Listed in the 1978 Lawsuit**
> Tommie's World-Famous Hamburgers
> Tammy's Original World-Famous Hamburgers
> Tom's No. 5 World Famous Hamburgers
> Tonnie's World Famous Hamburgers

Tom Koula & his creation

Dodgers, Lakers, and USC teams are playing home games, fans line up wearing their team colors to get their burgers.

For its seventy-third anniversary in 2019, Tommy's offered single burgers for 73¢ for one day, with a limit of five per person. Lines lasted for twenty-four hours, hundreds deep at all locations. Today, with thirty-four updated locations, some including drive-thrus and/or dining rooms, and a mobile unit, Tommy's is ready for the next generation. Its secret to success came not with franchising but from offering a simple, fairly priced menu of the same recipes from opening day. And today, you can even buy cans of the famous chili to take home! (And a T-shirt or baseball cap, too.) 🍔

The Original Tommy Burger

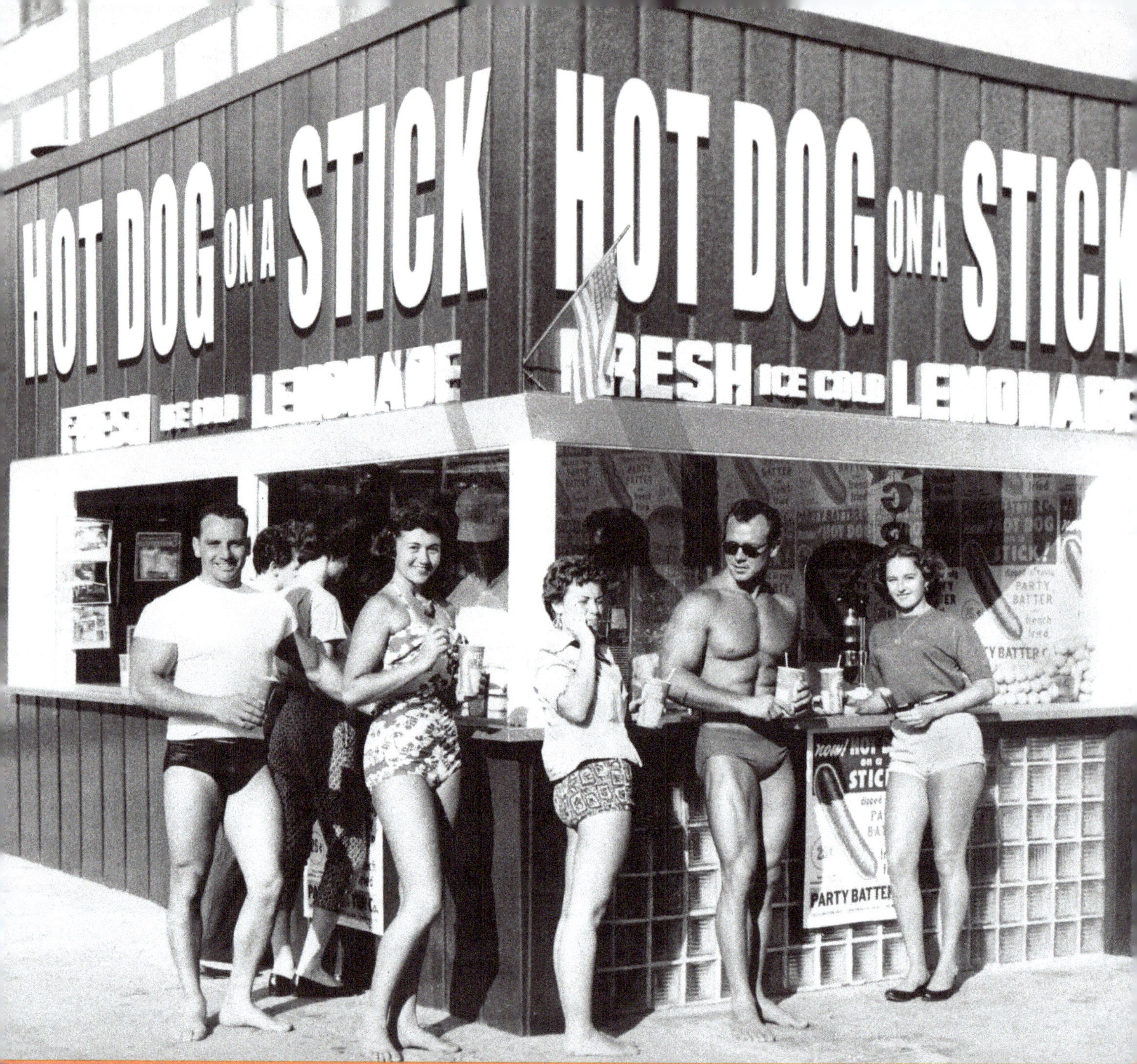
HOT DOG ON A STICK
FRESH ICE COLD LEMONADE
HOT DOG ON A STICK
FRESH ICE COLD LEMONADE
PARTY BATTER

CHEESE STICK 30¢
Fresh ICE COLD LEMONADE 25¢
ON A STICK

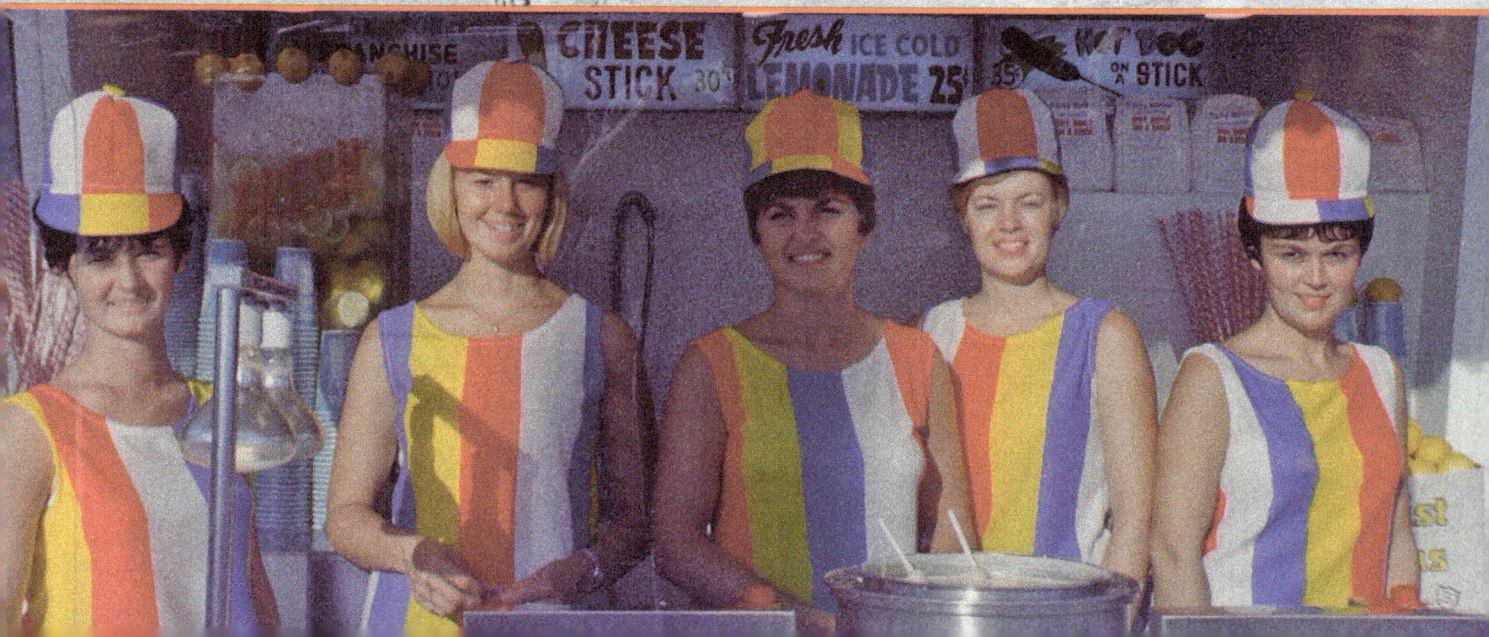

Party Puffs

NAME TODAY: Hot Dog on a Stick
ORIGINAL LOCATION: 1633 Ocean Front, Santa Monica

OPENED: June 1946
FOUNDER: Dave Barham
CURRENT OWNER: Global Franchise Group
CURRENTLY AT THE FIRST LOCATION: Hot Dog on a Stick

There are 44 locations in 5 western states and South Korea.

hotdogonastick.com

IN THE MID-1940S, Dave Barham worked the evening shift testing radar and radio equipment at Lockheed's Burbank plant. The war had ended, and hours were getting scarce. Dave was an avid beach-sports guy who spent his daylight hours playing beach volleyball and surfing. He'd been thinking about starting his own business when he found a 440-square-foot building on Ocean Front across from the famed Santa Monica Pier, at the end of the Mother Road, Route 66. An adjacent beach was popular with bodybuilders in those days, and it got the name Muscle Beach. Dave opened up a lemonade and ice cream stand and named it Party Puffs. He painted the roof bright red and the outside walls brown and white. With a location directly across from the sand volleyball courts, he figured that thirsty players would always be near. The business started out well, but he grew concerned that selling only beverages and desserts was limiting his market, so he came up with a new idea: dipping hot dogs into a watered-down version of his mom's cornbread recipe and frying them. Success! Dave changed the stand's name to Hot Dog on a Stick in 1948.

He dubbed the young women—it was only young women in those days—who worked for him "hotdoggers." The name stuck and is still used today. The uniform of the day was polka dot blouses with matching berets; later it changed to shorts, striped shirts and socks, and hats resembling ruffled lampshades. Suede boots also came into vogue for a while. The red or blue shorts are longer today than they were in the 1960s, and now they're worn by men and women alike, as are the striped collared shirts and caps. These caps are so coveted that hotdoggers are not allowed to take them home.

As iconic as the hats is the lemonade. It's the only fast-food beverage I know of that's "hand-stomped" for every order. The recipe combines tart Ventura County lemons, picked at their peak, sugar, and water. The hotdogger uses a specialty plunger in a large container sitting on the shop floor—with a downward rowing action, he or she pulverizes the fresh lemons into the sugar mixture. In the early days, the drink was made with local honey, but Barham later decided the flavor balance was better with pure cane sugar. Later he added cherry, lime, and a sugar-free "lite" lemonade.

Top: When Muscle Beach really was muscled • **Bottom:** Iconic uniforms

The hot dogs are Nathan's Famous all-beef dogs, dipped into the corn batter and fried in oil for three minutes to golden perfection. In 1988, the menu expanded to include veggie and turkey dogs. Fried cheese on a stick is also a favorite, made with American, spicy jack, or mozzarella that's dipped into the same batter as the corn dogs. A secret menu item: Order both a dog and cheese and you can have them layered and fried together.

This was obvious fair food, so it was not surprising that Barham started selling at county fairs in the 1950s, using the engine of his Lincoln Continental as a generator. Today, you'll see stalls offering their products at various county and state fairs, including a whopping eight locations at the L.A. County Fair. Dave's son, Gary, and Gary's wife manage the fair locations.

Milestones

1946:	Party Puff's opens
1948:	Name changes to Hot Dog on a Stick; created HDOS Enterprises
1950:	Products are sold at state and county fairs
1960s:	The iconic hotdogger uniform is created
1972:	First mall location in Torrance
1973:	First location opens in Utah; also first location to sell cheese sticks
1991:	Dave Barham dies
1999:	Lemonade is renamed Muscle Beach Lemonade
2000:	Juicy Lucy's is acquired
2004:	Juicy Lucy's is sold
2014:	Global Franchise Group acquires HDOS
2019:	First location in China opens

As the building of indoor malls exploded in the 1970s, Dave Barham saw opportunity, since his beach locations were dependent on nice weather. The Old Town Mall in Torrance opened just in time for the holiday season in 1972, and it became the first mall location for Hot Dog on a Stick. Dave then approached Ernie Hahn, a pioneer in malls throughout the west, to rent space in his locations. The food court had not yet been invented, and retailers didn't like customers carrying food into their stores. Hahn finally relented and gave Barham space in his upcoming Fashion Place Mall in Murray, Utah, south of Salt Lake City, which was also the first location to test the fried cheese on a stick. After the success of those first two outlets, Barham was able to persuade other malls to lease him space. Hot Dog on a Stick became very popular with shoppers, who could walk around while eating their lunch with one hand. A Hot Dog on a Stick franchise was easier to buy

Dave Barham at the County Fair

than other food brands at the time, because you didn't need a lot of ingredients and equipment to get started, so they began appearing everywhere.

March 1991 was a sad time for the company—Dave Barham died at the age of seventy-seven, just before opening his ninetieth location in the Galleria at Tyler Mall in Riverside. He had set up the business to be solely owned by the employees at the time of his death, becoming one of the first companies to be employee owned.

Lemonade Flavors
Original: 1946
Cherry: 1985
Lime: 1987
Lite: 1990

After Barham's death, Hot Dog on a Stick stayed with its winning formula, with the only real change being the 1994 addition of french fries to the menu. In 1998, however, the management began making some significant changes, starting with a rebranding effort. For decades the lemonade had simply been called Original Lemonade, but it became Muscle Beach Lemonade. They even considered changing the iconic uniform, much to the chagrin of employees. Fortunately, however, the only change was a new cap sleeve on the striped shirts. The company also entered into a co-branding arrangement with a pretzel chain, and in 2000, it bought the Juicy Lucy's hamburger chain, and later looked into developing frozen corn dogs and lemonade products to sell in grocery stores. It didn't really work out, though, and Hot Dog on a Stick abandoned the Muscle Beach concept and returned to focusing on its hot dog roots; it also sold Juicy Lucy's. In 2014, Hot Dog on a Stick was acquired by Global Franchise Group, which is working on a plan to expand the chain across the nation.

It did have real opportunity, however, with dessert items that could be fried fresh, in the spirit of its core business. At the fair booths, they launched funnel cakes on a stick, drizzled with chocolate sauce. As food trucks took off, Hot Dog on a Stick got on board—one of its trucks can serve up to 1,000 hungry people at one event.

At the Muscle Beach location in Santa Monica in the 1940s and '50s, celebrities visited often. In 2015, the world watched when Katy Perry headlined the Super Bowl wearing a hotdogger uniform while performing "California Girls," with backup dancers dressed like beach balls. In 2016, to celebrate the company's seventieth birthday, Mario Lopez took part in the Celebrity Stomp-a-Thon at the original location in support of the Leukemia & Lymphoma Society, and many other stars took over making lemonade and serving customers for a great cause.

Even as it expands nationally, the original Muscle Beach stand remains a local's treasure and a traveler's destination, serving the same corn dogs as ever.

The first location, in Santa Monica

Walsh's Hot Dogs

NAME TODAY: Cupid's Hot Dogs
ORIGINAL LOCATION: 11377 Burbank Boulevard, North Hollywood
OPENED: June 17, 1946
CURRENT OWNER: Cupid's Hot Dogs Ltd.
CURRENTLY AT THE FIRST LOCATION: Denny's (page 183)

There are 3 locations in Southern California—2 company-owned and 1 franchised and owned by a family friend.

cupidshotdogs.net

IN THE EARLY 1940S, Richard F. "Dick" Walsh came to California from Massachusetts to follow a dream: breaking into the movie business. He met a wonderful woman from Kansas, Bernice, who worked at Hughes Aircraft in Santa Monica. Dick and Bernice married and decided to go into business together by opening a hot dog stand in the San Fernando Valley called Walsh's. It was a little stand without running water, though, and the health department wouldn't let them open. Looking for a solid building instead of a stand, they found a small place in North Hollywood that fit the bill, and they were in business. Soon after opening, Dick changed the name to Cupid's, in honor of his loving nickname for Bernice, Cupid. Some felt that Cupid's had copied Pink's (page 75) in Hollywood, but Cupid's stayed in the Valley while Pink's branched outward into other cities.

Cupid's menu was very short, with just two types of dogs: regular and a smoky, juicy quarter-pound kosher. A creamy, subtly spicy chili topping on an all-beef dog in a fresh bun was the number one offering. Onions and mustard topped the chili dogs—they called this "The Everything" or "The Cupid." Paired with a soda for 35¢, this made a popular meal. Over the course of thirty-five years, the Walshes opened up five spots, mostly near busy street corners in the Valley—all walk-up stands with outdoor seating. Dick and Bernice's little hot dog stands were a hit. In 1964, they partnered with family friends to open another location, in Northridge.

The all-beef hot dogs are specially manufactured for Cupid's, and their natural casings provide a nice snap. The chili served today is the same recipe from 1946. Cupid's debuted a custom-made wooden "dog holder" that looked like a fraternity paddle with five concave wells to hold the dogs in the buns so the server could dress them more efficiently.

In 1981, the Walshes' surfer son,

Awards
The Daily Meal: One of the best hot dogs in America
Zagat: A Must-Try Hot Dog
L.A. Weekly: Best Hot Dog Time Warp
L.A. Weekly: 10 Best Hot Dogs in Los Angeles
Time Out: Best L.A. Hot Dog

The first stand

Walsh's Hot Dogs (Cupid's Hot Dogs)

Bernice & Richard Walsh

Rick, took over the business. He was a bit of a rebel and made the rash move to add bags of chips to the menu, along with cheese, relish, and ketchup as topping options, which at first infuriated Dick. According to the company history, however, when Dick actually tried the relish and ketchup on a dog, he realized it was a good idea. After Dick passed away, Rick continued to run the show, but he never made bold menu changes again. In 1994, when the Northridge earthquake hit, Rick went to the Van Nuys location, cleaned out the fridge, and fed everyone in the neighborhood.

The dogs are great, but it's the memories that bring many people back: Valley natives who met their high school friends at Cupid's after a Friday night football game, just like on *Happy Days*.

Rick's daughters, Kelly and Morgan Walsh, grew up at the stands, helping their dad with deliveries and working the counters when they were old enough. They'd planned on having different careers, but when Rick died suddenly in 2009, when the girls were twenty-one and twenty-seven, they had to jump in immediately to keep the stands open (by this point, there were two, one in Simi Valley and one in Winnetka). After hearing so many stories from longtime customers and seeing how important Cupid's

> **Ownership Timeline**
> 1946–1981: Dick and Bernice Walsh
> 1981–2009: Rick Walsh
> 2009–present: Kelly Walsh and
>   Morgan Walsh-Preciado ▼

Made in California

> **Menu Changes by Generation**
> 1st Generation: Chili dogs (onions, mustard, and chili) and sodas
> 2nd Generation: Added chips, relish, ketchup, and cheese
> 3rd Generation: Added sauerkraut

was to people who grew up in the Valley, they decided to stick with running the business. They haven't changed much at the stands, but they did add classic-car shows once a month, on Saturday nights, although those stopped during the COVID-19 pandemic. And though Cupid's still offers chips, if you purchase fries at Daglas Drive-in next door to the Winnetka stand, Cupid's will be happy to add chili on top.

Best of all, as I write this, the sisters have launched carhop service at the Winnetka branch on Thursday evenings, delivering dogs themselves on roller skates!

> **Locations**
> 1946: North Hollywood opens (now closed)
> 1956: Van Nuys opens (closed in 1997)
> 1962: Canoga Park (now called Winnetka) opens
> 1964: Northridge opens (now run by different owners)
> 1988: Simi Valley opens
> 1989: Chatsworth opens (licensed by different owners)
> 1995: Tarzana opens (licensed by different owners, now closed)

Top: First location
Middle: Classic chili dogs
Bottom: Northridge location

Mr. Fatburger

SLOGAN: "The Last Great Hamburger Stand"
NAME TODAY: Fatburger
ORIGINAL LOCATION: 3032 South Western Avenue, Los Angeles

OPENED: 1947
COFOUNDERS: Lovie Yancey & Charles Simpson
CURRENT OWNER: FAT Brands Inc.
CURRENTLY AT THE FIRST LOCATION: Jefferson Park Terrace Luxury Apartments, along with a small building where the footprint of Fatburger stood as a "re-creation" of the stand.

There are 171 locations in 16 countries, all franchised.

fatburger.com

AT AGE THIRTY-FIVE, Lovie Yancey came to California from Texas after a stint in Tucson, Arizona, where she had opened a restaurant. Realizing that hamburgers were growing in popularity, Yancey looked toward opening a very small stand in Los Angeles. She partnered with a professional boxer named Charles "Suitcase" Simpson, who worked for a construction company in his off time, and built a three-stool, walk-up "Refreshment Stand" from scrap materials, calling it Mr. Fatburger. Yancey felt a name like Mr. Fatburger would portray a big burger with everything on it—a full meal in one hamburger—and it did.

After five years with Simpson, Yancey dissolved her personal and professional relationship with him, keeping that original stand on Western and removing the "Mr." from the name, creating what is known today as just Fatburger.

Black entertainers from the area stopped by often for a customized burger. Other stands like Original Tommy's (page 103) across town catered to white college students, and many burger joints were not friendly to African-Americans. Yancey, who was Black, set out to change this. She worked around the clock, seven days a week, and was always there to greet customers, whether they were regular folks or such stars as Redd Foxx, James Brown, or Ray Charles. She'd go home for only a few hours and then get back to work. Yancey did not plan on running a twenty-four-hour stand, but the customers dictated the hours.

In 1973, Yancey wanted to open a second location. She found a 1948 former sandwich/hot dog stand with inside seating for about a dozen customers at a perfect location, on the corner of La Cienega Boulevard and Burton Way in Beverly Hills. There was plenty of traffic and great visibility. It was also closer to the homes of celebrities who were already Fatburger fans, including Elizabeth Taylor, Johnny Carson, and Muhammad Ali. Once, after an Emmy Awards show at the Hilton

Burger Sizes
Baby Fat: 2.67 ounces
Original: 5.33 ounces
King Burger: half pound
Double King: 1 pound
Triple King: 1.5 pounds

Top: The first location • Bottom: the East Hollywood branch today

Mr. Fatburger (Fatburger)

Lovie Yancey

in Beverly Hills, Yancey had to close the stand because the parking lot was so filled with limousines that there was no place for the tuxedoed and gowned attendees to eat their burgers.

In 1981, Yancey started selling franchises, and by 1985, there were fifteen Fatburger franchise sites, with more coming, as well as four company-owned locations. At one point, Magic Johnson's Burger Business LLC held a 70 percent stake in the chain, alongside David Spade and Janet Jackson. In 2001, Johnson sold his interest to Fatburger's management team. Other celebrities who have invested in Fatburger franchises include Pharrell Williams, Kanye West, Montel Williams, Cher, and Queen Latifah.

When asked about her competition by a newspaper called the *Wave* in 1985, Yancey said, "I don't worry about McDonald's, Burger King, or Wendy's. They may be more popular, but a good hamburger sells itself, and I don't think anybody makes as good a hamburger as we do." Her menu allowed for lots of customizing, with sizes ranging from small to massive. The largest, the twenty-four-ounce XXXL Burger, comes with a challenge: Customers who can down it in one sitting get a certificate and their photo on the wall. In 2014, Jay Leno accepted the challenge at the newly opened Beverly Hills location. His picture hangs on the wall, and it is said that he finished the XXXL in fewer than five minutes.

In March 1983, Yancey lost her twenty-two-year-old grandson, Duran Farrell, to sickle cell anemia. Three years later, she created a large endowment at City of Hope Hospital in his honor. Four years after that, in 1990, she sold Fatburger to an investment group, keeping the original property on Western as well as the second location, which her actress/boxing referee daughter, Gwen Adair, managed for several years. (The site was later sold.) Gwen had been a regular on the hit TV show *M.A.S.H.* as one of the nurses and was one of the first female referees in boxing. Yancey had taken her young daughter to the Olympic Auditorium to watch the fights.

On January 26, 2008, at the age of ninety-six, Lovie Yancey died from pneumonia at Olympia Medical Center, just six miles from where she made history.

The original stand on Western was never designated as a Los Angeles Historical-Cultural Monument, but when the property sold after Yancey's death, it was with the stipulation that the shack must be

Fatburger Layers
Bun (white, wheat, or gluten-free)
Mayonnaise
Lettuce
Tomato
Pickles
Onions (raw or grilled)
Relish
Mustard
Patty (beef, turkey, skinny, veggie, or Impossible)
Add-ons: Cheese, bacon, egg, onion rings, chili

Milestones

1946: 1 location
1973: Second location opened
1981: Franchises offered
1985: 19 locations (4 company-owned, 15 franchised)
2008: First location in a sports stadium (Arizona Diamondbacks)
      First international locations: Dubai and Beijing
2013: Opened 2 locations in Pakistan, with one being the largest flagship globally
2021: 117 locations in 16 countries

rehabilitated and incorporated into any new development. Today, a sixty-six-unit, lower-income-housing building stands on the spot, with the small shack incorporated into it. The word *Fatburger* is painted on the side, but the interior remains empty.

Fatburger is now owned by FAT Brands, with Andrew Wiederhorn as the CEO. Wiederhorn was highlighted on the 2013 hit show *Undercover Boss*, where he learned about many aspects of Fatburger from firsthand experience. FAT Brands also owns Buffalo's, a Buffalo-wing concept that started in Georgia in 1985, so they've paired the two to bring wings and burgers under one roof. More recently, FAT Brands acquired the retro burger chain Johnny Rocket's.

Besides four sizes of hamburgers (with perfectly layered extras), the contemporary Fatburger offers two types of french fries ("skinny" and "fat"), store-battered onion rings, hot dogs, chili, and hand-scooped milkshakes. In 2019, it added the vegan Impossible Burger to the menu.

Over the years, Fatburger has been memorialized on countless television shows, in films, and in song lyrics. Two notable examples are Ice Cube's song "It Was a Good Day" and the Notorious B.I.G.'s song "Going Back to Cali." When David Letterman returned to New York after his late-night show's run in Los Angeles, he shared his top-ten list of things he'd miss about L.A., and number seven was, of course, Fatburger.

The fancy new design

In-N-Out

SLOGAN: "Quality You Can Taste"
ORIGINAL LOCATION: 1276 Garvey, Baldwin Park

OPENED: October 22, 1948
COFOUNDERS: Harry & Esther Snyder
CURRENT OWNER: Lynsi Snyder, granddaughter of the founders

CURRENTLY AT THE FIRST LOCATION: 10 Freeway overpass
REPLICA OF THE ORIGINAL: 13752 Francisquito Avenue, Baldwin Park (does not serve food; food service at 13850 Francisquito)

Today, there are 363 locations in 7 states, with Idaho in the offing.

in-n-out.com

HARRY SNYDER began learning the burger business while working as the day manager at a burger stand in Seattle, where he loved his work and also met his future wife, Esther Johnson, who'd been a surgical nurse in World War II. They married in 1948 and moved to the city of Baldwin Park, a suburb of Los Angeles. Looking to establish a business close to their house, the Snyders opened a ten-foot-square burger stand. Harry had a hunch that people would want to stay in their cars to order, so he created a two-way speaker in his garage. A customer could talk into the speaker to the order taker, and after about four car-lengths, reach the pickup window and collect their burger, fries, and drinks. This was revolutionary at the time.

Because there was no need for dining space, the cost of building the stand was low. The location was next to a busy highway (it later became the 10 Freeway), and the stand's red and white neon sign—"In-N-Out ~ Hamburgers ~ No Delay"—was easy to spot by passing motorists. Every day before sunrise, Harry visited the meat and vegetable markets downtown to buy fresh ingredients. He took the orders and cooked himself, and Esther managed the books from their home a few blocks away on South Merced Avenue.

Business boomed, and three years later, the Snyders opened a second location, in Covina, only about eight miles away, to test if a location would work that wasn't near a highway. They also had to move the original location a short distance in order to make room for the 10 Freeway. They designed a new sign with a red arrow to imply speed, and dropped the "No Delay." By 1958, the Snyders had five locations. In those early years, In-N-Out sold six varieties of drinks in little bottles, but Harry was always looking to streamline the process, so he installed fountain machines.

To this day, when you order a meal in the drive-thru, the order taker will ask, "Will you be eating in your car?" Harry didn't want customers to drip onto themselves, so he gave them a "lap mat." At first they were made from the brown wax paper used to package the buns; later they were made from pink butcher paper to be more appealing. Today, the lap mats are printed with In-N-Out's history,

The arrow points the way

details about the food, or fun facts.

To make their burgers, the Snyders used hand-leafed iceberg lettuce and first-rate American cheese, onions, and tomatoes. The buns are still made with old-fashioned, slow-rising sponge dough. The burgers are not cooked until ordered. The french fries come from potatoes shipped directly from growers and cut in the stores before being cooked in sunflower oil. Shakes, first served at the Pasadena store in 1958, are made with real ice cream and are so thick that you have to eat your food first so the shake melts a bit. Stands have no freezers, heat lamps, or microwaves. In the early days, Esther made the beef patties herself with a manual press, using chuck that Harry had ground to his specifications, with no fillers or preservatives. As the company grew, they had to open a production facility, but they held to the same standards. Today there are several such plants.

Figuring out the secret menu is partly why In-N-Out seems almost like a cult. The menu is short and simple, but newcomers will overhear people ordering mysterious things like "Animal Style" or "Flying Dutchman." Where did these come from? The first secret menu item was the Animal Style burger in 1961. The beef patty is coated in mustard before grilling and is topped with extra spread (In-N-Out's "spread" is a variation of Thousand Island), grilled onions, lettuce, tomato, and pickles. (The rest of the secret menu is detailed on page 123.) A staple of the regular menu is the Double-Double, with double meat and double cheese.

Over the next thirty years, even as McDonald's (page 81) and other fast-food chains opened thousands of restaurants, the Snyders managed In-N-Out with a "slow-growth" philosophy, stressing quality and customer service over rapid expansion and constant cost-cutting measures. In-N-Out employees (called "associates") are still paid substantially higher wages than those at other fast-food operations, with an unusual array of benefits, and hourly employees are often promoted to management positions.

The first In-N-Outs had

Standard Menu Items
Combo #1:
+ Double-Double®
+ Fries
+ Soft Drink

Combo #2:
+ Cheeseburger
+ Fries
+ Soft Drink

Combo #3:
+ Burger
+ Fries
+ Soft Drink

Hamburger
Cheeseburger
Double-Double®
Fries
Shakes: Vanilla, Strawberry & Chocolate

Harry & Esther Snyder

Made in California

Locations Without Drive-Thrus
Glendale
Laguna Hills
Las Vegas (the Linq)
Mill Valley
Placentia
San Francisco (Fisherman's Wharf)

a kitchen stand in between two lanes of cars, known as a double drive-thru, with a walk-up window facing the parking area; many also had a metal awning shading a few tables. Only six locations have no drive-thru windows. The color scheme is red and white, including the uniforms worn by the staff. Many locations are also notable for crossed palm trees. As with everything that In-N-Out does, there's a story behind that: One of Harry's favorite movies, *It's a Mad, Mad, Mad, Mad World*, features characters racing to find treasure buried under four palm trees planted to resemble the letter *W*. Because he thought that each In-N-Out was a treasure, he started planting crossed palm trees in 1972.

A pickup truck with a grill served burgers at a cookout event for Badillo Elementary School in Covina in 1974. Today, In-N-Out has eleven trucks that provide food for parties, businesses, and fundraisers. The trucks are also used for school fundraisers in Southern California and Texas, while also helping abused children through the In-N-Out Foundation. Schools keep 75 percent of the money raised, and the remaining 25 percent goes to the foundation.

Harry loved his cars and the car culture of the Southland. He invested in the Irwindale Drag Strip when it was under construction in 1965. This started a lifetime association with drag racing and classic cars. In-N-Out burgers were sold at the concession stands to fans and racers. Harold "Guy" Snyder, Harry's eldest son, also began a lifelong interest in racing, and today, Harry's granddaughter, Lynsi, drag races competitively. Iconic cars have been featured on the In-N-Out T-shirts made every year, which many people collect. Harry designed the first shirt himself in 1975. These are sold at the locations as well as at the company stores in Baldwin Park and Las Vegas.

Harry Snyder died on December 14, 1976, at only sixty-six years old. His two sons, Rich and Guy Snyder, took over as president and vice president, respectively.

On the site of the Snyders' original home in Baldwin Park, Rich built In-N-Out University, where entry-level managers get trained in every detail, from how to fold the cheese on a patty (a little trick so the first bite is cheesier) to how to schedule staff. The university is on the upper floor; downstairs is the company store, where you can buy socks that look like the shake cups, shorts with a burger mo-

Drive-thru in Baldwin Hills

> **Leadership**
> 1948–1976: Harry & Esther Snyder
> 1976–1993: Rich & Guy Snyder
> 1993–1999: Esther & Guy Snyder
> 1999–2006: Esther Snyder
> 2006–2010: Mark Taylor
> 2010–present: Lynsi Snyder

tif, and the annual T-shirts. You can also buy the merch online and at two company stores in Las Vegas. Rich also created a toll-free customer-service line in 1991, and had the opening month and year engraved for each store into the granite counter you see in the drive-thru.

It took forty-two years for the company to open outside the L.A. metropolitan area, with store #57, which opened in San Diego in 1990. The first location outside of California was, not surprisingly, Las Vegas, store #80, just off the Strip—in the early days, the wait time for a burger was up to forty minutes. Another location opened only a few weeks later, eight miles east. Unlike the casinos, In-N-Out's Vegas hours are the same as they are at all stores, closing at 1 a.m.

Location #102 opened with a bang on Sunset Boulevard, a few blocks from Highland Avenue and Hollywood High School. If you want to see stars, you don't have to take one of those bus tours. After any awards show, like the Golden Globes or the Academy Awards, just pop over to the In-N-Out—even the paparazzi hang out there, waiting. After winning the Oscar for Best Animated Short in 2018, Kobe and Vanessa Bryant opted out of the *Vanity Fair* after-party for a Double-Double and fries. So did Julia Roberts and her husband, Danny Moder. Other locations also get their fair share of celebrity love. A few days before Christmas in 2018, Tom Hanks and Rita Wilson were enjoying a meal at the Fontana location when fans noticed them. Like a real star, he got up and took selfies and even paid for some of the drive-thru customers. The late Anthony Bourdain claimed that the best restaurant in Los Angeles was In-N-Out—he'd always go to the one by LAX as soon as he arrived

The first double-sided drive-thru location

in town. (So does almost every college student returning home for the holidays after a semester in an In-N-Out–free state.) Ina Garten says she's a fan of the Animal Style burger.

The management team had a longstanding rule that they would not fly together, but they made an exception in December of 1993, when Rich, his mother, Esther, and executive vice president Phillip West boarded a chartered jet at John Wayne Airport in Santa Ana to join in the festivities for the opening of location #93, in Fresno. After the opening, they stopped in Bakersfield to scout for new locations, and then at Brackett Field in La Verne to drop off matriarch Esther, who wasn't

The Secret Menu

Burgers
- Animal Style: Mustard-glazed patties with pickles, extra spread, and grilled onions
- Protein Style: Bun replaced with large lettuce leaves
- M x C: M = the Meat; C = the cheese. A 3x3 is 3 patties and 3 cheeses. A 2x4 is 2 patties and 4 cheeses, etc.
- Double Meat or 2x0: A Double-Double without cheese
- Flying Dutchman: A Double-Double with no bun and no condiments
- Grilled Cheese: Bun with two slices of cheese, spread, tomatoes, lettuce, and onions
- Veggie Burger or Wish Burger: Bun with only the vegetables, no meat or cheese

Burger Options
- Mustard Fried Patty: Cooked with the mustard on the patty
- Onions: Can be ordered whole fresh, fresh chopped, whole grilled, grilled chopped, or any combination of the 4
- Chopped Chiles: Yellow chiles on the bottom of your burger or on the side
- No Salt: No extra salt added to the patties
- Extra Salt: Added to the tomato layer of the burger
- Buns: Extra toasted, lightly toasted, or untoasted
- Extra Everything: All extra veggies and condiments without added charge

Custom Fries
- Fries well done: Extra crispy
- Fries light well: Just a little more done than regular
- Fries light: Almost limp, no color whatsoever
- Fries no-salt: No salt added after fried
- Cheese Fries: Fries with 2 slices of melted cheese
- Animal Style Fries: Topped with 2 slices of melted cheese, grilled onions, and spread
- Lemon Fries: Fries with lemon squeezed on top

Milkshakes
- Root Beer Float: This is really the only dessert—half vanilla shake and half root beer
- Neapolitan: Chocolate, vanilla, and strawberry
- Black and White: Chocolate and vanilla
- Large and Extra-large shake sizes

feeling well. After being cleared for landing by the tower back at John Wayne, the plane crashed, killing all on board. The smaller plane had been impacted by the turbulence from a nearby 757. After the tragedy, Esther took over as president and Guy as chairman of the board. Guy took the company to new levels; within six years, he had expanded In-N-Out from ninety-three locations to 140, many of which had full dining rooms and only one drive-thru lane. Stephen Kanner, the modern architect who founded the A+D Museum in Los Angeles, created an angular design as a tribute to 1950s jet-age architecture for the 199th location, in Westwood Village near UCLA.

Guy Snyder died only a few years later, in 1999. His legacy includes creating the not-so-secret menu item called the Flying Dutchman (page 123), along with a relentless focus on improving processes, procedures, and equipment.

While Esther ran day-to-day operations, Guy's daughter, Lynsi Snyder, the founders' only grandchild, took a job in In-N-Out's merchandising department, later rotating through departments to

Grateful States with In-N-Outs
Arizona
California
Colorado
Idaho (in progress)
Nevada
Oregon
Texas
Utah

The replica in Baldwin Hills today

> **Milestones**
> 1948: 1 location in Baldwin Hills
> 1955: 5 locations
> 1973: 13 locations in the greater L.A. area
> 1988: 50 locations in Los Angeles, Orange, San Bernardino, Riverside & Ventura counties
> 1992: 80 locations; first out of state, in Nevada, opens
> 1994: 100th location opens in Gilroy, California
> 2000: Arizona openings
> 2005: 200th location opens, the second in Temecula
> 2008: 215th location opens, the fourth in the state of Utah, in Washington City
> 2015: 300th location opens, in Anaheim
> 2020: Colorado presence established, and location announced for Boise, Idaho

learn the business. On August 4, 2006, Esther passed away, leaving a legacy of leadership and compassion, especially toward children. Along with her son Rich, she established the In-N-Out Burger Foundation, which provides residential treatment, emergency shelter, early intervention, and foster care for abused children. In-N-Out also founded the Slave 2 Nothing Foundation in 2016 to improve the lives of victims of human trafficking.

After Esther died, Mark Taylor, a longtime executive, served as president for four years before turning the role over to Lynsi, who took the job in 2010 at just twenty-seven years old. As we go to press, she is thirty-nine, owns 99 percent of the company, and is presumed to be worth about $3 billion.

The company celebrated its sixty-fifth anniversary in 2013 by building a replica of the first location very near that site, since the original had been demolished all those years before to make way for the I-10. It's not a functional restaurant (although there's another close by), but it's fun to tour it and see how tiny it is.

Cities, states, and developers regularly try to court the fast-food chain into coming to their regions. In 2014, L.A.'s mayor tried just that with tours of downtown and LAX locations that he wanted the company to consider. But since car culture is part of the brand, In-N-Out needed room to handle at least fifteen cars in a drive-thru line as well as forty-five parking spots, so you still can't get a Double-Double in DTLA or at LAX. But you can in Colorado—Colorado Springs is now home to a 100,000-square-foot distribution and burger patty–making facility, and the state has three In-N-Out locations as of this writing, with more in the plans. When the Aurora location opened in late 2020, fans waited up to fourteen hours in line just to get a burger.

Introducing new products is not part of the In-N-Out model. Simple is best. But in 2018, after about sixty-five years of absence, hot chocolate with marshmallows returned to the menu; on rainy days, it's given free to children under twelve. And arriving not long after this writing will be a sugar-free ginger beer that they worked with Coke to create.

A month does not go by without Lynsi Snyder receiving offers to take In-N-Out public or to sell completely. She refuses them all. As her uncle Rich told *Forbes* in 1989, "I would be prostituting what my parents made by doing that…. There is money to be made by doing those things, but you lose something, and I don't want to lose what I was raised with all my life." The family motto could very well be: "This company is NOT for sale."

Love's Wood Pit Barbecue

SLOGAN: "When you're in Love's, the whole world's delicious."
NAME TODAY: Love's BBQ
ORIGINAL LOCATION: 15758 Ventura Boulevard, Encino

OPENED: January 2, 1948
COFOUNDERS: Mike Love (father) & J. Dan Love (son)
CURRENT OWNER: Love's Barbecue Inc.
CURRENTLY AT THE FIRST LOCATION: Wells Fargo Bank

At its height, Love's boasted 45 locations in the western United States. While there are no longer any open restaurants, the famous sauce is available for purchase on the website.

lovesbbq.com

WHEN THE LOVE FAMILY moved from Missouri to the San Fernando Valley in the late 1940s, they discovered they'd left one thing behind: the taste of home. Unable to find Missouri-style barbecue anywhere in their new neighborhood, the father-and-son duo gathered $600, rented a tiny cottage on Ventura Boulevard, and opened shop. Formerly a real estate office, the cottage measured thirty feet by twelve feet and accommodated only fourteen diners. The massive brick pit in the rear was the Loves' secret weapon. They began to barbecue large, succulent sides of beef and pork, ham, chicken, and ribs cooked over slow-burning, smoky wood fires. The Loves used flavored woods like oak, hickory, fruit, and citrus to smoke and cook, a technique previously unheard of by California diners. Fans drove miles to enjoy the sweet and smoked barbecue taste of Love's meats.

By May 1956, the Loves found they were outgrowing the building, so they enlarged the kitchen and added a lobby and a takeout window. It didn't take long to realize that even the remodeled space was insufficient, and the Loves moved to another location a few blocks away.

But for true expansion, the Loves decided franchises were the way to go. A Los Angeles design firm came up with the unique bright red aluminum shingle roof with a real flame constantly burning in a cupola at the top. The masonry exterior was enhanced by brown driftwood and rock veneer, and the sign at the top featured a spinning heart with "Love's" in red and white script. These buildings were noticeable not just from the street but also from a nearby freeway.

Visitors entered through the main dining room or, depending on their priorities, through a separate entrance into the Lion's Den cocktail lounge. The main dining room was family-friendly, and Love's featured a special kid's menu. Diners had their choice of red leather booths with large tables or seats at the counter, which offered a view of the kitchen as the cooks prepared the savory meats. And, of course, takeout was always available from the host stand. The Love's style was unique: heightened coffee shops with cocktail lounges attached. They served great food for a price that a median-wage, working family could afford. It was a nice dinner out for a family or a date.

Top: Early days on Ventura Boulevard • **Bottom:** The Escondido branch in its prime

Owners
1963: Transcontinental Investing Corp.
1970: International Industries, Inc.
1983: Butterfield Savings & Loan Assn.
1985: Federal regulators
Late 1980s: BSB Foods Inc.
2002: Love's Barbecue Inc.

A lunch-time favorite was the (ironically named?) Heart's Delight sandwich, packed with more than twelve ounces of smoked, chopped beef, ham, and pork. Specials, such as St. Louis ribs, always included all the sides: barbecue beans, corn, steak fries, and coleslaw. Nothing was prepackaged; everything, including the popular salad dressings, was made in-house. The lightly wood-smoked back ribs came with seven ribs cooked in a delicious, slightly sweet basting sauce made from brown sugar, vinegar, cider, herbs, and spices. A cup of additional sauce was served alongside.

Love's expanded throughout Southern California—the red-roofed buildings popping up close to major highways and then in the suburbs—and into Arizona, Nevada, and Texas, which completed their portfolio. Rex Allen, a voice-over artist and actor, narrated the Love's commercials, with the deep voice reminiscent of the cowboys he played on screen. The two most popular and recognizable tag lines were "When you're in Love's, the whole world's delicious" and "We LOVE Children."

In the late 1970s, the Escondido newspaper regularly highlighted local Love's employees with a photo, the length of time employed, and facts such as their favorite meal and a description of their job. Love's made news in other ways, too—such as winning gold medals from the California State Fair for the best barbecue beans and barbecue chicken in Sacramento. "Gold Medal" BBQ Chicken was thereafter one of the most popular items on the menu; it included coleslaw, barbecue beans, french-fried potatoes, a kosher dill pickle, and cheesy toasted French bread. You did not go home hungry from Love's. Nor did you go home covered in barbecue sauce: Love's provided finger bowls with fresh lemon slices in water to clean your hands after indulging in those succulent meats.

Celebrating at Loves
Opposite: The exterior & interior of Love's Costa Mesa

In 1963, the Love family sold Love's Wood Pit to Transcontinental Investing Corporation and left the restaurant business. Ownership changed hands several more times; eventually, franchise owners operated on their own without guidance.

In January 1979, the original location on Ventura Boulevard became a Tony Roma's; the building was later demolished to make room for a multistory office building. The Los Angeles Pico Boulevard location became a Noonan's Ribs after Love's closed. That building is still intact and now houses a medical facility. Although the cupola is still visible above, there is sadly no longer a flame.

In 2002, with locations closing, franchisees not paying their royalties, and the corporate headquarters resolving lawsuits, the company stabilized by streamlining the product line and terminating the franchises. The last Love's Wood Pit Barbecue, in Chula Vista, closed its doors in 2007.

The most requested recipes from the Love's kitchens were always the famous baked beans and the barbecue sauce. Many claim to have the recipes, but all the recipes and methods are proprietary and are still owned by Love's Barbecue Inc. Today, there's only one way to get that original taste of Love's: by buying the sauce on the internet.

Marie Callender Pie Shop

NAME TODAY: Marie Callender's
ORIGINAL PIE SHOP LOCATION: 1400 Obispo Avenue, Long Beach
OPENED: 1952
ORIGINAL RESTAURANT LOCATION: 574 North Tustin Avenue, Orange
OPENED: 1964

FOUNDERS: Clarence, Marie & Donald Callender
CURRENT OWNERS: Marie Callender's LLC
CURRENTLY AT LONG BEACH LOCATION: Parking lot
CURRENTLY AT ORANGE LOCATION: Vacant former Marie Callender's building

There are 30 locations in 3 western states, and frozen foods are available nationwide.

mariecallenders.com

IN THE LATE 1940S, Marie Callender answered a want ad in Long Beach for a part-time job making salads and hot items in a delicatessen. Soon after, the owner, Mr. Black, opened a little snack bar and asked Marie to make pies. Since the oven at the deli was not up to the task, she made them in her home oven on Gardenia Avenue. Impressed with the results, Black suggested that she start a pie business and volunteered to be her first customer.

Marie Callender

So in 1948, without capital or a location, Marie and her husband, Clarence (known as Cal), sold their Chevrolet for $700. Their son, Don, found a Quonset hut to rent in the industrial area of Long Beach. And they started baking: three rolling pins, one oven, between twenty and twenty-eight pies a day, in eighteen different fruit and cream pie varieties. Cal worked at the American News Company during the day and helped his son and wife with the pies at night. They supplied three restaurants in Long Beach.

After four years as a wholesale operation, the Callenders looked for a small location where they could sell pies retail, strictly to go. They found the perfect spot off of an alleyway at 14th and Obispo in Long Beach. Lines of eager buyers, many of them customers of the restaurants that served Marie Callender pies, soon formed down the alleyway—and the lines expanded from there.

Don, who wanted to aim for bigger profits, had to persuade his reluctant parents to enter the restaurant world by creating a dine-in pie and coffee shop. It took more than a decade, but in 1964, Don opened Marie Callender's Pie and Coffee Shop on Tustin Avenue in Orange. He placed the

Top: The original location in Orange • Bottom: The Toluca Lake branch

Marie Callender's

ovens in the front window so everyone could see the pies baking fresh throughout the day, and he offered a free slice of pie and a cup of coffee to first-time visitors (how he could identify a first-timer remains a mystery). Sometimes the line stretched for three blocks, with many customers taking home whole pies. A clever sales technique that continues to this day: charging a deposit on the pie tin when customers purchase a pie and offering a refund when they bring the tin back. Many pie lovers collected the tins and returned to the shop with a stack tall enough to cover the cost of a full pie.

Two years later, Don expanded the menu by adding soups, sandwiches, hamburgers, and sides like coleslaw and french fries. Other items from Marie's recipes were added to the menu in 1967 when franchising began.

"Apple pie without some cheese is like a kiss without a squeeze" was the motto printed on napkins and utensils in the restaurants—conveying a persuasive subliminal message before the customer had even taken a bite.

Don worked for sixteen years to perfect techniques for mass pie production. He looked at every aspect, including formulas, flour mixes, shortening ratios to improve the crusts, and the best temperature for cooking the fruit, custard, and cream pie fillings. In 1966, Don hired Harry Franklin to assist him as a trainee pie baker for $1.25 per hour; after four months, Franklin's salary was increased to $175 per week.

Franklin worked for Callender's for a little more than two years before taking his pie-baking

Don Callender

knowledge to Harold Butler of Denny's (page 183), who was opening pie shops called Mother Butler Pies. For a new salary of $350 per week, Franklin duplicated the recipes, methods, and production systems of the Callenders' successful operation. Callender's sued for recipe and production infringement, and the court ruled in the company's favor. Mother Butler (Denny's) was not the only company to do this: Jan Dobbins Pie Shop in Pasadena, part of the McDonald's (page 81) chain, and a now-defunct chain in Oregon also started to use the Callender's recipes and systems.

By the mid-'70s, the Callenders had dozens of locations around Southern California. The restaurants had a cozy, old-fashioned look with early American furniture meant to invoke a visit to grandma's house: tables with tall wooden chairs, booths lined in leather, waitstaff in ruffled aprons over their dresses. Pies displayed behind the cash register and host station encouraged bill-paying customers to take a pie home. Many locations had full bars.

Beyond pies, Marie Callender's became famous for its All You Can Eat Salad Bar, a salad bar like no other in its variety and innovation—such as the hot bacon dressing topping fresh spinach leaves. In the 1970s, most spinach was canned; consuming it fresh was remarkable.

Milestones
- 1964: 1 location
- 1967: 13 locations
- 1970: 26 locations
- 1986: 120 locations
- Late 1990s: 156 locations and 56 franchises in 13 states and Mexico
- 2006: 138 locations
- 2011: 89 locations
- 2019: 26 locations in 2 states
- 2021: 30 locations in 3 states

Don opened in 1984 what in later years he would call an "ego trip": three Callender's Grill locations, in Manhattan Beach, Phoenix, and the Mid-Wilshire/museum area of Los Angeles. The Grill offered a full cocktail menu, California wines, a slow-roasted tri-tip Philly melt, and limitless displays of pies. The Manhattan Beach location closed after only a few years, and the Phoenix store closed in 2011 when all the Arizona locations were shuttered. But the Wilshire location lasted thirty-four years, causing an uproar among locals when it finally closed. Callender's attributed the closure to a doubling of the rent; the landowner insisted that rent had increased only 10 percent over thirty-four years.

Many food companies wanted to purchase the Marie Callender's Pie Shops, but Don felt the offers were too low. In 1986, Ramada Inns Inc. purchased the business and

Top: A burger to go with your pie • Bottom: Ready to take home

The pie case

hired Don Callender as an adviser for the struggling hotel food and beverage operation. Though he signed a five-year contract, Don consulted for only a few years before parting ways, and in 1989 Ramada sold the restaurant chain (to Wilshire Restaurant Group) and the frozen-food line (to Conagra Inc.). Though the Callender family no longer owned the business—which has gone through further changes of ownership—the restaurants have retained the Marie Callender name even as their numbers have declined.

In the 1990s, updated menu items included freshly roasted turkey, sweet roasted red peppers, and garlic mayonnaise on focaccia; vegetarian burgers; turkey Caesars; and "super-premium" pies such as pumpkin on a white chocolate silk base and peanut butter on a dark chocolate base. Marie Callender herself would eat weekly at one of the locations and let her son know how they were doing.

On a November day in 1995, Marie passed away in a retirement community not far from the first Marie Callender's Pie Shop. Clarence had died in 1984. On the day after her passing, Jay Leno paid tribute to Marie and her famous pies on *The Tonight Show with Jay Leno*.

When he wasn't flying his plane, named "Pie

Popular Marie Callender's Pies
Lemon Meringue
Apple
Razzleberry
Cherry
Strawberry
Peach
Banana Cream
Coconut Cream
Chocolate Cream
Custard
Pumpkin

in the Sky," to and from his three homes, Don Callender spent his retirement years refusing to retire. He created a new restaurant, Babe's Bar-B-Que and Brewhouse, in 2002, serving barbecue from all parts of the world, from Korea to Kansas. Boneless beef short ribs, skillet corn bread, fresh pies, and strawberry shortcake made at the in-house bakery are among the menu items, and the on-site microbrewery creates award-winning beers. Stepping into the restaurant, a visitor would spot three things: a warm, inviting cocktail lounge, an oversize fireplace, and a photo of Don's youngest child, Donald "Lucky" Callender, then about nine years old, standing in front of the US flag wearing a flight suit and saluting. Many of the items on the kids' menu are named after Lucky, such as Lucky's Root Beer Floats. Today, Lucky Callender is the owner and operator of Babe's. He has taken the location to new heights with new flavors and beers, just as his father would have done.

On May 31, 2016, the corporate owners of Marie Callender's closed the original restaurant location on Tustin Avenue in Orange that Don Callender had started as a pie shop fifty-two years earlier. It was the end of an era, leaving many locals disappointed. Financial problems continued to pile up, and many more locations have been shuttered. The good news is that the closings have stopped, and business at the thirty locations seems stable at this writing, even with the pandemic challenges. Perhaps pies help people get through lockdowns!

The very frst ad

SNACK SHOP

COCO'S
Bakery • Restaurant
WE BAKE FRESH DAILY

COCO'S
Bakery • Restaurant

The Oak Tree Room
BANQUET FACILITIES
(626) 446-5951

Snack Shop

NAME TODAY: Coco's Restaurant and Bakery
ORIGINAL LOCATION: 2305 East Pacific Coast Highway, Corona del Mar
OPENED: October 19, 1948
COFOUNDERS: John Reuben McIntosh & Audrey Forrow McIntosh
OWNERS: Shari's Management Corporation
CURRENTLY AT THE FIRST LOCATION: Ruby's Diner

There are 33 Coco's in 2 states.

cocosbakery.com

JOHN MCINTOSH was apparently destined to go into the restaurant business. During high school, John started working at Keller's Restaurant in Milwaukee, pouring beer and making sandwiches, to pay for college at the University of Michigan. When the United States entered World War II, John left college and joined the Marines, supplementing his pay as a private by washing dishes in restaurants near El Toro Marine Base in Orange County, where he was stationed. While at El Toro, he met Audrey Forrow, who was also a Marine, and they soon married. Following their marriage and military discharges, they spent three years doing odd jobs in Orange County restaurants so that John could resume college. He took extension courses at the University of California, but insufficient income forced him to drop out in favor of full-time work. In 1948, John became the cook and Audrey the waitress at the Snack Shop—and two weeks later, the owners decided to sell.

John and Audrey obtained a bank loan and purchased the shop for $3,000. The space was small, with only two tables and ten seats around the counter. The husband-and-wife team worked from 7 a.m. to midnight six days a week. At first, it was discouraging. After a good week, they would celebrate on Monday, their day off, by grabbing a six-pack and renting a boat to go fishing under the Coast Highway Bridge.

Hoping to turn the business around, John wrote manuals to help train new staff, while Audrey created many new recipes and designed the restaurant's uniforms and décor. Finally, the books started showing some profit. Two years later, they found a location where they could open another Snack Shop, in Santa Ana, which was success-

Top: The original Snack Shop
Bottom: Modern locations

Original Snack Shop Locations
2305 East Pacific Coast Highway, Corona del Mar
1717 South Main Street, Santa Ana
Ocean Boulevard, Huntington Beach
Waikiki Beach, Honolulu, HI
Chapman & Shaffer, Orange
17th & Flower, Santa Ana
19th & Harbor, Costa Mesa
3440 East Coast Highway, Corona del Mar

Snack Shop (Coco's)

ful from day one. The chain grew to eleven coffee shops by 1960.

In 1960, the McIntoshes created Far West Services as their new restaurant group. In 1965, they opened upscale Reuben's Steakhouse, which shared a wall with their newest coffee shop, Coco's Restaurant and Bakery. They had two price points and two types of restaurants within one building: Reuben's with white tablecloths and wine glasses, and Coco's, strictly a coffee shop—but with plenty of cookies, muffins, brownies, and flaky double-crust pies piled high with freshly whipped cream, all on tempting display at the bakery counter just inside the front door. John and Audrey soon changed the name of the eleven Snack Shops to the new Coco's brand.

In several different years, Coco's competed in the American Pie Council competitions, held in Florida, and won many blue ribbons with a variety of flavors and types of pies. After each blue ribbon, Coco's would add these pies to their menus.

Looking to expand their family of brands within the Far West Services company, John sought out a faux-paddlewheel boat that would look more appropriate on the Mississippi than on the Newport Coast. He found *The Pride of Newport* in 1965 and named his new seafood restaurant the Reuben E. Lee: a mash-up of General Robert E. Lee and McIntosh's middle name, Reuben. This successful restaurant floated in Newport Harbor, hosting many weddings, meetings, and banquets during its thirty years of operation. In 1995, the floating restaurant closed, and the

John McIntosh & Audrey Forrow

Pies Honored by the American Pie Council

Apple
Banana Cream
Berry
Caramel Apple Harvest
Cherry
Chocolate Cream
Classic Pecan
Coconut Cream
Dark Chocolate Chip Cheese
Dark Chocolate Raspberry Harvest
Double Chocolate Silk
Dutch Apple
Dutch Apple Cranberry Cheese
Fresh Peach

Fresh Pecan Cheese
Fresh Strawberry
Fresh Strawberry Banana Cream
Fresh Strawberry Cheese
Lemon Meringue
No-Sugar-Added Apple
Pumpkin
Pumpkin Harvest
Pumpkin Swirl Cheese
Raspberry Swirl Cheese
Signature Cheese
Signature Strawberry Chocolate Harvest
Summer Citrus Harvest

Snack Shop Jr. menu cover

Newport Harbor Nautical Museum opened in its place. For twelve years, the museum hosted 20,000 visitors annually, but the structure became too costly and was dismantled in 2007.

The McIntoshes started other types of branded restaurants as well. At their peak, they served 45,000 guests each day in seventy-two establishments coast to coast. Today, out of all of the brands, only Coco's is still in operation.

In 1985, the McIntoshes sold Far West Services to W.R. Grace and Company. The ownership continued to change hands, bringing Coco's under the same umbrella as another coffee-shop chain, Carrow's, now considered Coco's "sister restaurant." In 2018, the Coco's and Carrow's brands were purchased by Shari's Management Corporation, which also owns Shari's Café and Pies in Oregon. Together, the three brands are the number-one twenty-four-hour restaurants in six states.

Sadly, John and Audrey are not here to appreciate the status that their Coco's coffee shops have attained: They died within two weeks of each other in 2019.

The Far West Family of Restaurants
Snack Shop
Baxter Street Dinner Theater
Coco's
Isadore's
Lt. Robert R. Lee
Reuben E. Lee
Reuben's
The Moonraker
The Plankhouse
The Sandpiper
Whaler

Swensen's Ice Cream

SLOGAN: "From the place where happiness never melts."
ORIGINAL LOCATION: 1999 Hyde Street (at Union), San Francisco
OPENED: April 1948
FOUNDER: Earle Swensen
CURRENT PARENT COMPANY: International Franchise Corp., Markham, Ontario, Canada
CURRENTLY AT THE FIRST LOCATION: The original Swensen's

There are more than 375 locations in 17 countries, 3 of those in the United States, with development rights sold in another 22 countries.

swensens.com

EARLE SWENSEN knew his sweet spot. While serving on a troop transport ship in the South Pacific during World War II, he learned how to make ice cream. After the war, he returned home to San Francisco and became a deputy city assessor, where he kept his eye on locations that might house an ice cream shop. In the late 1940s, a storefront became available on the corner of Hyde and Union—the perfect place, with the famed cable cars rumbling past on Russian Hill. Earle launched his shop with $750 in his pocket and a small-business loan.

Earle Swensen

Swensen's Ice Cream was a family operation: Earle's wife, Nora, and his father-in-law were by his side as he created a high butterfat (14 percent) ice cream, richer and creamier than anything on the market at the time. Earle kept his day job with the city and made the ice creams at night and on weekends, while Nora tended to the scooping and serving. Earle's mother-in-law would bring dinner by so they'd have a warm meal from the hot plate in the back office. Earle named the first shop See Us Freeze Delicious Ice Cream until he left his city job to run the store full-time—against the counsel of friends, who urged him to keep the job for the benefits and the pension—when he changed the name to Swensen's.

Earle and Nora's three daughters also got into the act, taste-testing new flavors and learning to judge for graininess, aftertaste, mouthfeel, and creaminess. "Good as Father Used to Make" became the store's motto, with a drawing of a father making hand-cranked ice cream, a mother, and two daughters, one of the girls holding a doll. Patti, the youngest, liked to say that the doll was her; the drawing was created ten years prior to her birth. It still hangs above the menu board at the original San Francisco location.

Earle's original store was simple: takeaway ice cream with no place to sit. Ice cream was served in a cone; sundaes, in a paper cup. The only offering besides ice cream was Mother's cookies.

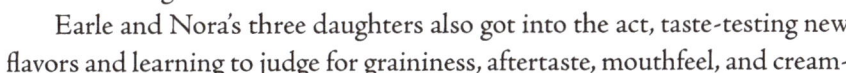

Swensen's first ad

The original San Francisco location

By 1977, Swensen's had been awarded seventy-six gold medals at the California State Fair for its premium ice creams. In fact, it won so many medals that the top of the store was lined with gold, silver, and bronze, until there was no more wall space.

The Russian Hill neighborhood attracted many movie and TV productions, and the stars came out for Swensen's. Vivian Vance, Tony Bennett, Brian Keith, and many others stopped in—but Earle never put their pictures on the walls. The ice cream was the real star. In March 1968, newly married Lynda Bird Johnson, daughter of then-President Lyndon Johnson, was on vacation in San Francisco. After Lynda ordered a double-decker butterscotch ice cream, she and her husband and their Secret Service escorts jumped on the cable car outside the shop. A few blocks later, she was kicked off for breaking an unwritten rule that you could not eat aboard the cable cars, and she refused to throw away her ice cream. In fact, the next day the group went back for more. Afterward, the President's social secretary asked that some ice cream be shipped to the White House for Lynda's return to Washington. Earle sent some, but he didn't have the heart to bill the President.

Before Swensen's, most ice creams fell on the mundane end of the flavor spectrum. Using locally sourced chocolate from Guittard in Burlingame, fresh fruit, and seasonal ingredients, Earle tested and created more than 150 innovative flavors, including Sticky Chewy Chocolate, Pistachio, Adam's Apple, Caramel Cashew, Thin Mint, Turkish Coffee, Fresh Peach, Pumpkin, Eggnog, and Cranberry.

An active participant in local events, Earle held an annual "Treat no Trick" Halloween stunt in the 1950s: Every kid who popped into the shop with a nice smile and no tricks received a free cone of "izekrim": orange sherbet and chocolate ice cream or pumpkin and licorice. As a sponsor of a tennis tournament at the Alice Marble Courts, Earle created a new flavor, Alice Marble Fudge (French vanilla, a ribbon of chocolate, and maraschino cherries), in honor of the local hero, a tennis player and spy for the Allies during World War II. In 1966, Swensen's provided Ghirardelli with ice cream for the new ice cream parlor at the famous Ghirardelli Square chocolate factory.

In 1959, while in high school, Dick Campana started working for Earle. He didn't realize this would be his career for life. He ultimately became the manager of the San Francisco location, and in the 1960s, when Earle began to franchise his concept, he helped Earle train franchisees in making the perfect ice cream using the forty-quart Emery Thompson batch freezer.

Earle was business savvy and taught Dick such tenets as: A smaller store will look busier with three or four people inside than a huge store, and the smaller store requires less upkeep and rent. Because the ice cream industry is small, don't talk smack about your competitors—a competitor may have to borrow something from you and you from them.

Earle's youngest daughters, Patti and Linda, drove all over California helping their dad with the franchisees. Earle traveled with his typewriter and index cards so he could type up recipe cards for each location. Every franchise had its own batch freezer, so the ice cream could be made in view of the customer. By 1964, there were 400 locations worldwide. But Earle always kept the rights to the San Francisco store.

Many franchisees wanted more than ice cream to sell, and full menus became part of the concept. Swensen's became a turn-of-the-century ice cream parlor with long wooden bar counters, tall brass and wooden stools, old-fashioned ceiling fans with Tiffany-style glass lights, marble-topped tables, and gingham uniforms. In one corner of the store, a large glass window painted with the word "Factory" allowed customers to watch the ice cream maker create those special flavors. If visitors timed it right, the maker would bring out a carton of freshly made ice cream to sample.

In the early 1970s, on a trip to an ice cream convention in San Diego, Earle and Dick and their wives drove to the San Diego Zoo. Earle had heard that Baskin-Robbins (page 93) had opened an ice cream shop on the grounds, with a new flavor he wanted to try: Pralines 'n Cream. Earle purchased four cones, one for each of them. He loved it so much, he told Dick, "We have to create a flavor like this!" Then he decided he wanted one more taste of the nutty, brown-sugary ice cream—but asked that someone else get it for him, as he didn't want anyone from the convention to see Mr. Swensen buying a Baskin-Robbins cone.

In the franchisees' stores in the late 1970s, many new sundaes were created and served in gigantic glass goblets. Patti recalls family vacations in Hawaii when her dad tasted ice cream from other companies. One had a Volcano Sundae, which gave Earle the idea of creating the Earthquake: eight scoops of any of the thirty-seven available flavors, covered with eight toppings, and completed with whipped cream, toasted almonds, and maraschino cherries. It became the dish to share with friends.

Brighter and more colorful ice creams were the most popular among kids. In 1977, Pink Bubblegum became a favorite. A few crazy flavors were introduced as publicity stunts to get people and the

> **Top 6 Swensen's Flavors Around the World**
> 1. Chocolate
> 2. Green Tea
> 3. Red Bean
> 4. Sticky Chewy Chocolate
> 5. Thin Mint
> 6. Vanilla

Swensen's Ice Cream

press talking about the new ice cream store in the neighborhood. Some of these included Dill Pickle (yes, it had dill juice in a vanilla base); Pink Squirrel, featuring crème de cacao and crème d'amande mixed in a strawberry base; and Golden Poppy, orange sorbet with sunflower seeds.

International locations feature flavors made with local fruits and ingredients not common in North America. Swensen's in Singapore, for example, has offered green tea and red bean ice cream since long before those were popular in the United States, along with Durian Supreme, Yummy Coconut, and Salted Gula Melaka.

In the 1980s, entrepreneur Karl Eller became the chief shareholder and chairman and moved the company to the Phoenix area. At the annual convention of franchisees, unbeknown to Earle, the corporation stated that each location would have thirty days to rid the locations of their batch freezers and start purchasing their ice cream ready-made from a new plant in Phoenix. During that thirty days, half the owners changed the names of their stores, and the company dropped to 200 locations overnight. Phoenix used Earle's original recipes, but the larger batches tasted different and the product was no longer stored according to Earle's standards. Many American franchises closed,

Artwork on the menu

The Miami location

Daniel Kobiolka & Kelli Pedroli at their Swensen's wedding

citing the prevalence of new high-quality ice cream products like Ben & Jerry's and Häagen-Dazs in grocery stores and the fact that the ice cream was no longer made at each location.

In 1982, Earle sold his percentage of the franchise, except for his original store. All around Northern California you could see Earle driving his royal blue Mercedes, with the personalized license plate ICE CRM.

In 1996, Earle passed away at eighty-six, leaving the San Francisco location in the hands of Dick Campana. Daughter Patti often visited the Napa location, which features a video loop of photos of her mom and dad working in their first location. When Patti's daughter Kelli got married, two huge goblets sporting the Swensen's logo were used as the newlyweds served each other ice cream instead of wedding cake.

Today, Swensen's operates in Brunei, Cambodia, China, Colombia, India, Laos, Malaysia, Maldives, Myanmar, Pakistan, Saudi Arabia, Singapore, Taiwan, Thailand, Vietnam, and the United States, which has just three operating ice cream parlors: Midland, Texas; Coral Gables, Florida; and San Francisco. Only San Francisco has its own in-store manufacturing.

And of all those hundreds of Swensen's flavors over the decades, which was Earle Swensen's favorite? Pure vanilla.

Earle making kids happy

Winchell's Donuts

ORIGINAL LOCATION: 9103 East Las Tunas Drive, Temple City
OPENED: October 1948
FOUNDER: Verne H. Winchell
CURRENT OWNER: A subsidiary of Yum-Yum Donuts
CURRENTLY AT THE FIRST LOCATION: PHD Hair Salon

There are 104 stores in 5 western states, Guam, Saipan, and Saudi Arabia.

winchells.com

AFTER STUDYING BUSINESS at Pasadena City College, young Verne H. Winchell leaped into work with two of the key qualities that make for a successful entrepreneur: ideas and enthusiasm. He just didn't have the success. His first two enterprises, Winchell's Music (selling jukeboxes) and Winchell's Used Motor Cars, both failed in short order. Searching for a new venture while talking with a friend about high profit-margin businesses, Verne lighted on...doughnuts. Since he already owned a piece of commercial property on Las Tunas and Hart in Temple City, Verne invested some money to turn it into a drive-thru doughnut shop.

The first shop was extremely successful, leading Verne to open two more, one in South Gate and another in Huntington Park. When these did not do as well, Verne decided that, since he could not personally be at every location at the same time, he needed to motivate his managers, create effective advertising, and ensure that his doughnuts were top quality. The two new stores soon turned around and became profitable. Verne expanded his operations throughout the state of California, taking out quarter-page ads in local newspapers to advertise that a new Winchell's store would be opening with special pricing. He also started the "Winchell's Dozen": fourteen doughnuts, one more than the baker's dozen most doughnut stores sold. When consumer trends showed that customers wanted more than a walk-up window, Verne opened a new type of doughnut shop in Redondo Beach, calling it a "coffee room," with seats and tables. The larger footprint meant higher construction costs, but the increased sales made up for it.

Five years later, Verne opened a corporate headquarters in Alhambra with a central production and distribution facility that could meet the stores' needs. This also enabled him to franchise.

The company went public in 1961 and expanded eastward into Arizona and Colorado. Mel Allison, director of quality assurance, spent time in the mountains

Left: Icing the doughnuts • Inset: A Winchell's matchbook cover
Right: Verne H. Winchell

to ensure that the doughnut mixes would work perfectly at higher elevations. Allison is still with the company in the same role, and one of the most popular doughnuts on Winchell's menu is his creation: the apple fritter—a large pile of dough and apples chopped together, fried, and iced with a sweet glaze. People traveled from all around the Southland to taste the treats created by Allison in his Westminster store.

In 1963, Verne experimented by branching into the frozen-food market with chocolate iced cake and cinnamon-topped varieties. But the chocolate icing stuck to the boxes, and the quality was not that of a real, fresh doughnut from the shops. The venture lasted only a few months.

Verne's franchises were much more successful: By 1968, there were more than 250 Winchell's locations, and Verne sold the company to Denny's (page 183) in exchange for stock. Verne remained in charge of his doughnut empire while also serving on the Denny's board of directors; he would later serve as Denny's chairman of the board, president, and CEO.

Under Verne's leadership, both Winchell's and Denny's expanded dramatically; Denny's sales quadrupled. During the 1970s, Winchell's grew to almost 1,000 units in six countries, with stores as far away as Asia and Europe. When, in 1980, the company announced it was closing 150 unprofitable stores, some enterprising entrepreneurs bought those closed locations, flipped the *W* to become an *M*, changed the *n* to a *t*, and announced the opening of Mitchell's Donuts. (But they had to find their own ingredients.)

Twenty-four-hour doughnuts

The twenty-fifth anniversary of the opening of the first Winchell's Donut House inspired a full year of celebrations in every store. The state of California awarded Winchell's a gold medal for product excellence at the California State Fair and Exhibition. And all stores celebrated with price savings on each dozen doughnuts. To add to the glory, twice in the 1970s Winchell's Donut House was awarded the Governor's Award for its float in the Rose Parade, televised to millions around the world.

Verne also made news for his longtime hobby: owning and breeding racehorses, a passion that started when he was a young man in the 1930s. His thoroughbred, the Donut King (which bore Verne's own nickname), was a favorite to win the Kentucky Derby in 1954, but he was injured a week before the race and had to be withdrawn. In 1978, Verne bought a 320-acre farm in Lexington, Kentucky, where he bred more than sixty stake winners and raced more than forty. He had twenty-five broodmares on the property. Three more of his horses—Classic Go Go, Sea Cadet, and Valiant Nature—ran in later derbys, coming in fourth, eighth, and thirteenth, respectively.

In 1980, Verne sold his interest in the company that he started and had managed. Later in the decade, Denny's returned to private ownership with Winchell's as a spin-off, more Winchell's stores closed in the Midwest and Texas, and Winchell's was sold to a variety of holding companies. Dunkin Donuts, launched in Massachusetts in 1980, had become the largest doughnut chain by far, but Winchell's still had the west coast markets with more than 466 stores in California alone.

Winchell's Prototypes & Ideas

1948: Winchell's Donuts
1989: Winchell's Express
1990: Winchell's N' More
1999: Winchell's World
2019: Win Win Fillin' Station

The company added new products, such as cinnamon rolls and bear claws. Since 70 percent of Winchell's sales occur before noon, Winchell's added muffins, bagel sandwiches, and blended smoothies. With coffee starting its stratospheric ascendancy, Winchell's introduced Legendary Gold, a high-end, dark-roast coffee. The coffee came in expensive, environmentally friendly cups instead of Styrofoam, and ads described the coffee as a premium alternative to the competitor they coyly referred to as "Big Bucks."

In 1998, for the fiftieth anniversary, the Pasadena store created the world's largest doughnut at the time, ninety-five feet in diameter and weighing 5,000 pounds. And Winchell's returned to its core principles of doughnuts and coffee. The logo and the company stores were redesigned. But competition from high-end coffee shops, supermarket bakeries, and rivals like South Carolina's Krispy Kreme proved tough for Winchell's to beat. Winchell's took a cue from Krispy Kreme and opened a 6,000-foot store in Pomona called Winchell's World, where you could see the doughnuts being made in front of you, but the store lasted only two years.

Win Win Fillin' Station

So Winchell's installed a red neon sign that said "Warm 'n Fresh" in each of its stores, which boosted sales by 10 percent in the morning hours while it was illuminated. Between 6 a.m. and 9 a.m., customers were guaranteed a warm doughnut right out of the fryer. This was part of the back-to-basics mindset. Consumers were becoming health conscious, so Winchell's introduced Light Side: the traditional doughnut, but 40 percent smaller. It was a hit. To increase visibility, Winchell's partnered with Lucy's Laundry Marts, opening small doughnut shops inside eleven locations around Los Angeles. It also conducted cross promotions with other companies, like Hershey's.

Verne H. Winchell died in 2002 at the age of eighty-seven. Since 2004, Winchell's has been owned by Yum Yum Donuts. At the time of the sale, Yum Yum purchased 111 company-owned Winchell's and sixty-seven franchised stores. Twenty-five Winchell's locations were converted to the Yum Yum brand.

Today in Southern California, you can find both the new and the old faces of Winchell's. Perfectly situated near the 10, 60, and 605 freeways in La Puente, a Win Win Fillin' Station opened in 2018, a twenty-four-hour, one-stop shop for fuel, food, and, of course, Winchell's doughnuts. More Win Wins are on the way. Then head to 555 South Glenoaks Boulevard in Burbank, where you'll discover the oldest continually operating doughnut store, #9311, one of the original Winchell's shops with a walk-up window. But proving that everything that rises must converge, it's now a Yum Yum.

Chris' & Pitt's

SLOGAN: "Home of the Live Wood Fire"
ORIGINAL LOCATION: 3226 Tweedy Boulevard, South Gate

OPENED: 1949
COFOUNDERS: Chris George Pelonis & Morris Pittman
CURRENT OWNERS: CGP Management Company, a privately held company
CURRENT MANAGER: Debbie Pelonis Berry (daughter)
CURRENTLY AT THE FIRST LOCATION: An empty lot

There are 3 restaurants remaining today

chrisandpittsbbqrestaurants.com

A GREAT BARBECUE sauce requires a great combination of ingredients, and Chris George Pelonis developed his with the most important ingredient of all: an incredible work ethic. Born in Chicago in 1922 to Greek immigrants, Chris moved with his family to Boyle Heights in L.A. when he was eight years old. During high school, he took a typing class because that's where the girls were; he then parlayed his typing skills into a career as a stenographer with the army. There he developed his capacity for hard work—and his dream of opening a barbecue restaurant.

After his discharge in 1949, Chris and his business partner, Morris Pittman, found a site in an unlikely location: a former dry-cleaning shop in South Gate. Pelonis borrowed $2,000 from his father to rent the space, then spent his days creating the restaurant (wooden tables, sawdust on the floors) and his evenings at home working out recipes for a Texas-style barbecue sauce. Chris' & Pitt's was launched. Business picked up quickly, so they opened a second location about five miles away in Downey, enabling each owner to manage his own location. Chris knew that marketing his barbecue sauce commercially would bring more customers into the restaurants, and by 1950, the bottles were on shelves in grocery stores. The sauce became a top seller in eleven western states.

Chris' & Pitt's restaurants offered full meals from day one, and at lower prices than their competitors. All dinners came with a "crisp tossed salad" or one of three daily soups, along with a wedge

Chris George Pelonis

Top: Early barbecue in South Gate • Bottom: The Bellflower location survives

Chris' and Pitt's

of garlic bread, barbecue beans, and french fries. For barbecue, customers had a choice of beef, pork, or chicken. Chicken breasts were cooked Hawaiian style with a sweet-and-sour glaze or plain, broiled without sauce. Diners also had a choice of toppings: peppers chopped together with scallions, bacon, and "au jus"; chicken gravy; or Italian cheese sauce. Steaks were a star attraction: sirloin steak in four sizes, rib steak, and porterhouse, all cooked in the famous wood pit. "That's Right—We're NOT Cooking with Gas" became the restaurant's motto. To attract the lunch crowd, Chris' & Pitt's introduced the "Merchants' Lunch": a salad to start, a main dish with a choice of side, and a beverage. This was popular from the beginning and is still served today.

In 1954, Chris married, and his wife, Andronikki, became his rock in the business. She managed a few of the locations until her death in 1993.

During the time Chris and Morris worked together, they expanded Chris' & Pitt's to seven locations. Many were iconic and highly visible, with big neon signs lighting the California sky and buildings painted to look like log cabins. Then in 1963, Chris became the sole owner of the chain in a friendly buyout. His family-minded sensibility set the tone. He hired close family members to manage the restaurants. He focused on providing great food at low prices, so more customers could afford to bring their families. He was dedicated to his employees and treated them like family. Norma Roman, a server/manager at the Downey location for thirty-six years, told the *Whittier Daily News* that Pelonis supported her when her daughter was in the hospital for three months. "If I had another job, I probably would have been let go," she said. "He kept my job and helped me with whatever I needed."

Over the years, fourteen Chris' & Pitt's locations opened in Orange and Los Angeles counties.

> **Chris' & Pitt's' Retail Products**
> Onion Bits Sauce
> Garlic Sauce
> Hickory Sauce
> Hot Sauce
> Regular Sauce
> Sweet & Sour Sauce (1972)
> Teriyaki Barbecue (1972)
> Cucumber Slices
> Small Kosher Dills
> Hamburger Slices
> Whole Sweet Pickles

The Garden Grove location, in business from 1957 to 1987

> A 1972 newspaper coupon advertisement: "There's only one reason why Chris' & Pitt's is the *best selling* barbecue sauce in the west: because it's the best *tasting*. We prepare Chris' & Pitt's without compromise—tomatoes of richest flavor, freshest herbs, and spices. And then our Chris' & Pitt's extra care cooking fully develops the deep-down flavor that active people crave."

Each one was numbered in succession, without a number 13. The last new Chris' & Pitt's opened in 1973 in Anaheim; it closed twenty-seven years later, and a Jollibee's, a Filipino fast-food chain, opened at the site. In 1968, Pelonis sold the rights to the barbecue sauces and a handful of other items to Durkee Fine Foods. Today, they're owned by the Flagship Food Group, marketed by Treasure Valley Specialty Foods.

On May 21, 2018, at the age of ninety-seven, Chris George Pelonis died. Debbie Pelonis Berry has continued her father's tradition at the three remaining locations. When a new Golden Corral Buffet Restaurant opened with a larger sign next to the Bellflower location in May 2016, Berry and the staff were concerned. Within a few weeks, however, Chris' & Pitt's again had lines—in fact, the lines were longer, since the buffet restaurant was too busy. But Chris' & Pitt's was ready to welcome all customers, and their families.

> **Remaining Locations**
> 9839 Artesia Boulevard, Bellflower (opened 1956)
> 11350 East Washington Boulevard, Whittier (opened 1956)
> 9243 Lakewood Boulevard, Downey (opened 1957)

The Downey restaurant, open from 1951 to 1977

McConnell's Fine Ice Creams

ORIGINAL LOCATION: 2001 State Street, Santa Barbara

OPENED: 1949
COFOUNDERS: Gordon ("Mac") & Ernesteen McConnell
CURRENT OWNERS: Michael Palmer & Eva Ein
CURRENTLY AT THE FIRST LOCATION: Garrett's Restaurant

There are 7 "scoop shops," and the ice cream is available prepackaged in many grocery stores.

mcconnells.com

IT IS UNHEARD OF for a food company to be in business for more than seventy years with only three sets of owners and maintaining the quality of the product. But that's what McConnell's Fine Ice Creams has accomplished since its founding in 1949 by the husband-and-wife team of Gordon ("Mac") and Ernesteen ("Ernie") McConnell.

Mac, a former health-food-store owner, wanted to create an ice cream like the ones he'd enjoyed in Europe during World War II: rich, pure, and natural, without any of the artificial flavorings, fillers, stabilizers, sweeteners, or colorings used in ice cream production at the time (and now).

The McConnells selected products from California's Central Coast to make their ice creams, including milk and cream from local grass-fed cows and nuts and fruits from nearby farms. And Mac created his own version of the French Pot method that had produced those ice creams he loved in Europe. As the pot spins, cream freezes to the sides. A blade scrapes the frozen cream back into the middle, preventing air from being whipped into the cream. This was the way all ice cream used to be made until large-batch, cost-cutting methods became the norm. When the McConnells opened their first shop at the corner of State and Mission in 1949, they made the ice cream on-site, and customers could watch the process. McConnell's still uses Mac's French Pot method today.

In 1962, after thirteen years of building the business, Mac died unexpectedly. Ernie sold McConnell's to Jim and Jeney McCoy. Jeney worked as the taste tester and quality-control person, while Jim, a former marketing man for Shell, became the scooper, public face, and big heart of the business, giving ice cream cones to children who brought in a report card with an A.

In 1975, the McCoys moved the headquarters and plant to the "Old Dairy," at the corner of Milpas and Cañon Perdido, which dated back to the mid-1930s. They had a life-size plaster cow placed on the roof, and it was soon dubbed the McConnell's Cow. Five years later, Jim hired Mike Vierra, a recent graduate of Cal Poly San Luis Obispo, to become a master ice cream maker. Mike developed such flavors as Brazilian Coffee Chip and Bordeaux Strawberry, and such seasonal flavors as Eggnog,

Ernesteen & Mac McConnell

Among the Many Awards
- NBC News: America's Best Ice Creams, 2008
- Best of LAist: Best L.A. Ice Cream Shop
- Specialty Food Association Sofi Award: Double Peanut Butter Chip
- *Time* magazine: Best in the World
- *People* magazine: The Dutchman Chocolate, Top Ice Cream for Summer
- The Daily Meal: The World's 50 Best Ice Cream Parlors, 2018

Pumpkin, and Russian Nesselrode (with dried fruit and chestnuts). Meanwhile, Jim and Jeney focused on introducing the ice cream to such chain stores as Whole Foods, Ralphs, and Bristol Farms. In 1987, the McCoys moved the original Santa Barbara ice cream shop from State and Mission a few blocks down to Mission and De la Viña.

When Jim bought McConnell's in 1962, he planned to run it for a few years. Nearly fifty years later, as he neared his eightieth birthday in 2011, Jim decided it was time to sell the company and retire. Husband and wife Michael Palmer (a winemaker) and Eve Ein (a chef) had recently lost their home in the Tea Fire and decided that rather than rebuild their house, they'd use the insurance money to buy McConnell's. Michael hired dairy veteran Charley Price to replace the Old Dairy's ancient machinery with state-of-the-art equipment.

In 2013, the Palmer-Ein team returned McConnell's to where it all began, with two scoop shops on State Street in Santa Barbara. One of the first orders of business was to bring back the legacy fla-

First location

French Pot manufacturing

vors that had started McConnell's, including peppermint, chocolate, and Turkish coffee. Next came new flavors: Toasted Coconut Almond Chip, Double Peanut Chip, Dark Chocolate Paso Brittle (using a smoked sea salt almond brittle made in Paso Robles), and Churros con Leche (described by one reviewer as "eyes-roll-to-the-back-of-your-head good"). Vanilla may outsell all ice creams in the world, but at McConnell's, the top contenders are Sea Salt Cream & Cookies, Eureka Lemon and Marionberries, and Salted Caramel Chip. They make their own jams, caramels, nut brittles, and baked goods to use in their ice creams, and they're always looking to improve. The molten chocolate chip–making process, for instance, is unique: While the ice cream is churning at 20–21°F, they heat the chocolate to over 100°F and pour it into the pot by hand, thus creating different-size chips for an incredible mouthful of textures and tastes.

Most ice cream makers do not make their base mix from scratch like McConnell's does, as it requires a pasteurizing center. McConnell's is one of the only small ice cream makers that does not start with a pre-mix—they create their own mix in their own plant, just like Mac McConnell did at the beginning. The mouthfeel is creamier, thanks to a milk-fat level of more than 18 percent (most gourmet ice creams are 14 percent). Today, they have seven company-owned shops, including one in downtown L.A.'s Grand Central Market, and their ice cream is available in thousands of markets and grocery stores.

Mac and Ernie would be proud.

Current owners Michael Palmer & Eve Ein

McConnell's Fine Ice Creams

NORMS Restaurants

ORIGINAL LOCATION: 6353 Sunset Boulevard, Los Angeles

OPENED: 1949
FOUNDER: Norman Roybark
CURRENT OWNER: CapitalSpring, a private investment firm
CURRENTLY AT THE FIRST LOCATION: An entertainment office building

Today there are 20 locations.

norms.com

Norman Roybark

HOLLYWOOD IN THE LATE 1940s: The war was over. The youth of the day were going out for the night. Dance places like the Palladium and Florentine Gardens were packed. And after an evening on the town, the next stop was breakfast. If you had a car that you wanted to show off, you'd head over to a drive-in like Tiny Naylor's, at La Brea and Sunset, or Delores, on the Sunset Strip. But if you were with a group and wanted waitress service, NORMS, at Sunset and Vine, was the place to be.

Norman Roybark, who had previously owned a used-car lot and a Nash dealership, found a great location to open his restaurant amid all the clubs in Hollywood. NORMS was different from the other coffee shops of the day. NORMS was open twenty-four hours, stayed local, and did not expand coast to coast like Denny's and Big Boy. Everything was made from scratch, from the soups to the salad dressings. Even today, a butcher works at each location, grinding meat for hamburgers and cutting steaks, roasting tom turkeys for Thanksgiving dinners and glazed hams for Easter.

Roybark referred to the original location as NORMS Hollywood. But the most iconic and longest-operating location is the NORMS at La Cienega and Melrose, a prime example of the space-age style of architecture known as Googie: cantilevered roof, glass and steel, vivid colors, and the unique signage spelling out NORMS on vertically arranged pennants. The location has operated consistently since 1957, even surviving a demolition threat by a new owner in 2015, until the Los Angeles City Council voted unanimously to have it designated as a "historic-cultural monument."

In 1963, Roybark opened SCOOPS, a diner in Studio City that later took on the NORMS name. Phil's Fast and Friendly was the third Roybark concept: a hamburger stand in San Gabriel next to the NORMS there.

Oldest standing NORMS, on La Cienega in Los Angeles

The now-gone Sunset Boulevard original

When Norm died in August 1969 after a long illness, the Roybark family continued to operate the chain just as he had for another forty-six years. Until the COVID-19 era, and like Denny's (page 183), each NORMS location had been open 24/7 continuously since 1950, with two exceptions: NORMS closed for two hours in 1963 for President Kennedy's funeral, and six years later for two hours for Norman Roybark's funeral.

In 1971, at the Sunset-Vermont location, NORMS president Sterling Bogart noticed a waitress wearing a smiley-face button given to her by a customer. Bogart ordered them for all the waitresses. Soon many customers were requesting them. Bogart launched happy-face balloons for the kids and buttons for the adults. In a year, nearly 1 million happy-face buttons were given away. They even incorporated it into their name as the O in NORMS for a time.

By 1980, fifteen NORMS dotted the Southern California landscape. The main office had few rules as to what the locations served except for the advertised specials. Unlike most chains, every NORMS location had different menus and pricing, but each had high-quality, great diner food at a lower-than-average cost.

Notice of breakfast specials and steak specials adorned the windows of NORMS. Breakfasts generally came with eggs, bacon, potatoes, coffee, and juice. Omelets (Spanish, Mexican, ham and cheese, etc.) came with toast and jelly, hash browns, and coffee or juice. A steak special, available any time of the day, featured one of seven different steaks (Salisbury, top sirloin, New York, T-bone, porterhouse, Delmonico, or chuckwagon sirloin), a big bowl of the soup of the day, a crisp green salad with house-made dressing (Thousand Island, blue cheese, or oil and vinegar), baked potato or mashed potatoes, hot roll, dessert, and a bev-

Ownership Timeline
1949–1969: Norm Roybark
1969–2015: Roybark Family
2015–present: Jim Balis

erage. You could top your steak with sautéed mushrooms or grilled onions and peppers.

In December 2014, the Roybark family chose to sell the chain—but

> **It's Still the 1950s at These Locations**
> La Cienega at Melrose, West Hollywood (since 1957)
> 2500 Slauson Avenue, Huntington Park (since 1959)

not the land that each of the locations sits on—to investor Jim Balis. NORMS continues its tradition of supporting the communities that it serves, with programs for fighting childhood hunger in local schools and with nonprofit organizations. During the COVID-19 pandemic, NORMS created care packages, such as eggs, milk, and other dairy products in short supply from local stores. NORMS even had a special: Spend $10, get a flat of eggs.

With its food, style, and customer service, NORMS has always had star power. The NORMS in Huntington Park has a full open-exhibition kitchen that allows guests to watch cooks in action. The West Hollywood location was used in an episode of *Comedians in Cars Getting Coffee* with Jerry Seinfeld and Carl Reiner. The former NORMS in Westwood, on West Pico, was used for interior and exterior shots for the 2015 film *Woman in Gold* starring Ryan Reynolds and Helen Mirren. The creator of *Mad Men*, Mattthew Weiner, wrote the notes for the beginning of the show at the NORMS West Hollywood location and supported the preservation of the restaurant as a historical location.

It makes sense that a restaurant chain that launched in the middle of Hollywood is always ready for its close-up.

Midcentury style inside NORMS Hollywood

The Red Onion Cafe

NAME BECAME: The Red Onion
NAME TODAY: The Original Red Onion
ORIGINAL LOCATION: 307 East Hillcrest Boulevard, Inglewood

OPENED: Fall 1949
FOUNDER: Enrique "Harry" Earle
CURRENT OWNERSHIP: Jeff Earle, grandson of the founder
CURRENTLY AT THE FIRST LOCATION: Aunt Emma's Popcorn Shop

There is 1 location remaining from a former high of 26. The remaining location is referred to as The Original Red Onion and is located in the Rolling Hills Estates neighborhood near Palos Verdes.

originalredonion.com

HARRY EARLE came to the food business naturally: His mother, Catalina, ran a kitchen preparing food for miners in a small town in Arizona, after moving from Sonora, Mexico, with her husband, Guillermo. (After Guillermo was killed in a hunting accident, Catalina married William Earle, who adopted Harry and his brother.) Harry moved to California, bringing his love for Sonoran food with him. He found work in restaurants and lunch counters around Los Angeles in the prewar years. He was a hard worker and took every position, considering each a learning experience.

In 1942, he opened El Rae (Earle spelled backwards) at 1149 South Western Avenue in Los Angeles. The flavors of the recipes came directly from his mother's kitchen—but the rationing and food restrictions demanded by World War II made it impossible to keep the restaurant open. Harry later opened the Red Onion Cafe on Hillcrest Boulevard, the second-busiest street in the Inglewood area. It was a small, step-down storefront diner with seating for only fifteen. The Red Onion was very much a family venture. Harry educated his two sons, Bart and Don, in the growing business.

In 1958, Bart opened his own Red Onion location in Hawthorne and dropped the word *Cafe*. The proximity to Los Angeles International Airport and the aerospace companies meant that his dining room was packed at lunch-time every weekday. He opened another location with great success during the summer of 1963 in the upscale neighborhood of Rolling Hills Estates, which had no restaurants at the time. It had a hacienda look, with a red-tiled roof and reclaimed bricks and, inside, colorful tile flooring, comfortable tomato-red leather booths, and sombreros and serapes on the walls. Bart purchased many doors from the famous La Posada Hotel in Winslow, Arizona, off Route 66, when it closed and installed them throughout the restaurant. This location became the company's flagship. Next came a Torrance location, between the Rolling Hills and the Hawthorne restaurants; all had a warm Sonoran look.

Bart's younger brother, Don, and his high school classmate Ronald Newman partnered to form a separate company, International Onion, Inc. Using the Red Onion name, they opened their first loca-

Top: The Inglewood original • Bottom: The red-tile roof in Rolling HIls Estates remains today

The rebranded "Original"

tion in a former Blue Chip stamp store in Westchester. By 1975, they had thirteen locations, each with a very different look and feel than Bart's. They were in higher-traffic locations and targeted a young, single crowd. Cash was king, cheap drinks flowed, and they charged a cover at the door. Food became secondary to an active bar scene and live bands. Some locations even held wet T-shirt contests. During the late '70s and early '80s, business boomed. In 1982, Don sold his interest to Newman.

To separate himself from the hard-partying other Red Onions, Bart changed the name of his places in Irvine, Hawthorne, Rolling Hills, Torrance, and Inglewood to Bart Earle's Red Onion. But the International Red Onion restaurants were in trouble. A number of factors led to their demise, starting with rent increases and a push from Mothers Against Drunk Driving to curtail drunken debauchery. Without admitting guilt, the partners paid heavy fines for health- and fire-code violations. With the large amounts of cash coming in at the door and the bars, the IRS got involved.

In May 1988, three independent Red Onion owners (not those of Newman's International Onion group), Bart Earle, Darrien Earle, and Rick Loomis, felt that their establishments had been tarnished by association. Bart changed his building name again, this time to the Original Red Onion. On many mornings, the mail would bring notices of lawsuits and legal papers, as people thought that the Rolling Hills Estates location housed the corporate offices of International Red Onion.

Bart sold his restaurants to Host International in 1973, keeping the Rolling Hills Estates location. Host International rebranded them as Casa Marias. Host International was later sold to Marriott Corporation, so thus, the Casa Marias became El Toritos (page 187). (At this writing, Ronald Newman and his son Greg control eleven food enterprises from Newport Beach to Santa Barbara; none are former Red Onions.)

Bart's son Jeff began working in the restaurant as a summertime dishwasher when he was thirteen. His passion was politics, and after graduating with a degree in history from USC, he worked for President Reagan as an assistant press secretary. After a close loss for California Assembly in 1994, Jeff returned to the restaurant business, and in 1996, he bought his father's

Harry Earle in the kitchen

The crew at the Rolling Hills location

interest in the Original Red Onion in Rolling Hills Estates. Bart passed away in 2011.

Jeff brought a fresher look to the menu, and healthier options. He also instituted a catering service, initially operating out of his Toyota 4Runner, and now composed of catering trucks grilling on aromatic mesquite and serving from copper chafing dishes; he can even provide mariachis.

Today, the Original Red Onion in Rolling Hills is the sole location left of the twenty-six restaurants that once operated under that name. Inside, almost every inch of the walls is covered with historical framed photos, menus, and mementos from the family and the restaurants. Jeff also has many of the original drawings of the stars of yesteryear from the Brown Derby (page 39) in Hollywood.

Jeff even managed to change the name of the frontage road on which the restaurant sits. It's now called Bart Earle Way.

Three generations of Earles, left to right: Bart, Harry & Jeff

Hamburger Hamlet

ORIGINAL LOCATION: 8929 West Sunset Boulevard, West Hollywood

OPENED: 1950
COFOUNDERS: Harry Lewis & Marilyn Friedman-Lewis
CURRENTLY AT THE FIRST LOCATION: Car dealership

At one point there were 24 locations in 3 states. The last branch, in Sherman Oaks, closed in 2018.

ACTOR HARRY LEWIS met his future wife, Marilyn Friedman, at the Pasadena Playhouse while he was playing Edward "Toots" Bass in *Key Largo*, a role he'd go on to play in the film. In fact, Marilyn came to the theater a number of consecutive evenings just to see Harry. You could say they were meant for each other like a hamburger and a bun.

When film jobs started drying up for Harry, his girlfriend Marilyn was the force driving him to open a restaurant. She spent her days off from work scouring the Hollywood area for a prime location. One day in 1950, she phoned Harry and said, "I found the perfect spot for our little place." She put a deposit down on 8929 West Sunset Boulevard, where they operated for eighteen years; the entire cost of opening was $3,500. Harry named the restaurant after the role every actor wanted to play: Hamlet.

The upscale hamburger/steak restaurant started a trend for casual dining with elegance. Harry was in charge of the kitchen, and Marilyn waited tables and trained the staff. Marilyn's training manual, which she wrote herself, could have been a textbook for all restaurant managers on how to treat and talk to diners correctly. She created what became known as the Nine Commandments. One was never to use the word *fried*; use *sautéed* instead (not that she knew about the health concerns of fried foods in the 1950s, but she knew that sautéed sounded more European and classy).

The antique-wood-paneled walls were hung with a coat of arms consisting of a crossed knife and fork behind a fat hamburger. Quasi-Shakespearean quotes decorated the menu: "Hamlet to the chef," "Much ado about something," "Eat the sides, I pray you," "To eat or not to eat, this is not the question," and "This above all, to cheese blintzes be true." John Barrymore Jr. contributed photos of his famous father, and papier-mâché miniature stage settings of Shakespeare's plays decorated the walls.

Given the name, the hamburgers and their wide range of toppings (Russian dressing was a favorite of Janet Leigh and Tony Curtis) took the spotlight, but burgers were only a fraction of the menu. Hamburger Hamlet was also famous for its lobster bisque, onion soup, sandwiches, fried-zucchini "zircles," and more.

Hamburger Hamlet on Sunset

The combination of upscale burgers, the Bard, and celebrities proved irresistible. Autograph hounds lined up on the weekends to catch a glimpse and possibly a signature. Shelley Winters, Arlene Dahl, and Joan Caulfield were among the regulars. Bette Davis loved the chocolate cheesecake, and Marlene Dietrich always ordered a burger-on-a-diet, a burger topped with sauerkraut without a bun. Ronald Reagan, Frank Sinatra, and Dean Martin were all seen enjoying the Hamlet's burgers. When Sammy Davis Jr. appeared at Ciro's down the Strip, he'd head to the Hamlet for dinner after his 1:30 a.m. closing, sometimes treating the late-night diners to a soft-shoe routine atop a table.

One late night in the early days, British actress Sarah Churchill demanded a glass of beer. It was after the legal time of 2 a.m. to drink, so Harry refused. She called him a "dusty American," though most British pubs at the time closed at 11 p.m. Someone at the next table called in the story to the *International Herald Tribune*, and it ran the next morning in every paper in the nation and even in some foreign countries. The publicity was golden for the Lewises and helped attract even more stars.

In fact, Hamburger Hamlet had so much of a good thing going that Marilyn had to call Sidney Skolsky, the Hollywood columnist, to ask him to stop writing about its success. The publicity brought more people than they could accommodate. The crowds overflowed outside and around the block. Some customers even sat on the front stoop to eat.

Two years after Harry and Marilyn opened the Hamlet, Tony Curtis, Sammy Davis Jr., and Jeff Chandler sat the couple down and suggested that it was time for them to get married. Both worked hours on end and never had time for anything except the business. The three stars handled the restaurant operation for two days, taking orders and broiling the burgers. They refused to sign even one autograph. They did this so the two lovebirds could drive to Las Vegas and get married. A few years later, the trio got back behind the counter to run the place when Marilyn gave birth to the Lewises' first son, David.

The first Hamlet

Competition grew fierce on Sunset. A former disc jockey opened a restaurant called My Own Place; it featured a live on-site radio show and started taking business away from Hamburger Hamlet. Harry and Marilyn were not going to let this happen. They installed a radio wire to broadcast from the Hamlet, negotiated with KGIL, and set up sponsors, from Muntz TV showrooms to Triumph sports cars. *Hollywood at the Hamlet* was broadcast from midnight to 2 a.m. Tuesdays through Sundays. Sometimes the Lewises would interview interesting customers, but mostly it was like peering into the life of a married couple—unscripted "reality radio" for the 1950s.

The Hamlet was the first Hollywood restaurant to break the color barrier, hiring many African-American employees during the

Hamlet's radio broadcast with (clockwise from top) the Lewises, Sammy Davis Jr. & Hugh O'Brien

segregated 1950s. The first chef was Marcelion Martinez, a Zapotec Indian from the highlands of Oaxaca, Mexico. As the Lewises expanded to two dozen locations, Martinez became director of the chain's kitchens at age twenty-four. He traveled across the country to help open locations in Chicago and Washington, DC, where he visited the White House.

In 1968, the Lewises moved the Sunset Hamlet to a new location, four blocks to the west. It was designed in the style of other upscale Hollywood establishments, like Chasen's and Scandia. Marilyn made another style statement in the 1960s, designing a clothing line called Cardinali that was carried around the world. Her fashions were worn by Marlo Thomas's character, Ann Marie, on the TV show *That Girl*. In 1968, the *Los Angeles Times* named Marilyn its Woman of the Year.

In the 1980s, the Lewises opened a more trendy restaurant, on Wilshire Boulevard, called Kate Mantilini (it's said she was a boxing promoter and the mistress of Marilyn's uncle). It became a hot spot for the entertainment industry.

In 1987, after nearly forty years in the business, the Lewises sold the entire company to a New York investment firm, with a deal that after five years they could repurchase the Kate Mantilini brand. For several years their sons David and Adam ran the day-to-day Kate Mantilini operations at the original Wilshire location and one in Woodland Hills; they closed both restaurants in 2014.

Harry Lewis died in 2013 at the age of ninety-three. Four years later, Marilyn passed away, leaving behind a 2004 memoir, *Marilyn, Are You Sure You Can Cook? He Asked*, referring to the question Harry asked her prior to signing the lease for their first restaurant.

The Pasadena Hamlet, one of the last two in the Los Angeles area, closed in January 2014 and became a Du-Par's (page 65). In September 2014, Kevin Michaels and Brett Doherty of Killer Shrimp Restaurant fame purchased the last remaining Hamlet, in Sherman Oaks, which gave fans great hope. But it closed in 2018, and the Hamburger Hamlet era officially ended for good, leaving behind a legion of brokenhearted fans.

Jack in the Box

ORIGINAL LOCATION: 6270 EL CAJON BOULEVARD, SAN DIEGO

OPENED: February 1951
FOUNDER: Robert Oscar Peterson
CURRENT OWNER: Jack in the Box Inc.
CURRENTLY AT THE FIRST LOCATION: Platt College Media Design

There are more than 2,200 locations in 21 states and Guam.

jackinthebox.com

AFTER WORLD WAR II, Robert Peterson became a successful traveling salesman for a milkshake-mixer company (similar to Ray Kroc, page 81). However, Peterson felt that there was more out there for him than just going door to door. In the late 1940s, Peterson opened one (and then several) Topsy's Drive-ins in the San Diego area. Always looking for the next better thing, Peterson obtained rights for an intercom concept for drive-thru windows from George Manos of Anchorage, Alaska, the owner of Chatterbox.

Peterson changed the name from Topsy's to Jack in the Box, eliminated the carhops, and reopened in 1951 with the "chatterbox" intercom system. Now things were *really* hopping. The intercom system sped up service and allowed multiple orders to be prepared in the time it used to take for one. The thoroughly modern business also got a modern, Mies van der Rohe–inspired look from architect Russell Forester—although van der Rohe couldn't have anticipated the clown heads atop the building and the intercom. Using what might have been the ever-innovating Peterson motto, Jack instructed drivers to "Pull forward." And drivers did, moving through the line quickly, helping the company rack up sales and keep prices low.

Soon Peterson had 180 locations in California and the Southwest. He was loathe to unionize, but he created a profit-sharing plan for his employees. In 1960, he formed Foodmaker as a holding company for the Jack in the Box brand. Eight years later, Peterson sold Foodmaker to the Ralston Purina Company. At the time, the menu was limited to fifteen items; today, Jack in the Box offers sixteen different hamburgers alone. Ralston Purina opened franchises and launched television commercials.

In the late 1970s, Jack in the Box ads featured three-and-a-half-year-old child actor Rodney Allen Rippy, who became a household name when he tried to take a bite of the new Jumbo Jack and

An early Jack in Southern California

said, "It's too big to eat!" The tagline was an instant success, and Rippy was loved by all. In 1980, Ralston Purina decided to update the Jack in the Box image and introduce new menu items, such as a chicken sandwich. A television commercial made the point with a bang: blowing up a Jack in the Box intercom. The company also temporarily renamed the locations "Monterey Jack's"—followed by a quick, sheepish return to Jack in the Box.

Robert Peterson

Dan Gilvezan became the face of Jack in the Box from 1981 to 1984. Originally hired to shoot two Jack in the Box commercials, he was signed to a three-year contract as spokesperson when sales skyrocketed after the first two commercials aired. He made more than eighty TV commercials, along with hundreds of radio spots, highlighting new menu offerings and apologizing for the name change to Monterey Jack's. Gilvezan's character sported "yuppie" outfits, from SCUBA wear to aerobic gear. He frequently attempted to compare Jack in the Box's food to that of other fast-food chains, hence the slogan, "There's No Comparison," which became Gilvezan's tagline.

In 1985, after eighteen years, Ralston Purina sold Foodmaker Inc. to an investment banking firm and to members of Jack in the Box senior management. Within two years, the company had almost 900 locations open, and Foodmaker became a publicly traded company.

The introduction of new international menu items (such as fajita pitas, chicken teriyaki bowls, and egg rolls) boosted sales. These and other offerings (chicken supreme sandwiches, salads, a large breakfast menu, mozzarella sticks, stuffed jalapeños, not to mention sixteen different burgers) skyrocketed Jack in the Box to new stardom.

An early Jack springs forth

> **Just a Few of Jack's Many, Many Discontinued Offerings**
> Bacon Ice Cream Shake
> Blueberry Muffin Oatmeal
> Exploding Cheesy Chicken Sandwich
> Frings
> H'angry Chicken Hash
> Hella-Peño Burger
> Hot Mess Burger
> Macaroni Bites
> Toasted Raviolis
> Wakey Bakey Hash

In 1994, the Jack character was back and starring in a new television commercial called, no surprise, "Jack's Back." He joked about being blown up and how he'd returned to change the company. Not a single menu item was featured in the new campaign—just a paper sack printed with the words "Jack in the Box." Over the years, commercials involving Jack, his wife Cricket, and son Jack Jr. hit the airwaves. Martha Stewart even played herself battling Jack during a Super Bowl commercial.

On April 19, 1994, Peterson passed away at his home in the Point Loma area of San Diego. He left a mark on San Diego not only as one of the most successful fast-food entrepreneurs, but also as a major benefactor of the arts, higher education, and liberal political causes. A lecture hall at UC San Diego bears his name.

In 1995, the "We don't make it until you order it" policy was enacted, with millions of dollars spent by franchisees to improve their kitchens. Sales jumped and food quality also rose steeply. Ironically, for all the changes and additions to the menu, the top-selling item continues to be...tacos, first introduced in the 1950s. About 554 million Jack in the Box tacos are sold in the United States each year, the same amount as Big Macs. The tacos are mass-produced in Texas or Kansas, shipped frozen to each location, and deep-fried on-site. This process creates the special taco shell: It remains soft in the meaty center and crunchy on the sides. After frying, the tacos are dressed with a slice of American cheese, lettuce, and a mild hot sauce. Twice, in 2009 and 2019, Jack in the Box offered a larger taco, calling it "Monster Taco," only to discontinue it. Two regular tacos are larger than one monster taco and less expensive. But don't be surprised if they try to bring it back in 2029. Recently, a fifteen-count mini-taco pack was introduced with an avocado-lime dipping sauce.

Jack in front of HQ in San Diego

In 2004, Jack in the Box took five locations and revamped them into casual restaurants, test-marketing the JBX Grill concept. The drive-thrus remained, but for customers who ordered inside, a staff member brought the meal to the table. The design and décor of the JBX Grills were hip and trendy. They even had a firepit in the front. But the test proved unsuccessful, and after two years the grills reverted to traditional Jack in the Boxes.

In 2015, Jack in the Box unveiled what Guinness World Records deemed the World's Largest Coupon: an eight-story-high banner promoting the new Buttery Jack Burger, with a buy one, get one free offer. A photo of the coupon was acceptable for redemption.

Jack in the Box seems to reinvent itself every few years with new marketing, new menu items, and the return of past icons and items—so stay tuned for a trip back to the future.

Baker's Burgers

NAME TODAY: Baker's Drive-Thru
ORIGINAL LOCATION: 164 West Highland, San Bernardino
OPENED: November 1952
COFOUNDERS: Neal T. Baker and Carol Baker
CURRENT OWNER: Baker's Burgers, Inc.

There are 39 locations, all in Southern California and all company owned.

THERE'S A STORY here of five friends with much in common: fast food, friendship, location, and entrepreneurship. Those friends are the McDonald brothers, Richard and Maurice (page 81); Glen Bell of Taco Tia and Taco Bell (page 229); John Galardi of Der Wienerschnitzel (page 219); and Neal T. Baker of Baker's Burgers. To explain the relationship of these men nearly takes a flowchart.

Neal Baker, a carpenter and builder by trade, helped the McDonald brothers after they moved their hexagonal building from Glendora to San Bernardino in 1940 (see page 81); this was before they closed for a few months and implemented their "Speedee Service." Neal made a mental note after seeing how the food industry was transforming to serve more people and faster.

In 1946, Neal and his brothers built a family home with bricks that they had made themselves from clay soil mixed with straw. The three brothers opened an adobe brickyard in Riverside County that sold heavy earthen bricks for 13¢ apiece. Looking for someone to haul their product, Baker asked his best friend from high school, Glen Bell. For 5¢ per brick, he agreed.

Many afternoons, Neal and Glen would meet up at the McDonald brothers' hamburger stand, planning a course of action. After watching the former military men who worked in the nearby factories wait in line for burgers, they both knew that the San Bernardino area was ready for business expansion.

In 1948, Neal helped Glen build a hamburger stand across from Milta Café, which served tacos (page 229). This was the beginning of Taco Bell. With now two of his friends in the food business, Neal found an empty lot on Highland in San Bernardino and decided to build Baker's Burgers. It was less than a mile from the McDonald brothers, and a few miles from Bell's burgers, but Neal felt he had something different.

Opposite Top: The first Baker's • Bottom: The Corona branch today
Right: Carol & Neal Baker

Neal built the building himself, saving on labor, time, and added costs.

After the building was erected, Neal looked into the equipment needed. Burton Murray, of Murray Hotel & Restaurant Supply in Colton, financed Baker's stock for nothing down, just a handshake. This is how it was done in that place at that time. Neal paid everything back on schedule.

Neal's wife, Carol Baker, had a successful interior design business called Baker's Interiors. The two of them worked as a team: After Neal's construction company finished the building details, Carol created the interior design.

When Bell started opening more food establishments in the area, Neal paid attention. Bell was creating Mexican locations, while the McDonald brothers' focus was hamburgers. Neal was ready to open his second location, but with a change: two in one. Two cuisines in one location. Neal opened the location in 1955 as a twin-kitchen restaurant in Rialto on Foothill Boulevard. One side had a window for burgers; the other, Mexican fare. The customers complained that if they wanted a taco *and* a burger, they had to wait in both lines. Today, this is the oldest continually operating location.

John Galardi worked eighteen-hour days at the Taco Bell commissary. When Bell hired a consultant to streamline the commissary, part of the recommendation was to cut Galardi's pay by half. Galardi gave notice and got hired at Baker's for fifty dollars more a month and with fewer hours than he'd put in at Taco Bell. In 1961, Galardi moved on to open Der Wienerschnitzel (page 219).

Neal's friends Bell, the McDonald brothers, and Galardi all had successful companies that they greatly expanded. Neal was once asked why he did not expand like his friends. He said that he was content to allow Baker's Drive-Thru to remain a regional chain in Riverside and San Bernardino counties. Baker was also claustrophobic, which prevented him from flying and led him to keep the locations close to home.

Bell and Neal would often golf at the country club in San Bernardino. Many were impressed that two food entrepreneurs were friends in their everyday lives. Competitors, but friendly competitors.

In 1968, the family-minded Neal created an affordable family-friendly experience, "Taco Fridays": five tacos for 75¢. This was followed by "Taco Tuesdays" in 1976, although many other companies tried to lay claim to having created the catchy midweek sales promotion.

Alta Loma has a large concentration of vegetarians, but in the early 1970s, it was difficult to find vegetarian menu items beyond salads, let alone an entire vegetarian restaurant. So Baker's Drive-In created a specific vegetarian menu. It took a little time, but today all locations serve the vegetarian menu as well as their regular menu. Neal called this the "Loma Linda Kitchen."

Logos then & now

In 1987, Neal returned to the roots of the burger business. At the time, he was offering four varieties of burgers, trying to keep up with the large chains. He decided to return to the burger that helped him get his start thirty-five years earlier: a great burger with tomato, lettuce, sauce, and cheese. And while most shakes in the industry were made with frozen ice milk, Neal returned to hand scooping ice cream and using a blender to make the best shakes possible. It was time-consuming and costs were greater, but this was his way of beating the multi-unit competition. Neal confessed that he could never have the funds for television advertising like the others, so he opted for radio ads that were less expensive, and he could control the areas where they played.

In the five years between 1989 and 1994, Baker's almost doubled its locations, from sixteen to twenty-nine. They opened within half a mile from a freeway off-ramp in the Riverside and San Bernardino areas.

Baker's Drive-Ins do not have a central commissary. Each restaurant kitchen prepares its own ingredients, shreds its own cheese, and chops its own tomatoes so they taste of a tomato and not of a plastic bag. Customer service is very apparent in the restaurants: Unlike other fast-food outlets, Baker's will deliver your food to your table and refill your drinks.

Neal was awarded the 2004 Lifetime Award from Spirit of the Entrepreneur. He and Baker's participated in many philanthropic efforts in the community, including the Easter Seals and Children's Fund. Neal donated a piece of land that he owned in San Bernardino, stipulating that it must be put to use for the community. It now houses the Baker Family Learning Center, with a public library and a preschool.

Neal worked right up to the end, visiting the office daily at the age of eighty-four until a few days before he died in 2008. His beloved wife of sixty-two years, Carol, took over her husband's role as president of Baker's Drive-In and remained involved for many years. In 2011, Neal was inducted into the Hall of Fame of California State University, San Bernardino, for all of the time and financial support he'd provided for the athletic department.

Neal believed in keeping his businesses close to his community, and his community was the better for it.

Big Do-Nut Drive-In

NAME TODAY: Randy's Donuts
ORIGINAL LOCATION: 805 West Manchester Boulevard (at La Cienega), Inglewood
OPENED: July 1953
CURRENT OWNER: Mark Kelegian and family

There are currently 8 locations, in Southern California and South Korea.

randysdonuts.com

OTHER THAN THE BROWN DERBY (page 39), Randy's Donuts is probably one of the most famous examples of novelty architecture in the country. Atop the midcentury building is a large—very large—doughnut, made of steel, gunite, cement, and sand sprayed onto a steel round frame, standing more than thirty-two feet high. It can be seen from the 405 Freeway and even from the sky, when on approach to runway 24R at Los Angeles International Airport.

Most people today, many of whom know Randy's Donuts only from its TV and film appearances, probably assume it was started by a guy named Randy. It's a little more complicated than that. Randy's Donuts was originally built as the second of ten Big Do-Nut Drive-Ins designed by architect Henry J. Goodwin for Russell C. Wendell, a doughnut-machine maker. In the late 1960s, Wendell, who also opened Pup 'n' Taco (see page 241), sold the first two locations (10003 Normandie Avenue at Century and 805 West Manchester at La Cienega) to Robert Eskow, who renamed the businesses Randy's Donuts and Sandwiches after his son, Randy. In 1977, Eskow sold his Normandie location to Gary Kindle, who changed the name of his doughnut store to Kindle's. (It also has a giant doughnut on the roof, reading Kindle's Do-Nuts, but it never achieved the same star status.) Randy's retained its name when Eskow sold the business to his cousins, Ron and Larry Weintraub in October 1978. Of the more than one dozen Big Do-Nut locations, six are still in operation, but none bears the original name.

The Weintraubs put Randy's on the map outside of Los Angeles by making it available for filming in many movies, on television shows, and on multimedia platforms. In *Iron Man 2* (2010), main character Tony Stark can be seen sitting in the center of the giant doughnut, eating (what else?) a doughnut. The disaster film *2012* shows the large doughnut rolling down the street as the city of L.A. is destroyed by a 10.9 earthquake. In Tim Burton's film *Mars Attacks* (1996), Randy's Donuts was named Donut World and included fake interior shots that were filmed on a soundstage, since Randy's does not have inside seating. Randy's Donuts is also well known for its television appearances on *The*

One of L.A.'s most-Instagrammed sites

Big Do-Nut Drive-in (Randy's Donuts)

Opening day, July 1953

Tonight Show with Jay Leno, *The Big Bang Theory*, *The Simpsons*, *Arrested Development*, and many others. It has also been highlighted in music videos, including the Red Hot Chili Peppers' "Californication," Becky G's "Becky from the Block," Randy Newman's "I Love L.A.," and Justin Timberlake's 2016 hit "Can't Stop the Feeling."

Because Randy's is so close to an international airport, it is one of the first places visitors stop after retrieving their luggage, besides nearby In-N-Out (page 119).

The Weintraubs upheld the quality of the doughnuts and also brought media attention to the huge doughnut in the sky with clever promotions. Weeks before the October 2012 move of the Space Shuttle *Endeavour* from LAX to downtown L.A., the brothers prepared for the move. All of the streets around Randy's were going to be closed, so Randy's changed its hours and closed the night before. It placed a small model of the shuttle into the center of the iconic doughnut on the roof and sold "iced space shuttles," shuttle-shaped doughnuts with "USA" in chocolate. Some of the best photos of the building from October 12, 2012, show the shuttle next to the building, since Randy's was one of the shuttle's resting spots on the way downtown and was there for almost seven hours. Crowds came to take pictures and eat doughnuts.

In 2015, the Weintraubs decided to sell Randy's to someone who would keep the tradition alive and also move it forward. The historical doughnut-making process was passed to former lawyer Mark Kelegian (who had retired in 2005 after gaining a national reputation representing victims of sexual assault) and his three daughters. Kelegian grew up visiting Randy's after Loyola High football games.

The sports promotions continued. In January 2019, the Big Donut was repainted with "L.A. Rams" and "Donuts" in honor of the newly returned team going to the Super Bowl in Atlanta. The colors of the Rams (blue and yellow) adorned the building for a few months. Also, a special Rams doughnut was featured on the menu. On game day, the line had about 200 customers, who created traffic problems by posing out in the street with their boxes of doughnuts with the giant doughnut in the background. Whatever pop culture phenomenon is happening, you can be sure that Randy's will be in the picture.

Randy's has racked up the awards and "top spot" titles for more than fifty years, including ranking No. 1 on *Bon Appetit*'s "Top 10 Best Places for Donuts" list and *USA Today*'s "12 Best Donut Shops." Randy's Apple Fritter is often listed as a must-try.

National Doughnut Day is the first Friday of June every year, and Randy's has given away thousands of

Most Popular Doughnuts
Glazed Raised
Chocolate Raised
Texas Glazed
Glazed Buttermilk
Apple Fritter

glazed doughnuts and doughnut holes to honor the occasion. (National Doughnut Day started in 1938 to honor the Salvation Army Donut Lassies, women who brought doughnuts to soldiers during World War I.) Randy's has donated frequently to Southland nonprofits and has long supported the Salvation Army and its mission to aid veterans. In doing so, Randy's won the highest award for support on National Doughnut Day in 2016 and 2017. Randy's estimates that it has given away more than 1 million doughnuts in the last twenty years.

Randy's bakers produce more than forty different varieties daily. They have been making every doughnut by hand since 1953, so no two are exactly alike. The secret recipes lead to doughnuts that are fluffier, airier, and fresher than most, and toppings are applied generously. Most of the doughnuts cost less than $2.

Doughnuts for the Inglewood Police Department

In 2017, a new premium line introduced such varieties as Red Velvet with Ganache, S'mores, and Matcha Tea Raised. This line is more indulgent, with fanciful toppings that can be consumed any time of the day or as a dessert after a meal.

Randy's opened its second location in August 2017, at the Westfield Century City Shopping Center; a third location opened a year later, at the Apollo Landing Center in El Segundo; followed by a fourth next to the historic Grauman's Chinese Theatre on Hollywood Boulevard. Alas, the COVID-19 pandemic led to the closure of both the Hollywood and Century City locations.

The global popularity of Randy's—thanks to Hollywood films, tourism and travel videos, and promotional materials on behalf of the Los Angeles Tourism Board—has created constant demand for franchises all over the world. A national and international program has been launched with the help of experts, and the goal is to have 1,000 stores within the next ten years. The first international Randy's opened on Jeju Island, South Korea, in 2019. Hundreds of customers lined up for the doughnuts.

A new Downey location opened in late 2019 with a huge doughnut erected on the roof. Some locations, where local ordinances forbid the installation of a giant plaster doughnut, find other creative ways to catch the eye of passersby, like making the doorway the "hole" of a large doughnut. Six to ten additional locations are slated to open in the greater L.A. area in the near future—because you can never have too many doughnuts. Or donuts.

The grand opening of the South Korea outpost

Danny's Donuts

NAME BECAME: Danny's Coffee Shops
NAME TODAY: Denny's, Denny's Diner, and The Den
ORIGINAL LOCATION: 4917 Bellflower Boulevard, Lakewood

OPENED: 1953
COFOUNDERS: Harold Butler & Richard Jezak
CURRENT OWNER: Denny's Corporation
CURRENTLY AT THE FIRST LOCATION: Kentucky Fried Chicken

There are 1,707 Denny's in 50 states and 14 countries, including 46 Denny's Diners and 15 Dens.

dennys.com

An early Denny's

AFTER TAKING a doughnut-making class in 1953, Harold Butler and Richard Jezak decided to open a twenty-four-hour doughnut shop in Lakewood, a fast-growing new postwar suburb southeast of Los Angeles. They found a location on the busiest street in Lakewood, Bellflower Boulevard, just one block from the new indoor mall, Lakewood Center, and close to the aerospace industry in neighboring Long Beach. One evening before the grand opening, while driving around, Richard and his wife, Frances, started brainstorming names for the shop. Frances thought that using Richard's or Harold's first name wouldn't work. But she felt that a simple male first name would, so she came up with "Danny."

The motto at Danny's Donuts was "To serve the best cup of coffee, make the best donuts, give the best service, offer the best value, and stay open twenty-four hours a day." With so many aircraft company employees working shifts through the night, the shop was a huge success almost immediately, with lines into the wee hours.

They set up their headquarters a few blocks from the second location, in Garden Grove, only a few miles from the Anaheim spot where Walt Disney would soon start construction on Dis-

Left: Danny's Donuts · Right: Richard & Frances Jezak

Danny's Donuts

You can't get any more '70s than this Denny's

neyland. Frances worked in the main office handling payroll, bank deposits, bill paying, uniform design, and when needed, substituting as doughnut maker and waitress. After the sixth location opened, Richard tired of traveling among the shops and left the company.

When customers began requesting more than good coffee and doughnuts, Butler opened an eighth location, in 1956, the first to be named Danny's Coffee Shop; it served sandwiches, soups, salads, and more. As the coffee-shop chain expanded, Butler looked eastward for help and found it in Edward C. Field, former president of the successful Child's Restaurant chain in New York. Field stayed with Denny's for more than twenty years.

In the early 1960s, confusion arose between "Danny's" and "Coffee Dan's," a longtime twenty-four-hour San Francisco club that had locations in Hollywood and downtown L.A. This necessitated a name change, but not a major one. By replacing just one vowel, Danny's Coffee Shops became "Denny's" in 1961; the menus briefly used both vowels, the *e* above the *a*, to familiarize customers with the change. The first Denny's non-conversion was built in Marysville, California. Designed by the Armét & Davis architecture firm (which also created the distinctive Googie style of NORMS restaurants, page 159), this Denny's location was the prototype of the iconic "boomerang"-shaped roofline. The building still stands and has been serving customers daily for six decades.

Investors watched the expansion of Denny's and wanted to franchise the concept. In October 1967, Butler and Field attended the Great Franchise Show in downtown L.A. and walked away as a franchising powerhouse, having sold existing company locations in Seattle, Las Vegas, Spokane, and Blythe, along with new locations across the western states. A year later, the first international franchised restaurant opened in Acapulco, Mexico. Now Denny's was a global brand.

Denny's got back into the doughnut business in 1968 when it acquired 425 Winchell's Donut Houses (page 147). Denny's kept the doughnut houses completely separate in their portfolio for almost twenty years.

In the fall of 1971, Butler stepped down as chairman and sold off his stock in Denny's, but the brand continued to expand, opening Mother Butler Pie Shops. These were similar to Marie Callender's (page 131)—perhaps a little too similar. The lead baker at Callender's was offered a higher wage and moved over to Denny's to manage the newly built pie-manufacturing business in Santa Fe Springs. The Callender's company went to court with a slew of lawsuits against Denny's and the baker for pilfering everything from Callender's pie formulas to its production methods. The outcome was that Denny's could not use the exact recipes. Mother Butler Pie Shops opened, with slices offered after your meal. The hostess stands in the existing Denny's were even retrofitted with display cases for whole pies that you could take home on your way out. Today, except for during the holidays, pies are no longer on the menu at Denny's.

Throughout the 1980s, Denny's converted more than a hundred former Sambo's (page 195) to the new national Denny's brand. Some Denny's locations began to change their hours. During the holiday season in 1988, managers had to scramble to find locksmiths, as for the first time, all but six Denny's were closing on Christmas Day. Many locations did not have locks or, if they did, no one knew where the key was.

Denny's has earned a worldwide reputation for its catchy names for menu items and its customer promotions. In 1977, Denny's introduced the Grand Slam (pancakes, eggs, bacon, sausage) in honor of Atlanta Braves star player Hank Aaron, the MLB home run record breaker. Denny's hit a milestone in 1981, with Slams served in every one of its more than 1,000 restaurants in every state coast to coast, border to border. Moons Over My Hammy (a sandwich of ham and scrambled eggs) was meant to be a temporary menu item in 1992, but it became an instant hit and is still on the menu today.

> **Denny's "Slams"**
> All-American Slam
> French Slam
> Grand Slam
> Grand Slam Slugger
> Jr. Grand Slam
> Lumberjack Slam
> Play It Again Slam
> Senior Belgium Slam
> Slam
> Slim Slam
> Southern Slam
> Super Slam

Marketing campaigns are unforgettable with Denny's. For three years, from 1990 to 1993, Denny's created a massive marketing event: a free meal on your birthday—until Liesel Long of St. Charles, Missouri, celebrated her eighteenth birthday by consuming fifteen meals at various locations during the twenty-four hours of her birthday: twelve BLTs, one omelet, one grilled cheese, and fifteen desserts. One memorable television ad in the late '80s and early '90s featured the senior Corlick sisters, Rose and Edith, bickering about life and correcting each other with the memorable line, "It's Denny's, not Lenny's."

Denny's has experimented with a number of concept designs, including the '50s-style Denny's Classic Diners, which looked like East Coast diners on the outside, featured a retro design on the inside, and offered homestyle favorites like meatloaf and thick shakes. The Las Vegas location began offering a wedding package: Get married in Denny's chapel (installed with a photo booth lined with silk flowers), enjoy a wedding pancake-and-champagne meal, and take home gifts of T-shirts and Grand Slam coupons. Not to be outdone, the New York Denny's in Lower Manhattan, with its tin ceiling, brown leather booths, and full bar and liquor license, offered a $300 Grand Cru Slam: a bottle of Dom Perignon with a Grand Slam meal. Unfortunately, the location lasted only three years. However, you can still get the wedding pancake in Las Vegas!

A new look and dining experience launched on college campuses: The Den, catering to students. Its interiors look more fast-food-ish than Denny's, and it serves the most popular dishes, like Grand Slams and Moons Over My Hammy, all day, along with newer items, such as wraps and seasoned burgers.

Cofounder Richard Jezak passed away in 1994, not far from Danny's Donuts' first location. Harold Butler died in 1998 at his resort in La Paz, Mexico. Starting with humble handmade doughnuts, the two men left a food legacy with a global impact, one that shows no sign of ending.

El Torito

ORIGINAL LOCATION: 16268 Ventura Boulevard, Encino

OPENED: Fall 1954
FOUNDER: Larry Cano
CURRENT OWNER: Xperience Restaurant Group
CURRENTLY AT THE FIRST LOCATION: Encino Medical Tower

There are currently 30 locations.

eltorito.com

First newspaper ad

LARRY CANO was a law student before entering the Air Force to become a fighter pilot. At thirty, he arrived in Van Nuys with the Air National Guard, and he took on a second job working for Mr. and Mrs. Frazer Wu at the Bali Hai, a South Seas–themed restaurant serving exotic Chinese fare. Cano fell in love with the food industry, ending his ambition for a career in law. When the Frazers closed Bali Hai in early 1954, Cano bought the restaurant, all of the equipment, and the building.

With Mexican-American roots and a love for the flavors of Mexico, Cano transformed the restaurant into El Torito ("the little bull"). But one of the major contributors to the restaurant's success wasn't a food item at all: It was the margarita he made with blended fresh ingredients and high-quality imported tequila. When El Torito opened, the margarita was an obscure cocktail, but its popularity quickly grew, and Cano started adding new flavors to the expanding margarita menu. El Torito would later claim to be buying more tequila than any other restaurant chain in the country.

When Cano began building his menu of Mexican Sonora-style food, he designed the building to match. The structure was similar to that of the California missions and Mexican villas, including a central courtyard, Mexican tile floors, and pottery. Brightly colored tablecloths covered tiled tables. Palm trees were planted in the front; floral baskets hung in every corner and above every balcony. A cantina and several smaller dining rooms for groups circled the central courtyard. Fireplaces and hand-painted wall scenes added to the ambience. The presentation of the food was equally important; El Torito was not the kind of place to serve puddles of melted cheese or allow sauce drips on the rim of the plate.

Within three years, Cano opened a second location, in Toluca Lake, and added a third a year later, in Hollywood. All three had regular visits from stars. Roy Disney came to the Toluca Lake branch near his Burbank studio many nights after work, sitting alone in a booth. Jack Webb had a regular

Top: The first location in the Valley • **Bottom:** A contemporary El Torito

booth. Gregory Peck, Lana Turner, and John Wayne dined at El Toritos often. Anthony Quinn was known for demanding his own bottle of tequila and for becoming aggravated whenever one of his dates wouldn't order rice.

One day, Cano noticed a car parked outside his Encino restaurant with a man sitting inside. A week later, Cano saw the same car with the same man, who sat there for quite some time. Cano went over and asked why he was there. The driver introduced himself as Glen Bell and admitted that he was watching the restaurant because he wanted to open his own place. Bell would go on to start Taco Bell (page 229), the largest chain of Mexican fast-food restaurants in the world.

Cano opened yet more restaurants, always focusing on prosperous communities with ample disposable income and a fondness for casual-but-upscale Mexican food. He opened the first Mexican restaurant inside a mall, in what is now the Lakewood Center, followed by a new restaurant, La Fiesta, at the Orange Mall, his first Orange County foray. Cano's next OC opening was an El Torito in Newport Beach in 1973.

Cano was always looking for new ideas. He claimed to have invented the Sunday brunch at his Marina del Rey branch, and he came up with a "Taco Tuesday" promotion in Rancho Mirage in the early 1970s to boost midweek sales. (To be fair, others, including Neal Baker of Baker's Burgers—page 175—claim to have invented the now incredibly popular Taco Tuesday.)

El Torito expanded outside California, though some locations (looking at you, Indianapolis) needed to have cilantro shipped from the west coast, since none could then be found, or had even been heard of, in Indiana produce departments.

The El Torito Original Tostada that Cano and his staff invented has been imitated across the nation. It's a mammoth meal of shredded beef or chicken layered with refried beans, shredded lettuce, diced tomatoes, cheese, guacamole, and sour cream in a fried tortilla bowl. El Torito was one

Left: Larry Cano & daughter Lisa Cano at an El Torito Grill • Right: Larry Cano in later years

> **The Many Margaritas of El Torito**
> - Black Diamond (with Hennessy cognac)
> - Cadillac (with Cointreau; can add mango, strawberry, blackberry, pomegranate, or Midori melon)
> - Cilantro Cucumber Skinny
> - El Dueño (served in a schooner)
> - Patrón Citrus Cadillac (with Cointreau Noir)
> - Roca Skinny
> - Signature (can add the fruit flavors above)
> - Spicy Jalapeño Cucumber

of the first Mexican restaurants to make tableside guacamole from scratch, prepared to the guest's specifications and served in a traditional stone *molcajete*. Another dining room showstopper: the fajitas that arrived tableside in a sizzling cast-iron skillet and included all the sides, even handmade tortillas. The menu offered tamales, enchiladas, tacos, traditional Mexican combination platters, and the trademark selection of margaritas. The desserts, such as Kahlua Mousse and Chocolate-Glazed Churros, were also inventive.

Cano focused on building a loyal and talented staff, many of whom were Mexican immigrants. They went through a demanding nine-day training program, and they appreciated a company culture that seemed family-like. The 1980s saw a huge expansion of the El Torito restaurants, and hiring good talent was challenging. In 1984, El Torito announced that it would pay for part of the college expenses of its management-training workers, and it paired with a local community college to allow the job training to count toward a business degree, in the hope that the trainees would stay for a career after receiving their degrees.

The company grew to more than 225 locations throughout the world, including the acquisition of twenty-four Casa Marias and Casa Gallardos. In 1982, *Time* magazine named Cano as one of the "Enchilada Millionaires" in a story on the new and upcoming Mexican food chains that were hotter than chile peppers. In May 1988, Cano stepped down as chief executive.

In the early 2000s, Pepe Lopez became the master chef for the entire El Torito chain, as well as for the other restaurants that fell under the umbrella of the parent company. Using locally grown ingredients with an emphasis on high-quality meat and vegetables prepared in the traditional Mexican style, Chef Lopez created regional Mexican dishes.

Larry Cano died in December 2014, and in 2018, Xperience Restaurant Group took over ownership, adding the El Torito restaurants to a roster that included Chevy's, Acapulco, Las Brisas, and other Mexican chains. But El Torito has kept its identity, menu, and style, carrying on Cano's vision.

Shakey's Pizza Parlor

ORIGINAL LOCATION: 5641 J Street, Sacramento

OPENED: April 15, 1954

COFOUNDERS: Sherwood "Shakey" Johnson & Ed Plummer

CURRENT OWNER: The Jacmar Companies

CURRENTLY AT THE FIRST LOCATION: Mimosa House Restaurant

There are more than 500 locations around the world, with 50 in the United States (47 in Southern California, 1 in Northern California, and 2 in Washington).

shakeys.com

FOR MORE THAN half a century, Shakey's has been the place to go after a game or to take the family on a Friday night, to enjoy big pizzas and never-ending soft drinks for the kids and beers on tap for the adults.

Sherwood "Shakey" Johnson suffered from malnutrition while serving in the navy during World War II. His condition resulted in tremors. There were eight Johnsons on his ship, so to differentiate them, they all got nicknames. The short guy became "Shorty," the redhead became "Red," and Sherwood became "Shakey."

In 1954, Johnson and his World War II friend Ed Plummer each put in $850 to turn a Sacramento grocery store space into a beer joint called Shakey's Ye Public House; after just a few weeks of serving nothing but beer, they decided to add pizza, so they put in ovens and called the place Shakey's Pizza Parlor. Before Shakey's, nobody in Sacramento had heard of a pizza "parlor." Johnson wanted to be different and not call it a pizzeria, because he envisioned a place that was about more than just grabbing a slice.

The recipe for the crust came from Johnson's childhood. It was a combination of his Swedish mother's and Italian neighbor's recipes. Johnson was the only Swede in his Italian neighborhood and learned to translate the recipes that were given to his mom. Shakey's dough was sparked with European spices, unlike other pizza doughs.

After opening in Sacramento, Johnson opened the next two locations in Oregon. The third one, in Albany, was the first built from the ground up to his specifications. He wanted a distinct style, with dark woods and large seating areas with picnic tables so families and sports teams could sit together. He also called for a separate kids' zone. Large windows to the kitchen were a favorite for the kids, as they could watch their pizzas being made. Next came franchises—Shakey's became the first franchised pizza chain in the United States. Johnson started placing Shakey's locations near or close to the popular Kinny's shoe stores of the time.

Sherwood "Shakey" Johnson giving advice to a pizza maker

Johnson was a large, jovial man with white mutton-chop sideburns. He looked like a singer in a barbershop quartet. In fact, he was a banjo player who loved ragtime and Dixieland jazz and featured live ragtime performances in the restaurant. It's hard to believe if you only know today's Shakey's, but jazz historians have credited Johnson's showcasing of player pianos, banjos, and live music for helping inspire a revival of jazz in Sacramento. He was even honored at the American Banjo Museum in Oklahoma City for promoting banjo music at his pizza parlors. Live music was featured on weekend nights, with some locations hiring award-winning banjo and piano players. If a ball game wasn't on the overhead TVs, they'd display the lyrics to the song being performed, with a "bouncing ball" following the words so all could sing along.

> **Milestones**
> 1954: 1st location, in Sacramento
> 1956: 1st Oregon location, in Portland
> 1968: 1st Canadian location, in Winnipeg
> 1975: Expansion to the Pacific Rim (Japan and the Philippines)

The kids' areas expanded to become "Fun Zones" filled with arcade games and prizes, keeping families happy while they waited for their pizzas. They were decades ahead of places like Chuck E. Cheese.

When the chain hit 272 branches in 1967, Johnson sold his interest to Colorado Milling and Elevator (!) and retired on his 105-acre ranch in the low Sierras to raise Black Angus cattle, although he remained a public face of Shakey's for some time. Messaging did not seem to be his forte. In a 1974 story about the opening of a branch in Atlanta, Georgia, Johnson was asked what made his restaurant different. His answer: "We don't hire sexpots for waitresses…we like them a little plump and mature." If Johnson was hiring staff today, he'd have a little problem. Plummer sold his half of the business two years later for more than three times what Johnson got.

In 1974, Colorado Milling sold the booming operation to Hunt International Resources, a huge conglomerate run by Texas oilmen Nelson and Herbert Hunt. They didn't appear to put much effort into overseeing Shakey's, other than overhauling the menu and adding all-you-can-eat lunch opera-

The first home in Sacramento

Left: A typical franchise location in the 1960s • Right: Not just pizza at Shakey's

tions. This did well in major cities near business hubs but flopped in the suburbs, with a lot of wasted food.

In 1975, the San Miguel Corporation bought the rights to run Shakey's in the Philippines, mainly to serve its own draft beer. San Miguel owned and grew the franchise for twelve years before selling it to International Family Food Services. By 1992, the brand had mainly changed to fast-food, non-dining locations. Ten years later the company reengineered the brand once again into a family-oriented, casual-dining concept, and today the chain is huge in the Philippines. In 1999, International Family Food Services acquired the trademark rights for the Middle East, Asia (except Japan and Malaysia), India, China, New Zealand, Australia, and Kuwait, and it plans more expansion.

The American restaurants didn't fare as well. A couple of investors bought the chain from the Hunts (who were soon to go bankrupt) in 1984 and gave it a new boost of life, but it didn't last, and branches closed by the dozens. By the time they sold it to a Singapore-based company called Inno-Pacific in 1989, the number of US locations had dropped from more than 500 to 221. The decline of the US operation continued, with many franchisees blaming Inno-Pacific and filing lawsuits. In 2004, the Jacmar Companies in Alhambra, California, bought the remaining American branches, mostly in Southern California, and fortunately those have remained steady ever since. Local ownership seems to be what Shakey's needed. And the restaurants still cater to families, just as Shakey Johnson envisioned.

Shakey's today

Sambo's Restaurants

NAME BECAME: Chad's
ORIGINAL LOCATION: 216 West Cabrillo, Santa Barbara
OPENED: June 17, 1957
CLOSED: July 2020
FOUNDERS: Sam Battistone & Newell "Bo" Bohnett

From 1,450 locations in 1985 to 1 Chad's restaurant today.
chadscafe.com

"ONCE UPON A TIME there was a little boy in India named Sambo who was overjoyed with the new outfit his mother and father had given him. One day while he was walking through the jungle, he met a great big tiger who told Sambo he would eat him up if he didn't give him his pretty red coat. Sambo gave the tiger the coat and went on through the jungle where he met three more tigers. He had to give the first his beautiful green umbrella, the second, his blue pants, and the third tiger demanded his pretty purple shoes. Poor little Sambo started for home and he was very sad because the cruel tigers had taken away all of his fine clothes. But on the way home he heard a strange noise and when he peeked through the tall jungle grass, he saw the tigers chasing each other around a tree. They were growling and fighting over Sambo's pretty new clothes. Little Sambo went up to the tigers and told them that if they stopped fighting and gave his pretty new clothes back, he would treat them to the finest, lightest pancakes they ever ate. So they gave back his beautiful red coat, his green umbrella, his blue pants, and his pretty purple shoes. Then they all went to a Sambo's Pancake House where each tiger ate seventy-five pancakes...but Sambo ate 169 because he was soooo hungry."

This story was printed in the center of Sambo's menu, and parents often read it to their children while waiting for their food to arrive. On the walls were drawings of Little Sambo and tigers.

Sam Battistone came to the United States from Italy with his mother at the age of six. His father had come ahead, worked long, hard hours in the coal mines, and sent for his family after securing housing in Bentleyville, Pennsylvania. After high school, in the depths of the Depression, Sam hopped a freight

Sam Battistone in Santa Barbara

Milestones
- 1958: 2 locations
- 1962: 15 locations
- 1967: 59 locations in 6 states
- 1972: 257 locations
- 1979: 1,117 locations in 47 states
- 1982: 1,450 locations
- 1989: 1 location (the first)
- 2020: Last remaining location changed its name

First location

train west in search of work and ended up as a dishwasher in Glendale. He and a waitress, Ione, fell in love, married, and had three children. During World War II, the family moved to Ventura, where he worked on the naval base unloading and loading ships. After the war, Sam knew his passion was the restaurant business. He bought his own place in Santa Barbara, at 511 State Street, and named it Sammy's Grill. It was open twenty-four hours a day; Battistone cooked the 6 a.m.–to–6 p.m. shift, while Ione worked the graveyard shift, coming home just in time to get the children off to school.

In the mid-'50s, a breakfast place opened in Santa Barbara and became very successful. This intrigued Battistone, as selling pancakes by day seemed a lot easier than having a full menu twenty-four hours a day. He and his friend Newhell ("Bo") Bohnett, a restaurant developer and equipment salesman, found a perfect place across from the marina on Cabrillo Street. Combining their names, Sam and Bo, they named their new place Sambo's. The low prices and good food brought in a lot of customers—there was a long line every morning.

A year later, in 1958, Battistone was introduced to the children's story *Little Black Sambo*, first published in 1899 by Helen Bannerman. Sambo is an Indian boy who goes into the jungle and loses his fine clothes to bullying tigers. The tigers chase one another around a tree and melt into butter, which Sambo puts on his pancakes

Prices in 1960
- Buckwheat Pancakes: 45¢
- Pineapple Pancakes: 45¢
- Banana Pancakes: 75¢
- Danish Pancakes with Sour Cream: 90¢
- Papa Jumbo's Special (juice, 2 eggs, ham, bacon or sausage, 6 Sambo Cakes): $1.25
- Mama Mumbo's Special (juice, 1 egg, 4 Sambo Cakes): 65¢

First location in modern times, before becoming Chad's

and eats. Battistone and Bohnett decided to theme their restaurant around the story. They redecorated to match the art in the book, and pancakes became the signature dish. The first menu offered six fluffy pancakes for 40¢, served with "tiger" butter and maple or boysenberry syrup.

Immediate success inspired expansion. To build a strong management team, Battistone and Bohnett adopted an innovative concept called "Fraction of the Action"—managers had the opportunity to invest and become partners in the restaurant they ran. This system helped Sambo's grow quickly, and it was copied by many other companies over the years. A year later, Battistone and Bohnett found a manager-partner in west Sacramento and opened the second Sambo's there. The next year brought four more locations in California. The star at each was the pancakes, and people lined up for a chance to enjoy the food. Offering such a good value was a big part of the restaurant's success. Sambo's didn't raise prices during the first six years of its expansion. In the 1960s, its advertising slogan was "What this country needs is a good ten-cent cup of coffee." It sold ten wooden nickels, each worth one cup of coffee, to customers for a buck. And it invested in lots of billboard advertising along key highways.

By 1967, there were fifty-nine Sambo's in six states. At that time, Battistone and Bohnett decided to retire from active management. Sam's son, Sam Jr., was a natural to take over as president, even though he was only twenty-seven. He'd moved first to Oregon to open the first out-of-state branch, and then to Miami to start the expansion in the eastern part of the country. The company grew rapidly and went public in 1969, bringing capital that led to even more growth—during the next ten years, more than 1,000 new Sambo's opened, and the chain had more than 55,000 employees nationwide. It had also built a major distribution facility just outside of Santa Barbara, the most extensive in-house operation in the industry, with more than a hundred semitrucks delivering food and supplies

Sambo's Restaurants

to restaurants across the country every week. Bohnett and architect Jack Barlow, a star in the restaurant-design world, created the flagship restaurant and offices off of State Street in Santa Barbara.

In the mid-1970s, Sambo's was the fourth-most-franchised restaurant chain in the United States, with more than 1,400 locations and 200 in Canada. Sambo's started advertising for people to stop by for pancakes after church. Each location had a community room for church groups, service clubs, and nonprofit organizations; many could serve up to seventy patrons. With the money that came in from such success, Sam Jr. cofounded the Utah Jazz basketball team.

The name Sambo's, however, had become controversial. It was a common slur for African-American men and had strong negative associations for Black people. In 1966, the Colorado Springs chapter of the NAACP called for the *Little Black Sambo* book to be banned from all school and city libraries, and lawsuits over the name started getting filed. The founders insisted that the name was a combination of their names, but the controversy didn't go away. The chain struggled to rebrand with new names such as Sam's, The Joy Tiger, and No Place Like Sam's.

In 1979, a large hospitality company purchased the chain and combined it with other companies it was buying, including Motel 6, which was also founded in Santa Barbara. To address the name issue, it changed all the restaurants to Seasons. It also switched to a more remote management system, which hurt operations significantly, and within four years, it took the company into bankruptcy. Hundreds of locations closed. In 1983, the

Left: Uniform patches • Bottom: A typical 1960s design

On supermarket shelves back in the day

618 remaining spots were rebranded as Season's Friendly Eating. In 1984, the company sold 175 outlets to Vicorp Restaurants (Village Inn and Bakers Square) and later sold 600 to Denny's (page 183), which rebranded them as Denny's.

By 1989, only the original Sambo's remained, then called Sam's. The following year, owner Chad Stevens, Sam Battistone Sr.'s grandson, renamed it Sambo's. But then, following the intense national conversations on race after the murder of George Floyd in 2020, Chad changed the name on the sign atop of the red terra-cotta roof to read "& LOVE" and released a statement: "We are changing the name of our restaurant, what the future name will be is still uncertain, however it will not be Sambo's. Our family has looked into our hearts and realize that we must be sensitive when others whom we respect make a strong appeal. So today we stand in solidarity with those seeking change and doing our part as best we can…. Please join us in this message of peace and love. Also please know we do not tolerate racism or violence. We are committed to being part of a long-term solution. And we ask our customers and neighbors to join us in that pledge."

You still get the fluffy pancakes of yesteryear, but today they come with more awareness and they're served at a restaurant called Chad's.

Pancake Flavors
Applesauce
Banana
Blueberry
Buckwheat
Buttermilk
Chocolate
Coconut
Danish with Sour Cream
French
Peach
Pecan
Pineapple
Potato
Strawberry

The Copper Penny

Copper Penny Family Restaurants

SLOGAN: "Find a Copper Penny. Have a Lucky Day."
ORIGINAL LOCATION: 3639 Riverside Plaza, Riverside

OPENED: 1958
COFOUNDERS: Merle & Paula Afflerbaugh
CURRENTLY AT THE FIRST LOCATION: A shopping center

At its peak, there were 51 locations, although none remain today.

AFTER WORLD WAR II, Merle and Paula Afflerbaugh became proprietors of food establishments up and down the Southern California coast, from Ventura to Newport Beach. Merle's focus was coffee shops and drive-ins, knowing that the returning servicemen would want fast cars and good food. Merle's Coffee Shop in Port Hueneme was the couple's first location; their want ads sought out newly returned servicemen and navy wives as cooks and staff.

In 1952, the couple opened Beany's Drive-In, on the corner of Pacific Coast Highway and Ximeno Avenue in Long Beach, with lots of space for cars and a small dining room. Featuring Beany from the *Beany and Cecil* comics and cartoon show, the spinning sign could be seen from blocks away. On opening day, the Afflerbaughs gave flowers to all the ladies in attendance.

Moving southward to Newport Beach, they opened their namesake, Merle's Drive-In, on the corner of MacArthur Boulevard and Pacific Coast Highway. It featured a remarkable cantilevered roof that extended from the building like an airplane wing; carhops delivered malts, fries, and burgers to some of the fastest hot rods in the area. After a few years, it was sold and renamed The Zoo; today, the location houses the Gulfstream Restaurant, which for years maintained the distinctive roofline.

After moving from the coast to Palm Springs, the Afflerbaughs started looking at places between the beach and the desert to open a restaurant. In 1958, they chose a space in the newly built Riverside Plaza Shopping Center for their sit-down coffee shop, which they named Copper Penny Family Coffee Shop—the word *family* invoking a positive image for an area in the midst of a postwar building boom of houses and neighborhoods. The coffee shop's symbol was that of the Lincoln-head penny, bearing the inscription "In our food you can trust."

The Afflerbaughs opened three additional Copper Penny locations within eighteen months, all in shopping malls rather than freestanding. This kept the building costs low and the opening time-

Top: The first location, in Riverside • Bottom: The Burbank branch

frame short. These locations were free of carhops and hot rods and instead had waitress service.

Only a few months after the fourth Copper Penny opened, Merle passed away at the young age of forty-seven. Paula kept the company intact for two years before selling the restaurant chain to International Industries, the parent company of International House of Pancakes (page 209), in September 1962.

In 1969, International Industries purchased twenty-six Hyatt Coffee Shops and converted them to Copper Penny locations, bringing the total to fifty-one locations, half of them in Southern California. Today, most of the buildings and locations have been morphed into other brands that International Industries once held.

One iconic location, on the corner of La Brea and Sunset in Los Angeles, is now a Burger King. When one of the last intact Copper Penny buildings, on Geary and Masonic in San Francisco, was sold, the new owner changed the name to the Lucky Penny. It closed in 2015 to make room for a new multipurpose, seven-story building.

"Find a Copper Penny. Have a Lucky Day" was the motto. Today it is difficult to find a great diner like the Copper Penny.

Right: An early ad
Bottom: Riverside Plaza, home of the first location

Early menu cover

Sizzler Family Steak House

NAME TODAY: Sizzler
ORIGINAL LOCATION: 6107 South Sepulveda, Culver City
OPENED: January 27, 1958
COFOUNDERS: Delmar & Helen Johnson & Jim Collins
CURRENT OWNER: Sizzler USA Restaurants, Inc.
CURRENTLY AT THE FIRST LOCATION: 405 and 90 freeways

There are 76 locations in the western United States and 13 in Puerto Rico.

sizzler.com

DELMAR JOHNSON WAS BORN in 1914 above his family's restaurant in Farmer City, Illinois. After moving west, Johsson became a successful ice cream salesman. In the mid-'50s, he worked a territory on L.A.'s westside. While reading *The Wall Street Journal* in 1957, Johnson saw that Tad's Steak Houses in New York, Chicago, and San Francisco offered a complete meal of salad, baked potato, and a steak for $1.09 (the equivalent of $10.10 in 2020). The low price inspired him to open his own steakhouse.

While on his ice cream route, Johnson had befriended Jim Collins, who owned a hamburger stand at Sepulveda and Centinela in West L.A. Together, they established Sizzler Family Steak House in a garage they remodeled themselves. Del's wife, Helen, sewed curtains out of red-and-white-checkered tablecloths, and they covered the floor with sawdust, hoping to add carpeting when they could afford it. Creating a good, affordable menu and keeping labor costs down were their priorities. They served only four items: steak and ground round burgers for 69¢, top sirloin with potatoes for $1.19, and salad for 19¢.

Franchising came fast, and within ten years Del and Helen had franchised 156 locations and had four of their own. Del gave Jim Collins the opportunity to buy him out in 1967, and Collins created Colbee Inc. to purchase the chain under the Collins Foods International umbrella. Collins Foods also became the largest franchisee of Kentucky Fried Chicken locations from San Luis Obispo to the Mexican border. Del and Helen eventually retired to Indian Wells, and he passed away there in 1992.

Collins opened a flagship location on Hollywood Boulevard to so much fanfare that it was compared to a movie opening. That's where he launched the parmesan cheese toast that is still served today, more than sixty years later. (Now there's even a National Cheese Toast Day: September 15.)

During the late '70s and early '80s, Sizzler promoted a combination steak dinner that included a salad bar. To give customers the feel of a full-service restaurant at a lower price, they opted for counter service—not completely full service, but almost. They also used in-house meat cutters to help control

Top: Second steak for a penny! • **Bottom:** A location in 1975

costs. Around that time, Dan Blocker, the actor who played Hoss Cartwright on *Bonanza*, opened Bonanza Steakhouses and Ponderosa Steakhouses, with backing by investors, and they provided stiff competition for Sizzler.

More challenges came as Americans cut back on eating red meat, and beef prices rose steeply. Sizzler countered with all-you-can-eat salad bars and "Ultimate Value" meals, but profit margins suffered. The company then tried launching a more high-end concept with full waiter service, Buffalo Ranch Steak Houses, which struggled to find traction. Collins closed the 130 company-owned Sizzlers in 1996 and began a reorganization while under Chapter 11 bankruptcy protection, keeping the franchises open during that time. This helped the company escape costly leases on unprofitable locations. Within a year, Sizzler emerged from bankruptcy.

Collins then created Sizzler's American Grill, which offered more health-conscious fare, including a larger salad bar (called the "Buffet Court")

Bestsellers That Aren't Steak
Cheese Toast
Craft Salad Bar
Double Malibu Chicken
Fried Shrimp
Steak and Malibu Chicken

A bustling Sizzler dining room, 1975

with lighter dressings, pastas, and broth-based soups. The public didn't really take to the new idea and sales stayed flat, but it did help slow the closing of more locations.

Collins Foods International sold off the Sizzler part of the conglomerate in 2005 to the Australian-based investment firm Pacific Equity Partner, but the CEO, Kerry Kramp, bought back the 178 US restaurants in 2011. He revamped the menu, remodeled the restaurants, and closed underperforming locations. Prices remained the same, but the kitchens stopped using prepared foods and made more from scratch, with old recipes brought back and chefs trained to be grill masters. COVID-19, however, took a terrible toll on the restaurants, with most of the locations in California having to close for a year, and in the fall of 2020, Sizzler filed for bankruptcy protection a second time.

Here's hoping that the remaining seventy-plus US locations recover from the pandemic shutdowns, and Sizzler can continue Del Johnson's mission of providing a tasty, honest steak dinner at an affordable price.

The International House of Pancakes

NAME TODAY: IHOP

ORIGINAL LOCATION: 4301 West Riverside Drive, Burbank

OPENED: July 1958

COFOUNDERS: Al Lapin Jr. (president) & Jerome M. Lapin (executive vice president)

OWNED BY: International House of Pancakes, LLC, a wholly owned subsidiary of Dine Brands Global

CURRENTLY AT THE FIRST LOCATION: Le Pain Quotidien

There are 1,678 locations in the United States and its territories, and about 200 more internationally, although up to 100 were closing permanently because of COVID-19.

ihop.com

AL LAPIN, A NEW YORK NATIVE, set out to make movies, not pancakes. After serving in the US Army, he studied filmmaking at USC, got work in early television, and produced civil-defense films on surviving atomic attacks. But he had an entrepreneurial streak, and he cared about food and drink. His first venture was a coffee-cart company called Coffee Time, aimed at the office market. For years, Al and his younger brother, Jerry, noticed the lines down the sidewalk in front of Bob's Big Boy (page 59) on Riverside Drive on the weekends. Bob's was known not for breakfast but for hamburgers, and the Lapin brothers thought if they could lure the same crowd for breakfast, they'd have a hit. A location became available across Rose Street, a small street that was the only dividing line between Bob's and the Lapins' dream. They used their mother Viola's nearby kitchen to test waffles and buttermilk pancakes for hours, until they found the taste, texture, and look they wanted. Albert and Trudy Kallis invested $25,000 to get them started. A hired chef got to work creating such inventive pancake flavors as Tahitian Orange Pineapple and Kauai Coconut. Opening on the Monday after the Fourth of July weekend in 1958 proved to be very successful.

Marilyn, Al's wife, would run the cash register as well as perform hostess duties while four-month-old Randy Lapin slept under the register in a bassinet. It was a family restaurant from the beginning.

Al was a perfectionist for presentation, both personally and when it came to food. He was quoted in *The New York Times* as saying, "You have to look like a dollar to borrow a dime" and "People eat with their eyes before they eat with their hands."

While driving around the Southland, the Lapins noticed the bright orange–roofed, small house–looking buildings that housed the popular Howard John-

Pancake Flavors in 2021
Buttermilk
Chocolate Chocolate Chip
Cupcake
Double Blueberry
Gluten-Free
Harvest Grain 'N Nut
Mexican Tres Leches
New York Cheesecake
Strawberry Banana

The iconic pitched-roof design of the early restaurants

The Lapin family at the first location in 1963

son's restaurants. *When you drive down the street, your business needs to be noticed*, Lapin thought. When building the Ventura Boulevard location of his restaurant in the Valley in 1960, Lapin knew he wanted something that stood out just like Howard Johnson's orange roof. He used an A-frame, chalet-style building topped with what he called the "International" blue roof you could see from miles away. For more than forty-five years, you could recognize an International House of Pancakes location from afar. The last A-frame to be built was in 2006 in Vero Beach, Florida. Today, you can still spot the iconic buildings; about 140 remain intact.

Besides pancakes, every table in the place has a "never empty" pot of coffee, dropped off almost as soon as you sit down. This was a policy from the start, so that guests could drink all the coffee they wanted without waiting for the waitress to get them a refill.

Another policy was to have at least four types of pancake syrups on your table that customers normally would not have at home. Boysenberry, blueberry, strawberry, and maple pecan have been some of the favorites over the years. Only one location serves real maple syrup; not surprisingly, that one is in Vermont. To get it approved, the location agreed to sell the serving at an additional cost.

In 1960, the Lapins began fielding requests to purchase franchises with International House of Pancakes. Soon franchises were popping up like blueberries in a pancake, expanding the brand all over the west coast and then into Midwest and East Coast locations. In 1961, the company went public, trading under the name International House of Pancakes.

Three years later, the company acquired several other franchised brands—including Orange Julius (page 45), Love's Wood Pit Barbecue (page 127), House of Pies (page 245), and the Copper Penny (page 201)—and changed its name to International Industries. In 1966, Al Lapin Jr. bought out his brother and cofounder, Jerry.

A new marketing campaign in 1973 introduced the acronym IHOP, and that's what everyone has called it ever since.

Television, theater, and film actor Cliff Bemis, playing an all-American guy who loves IHOP, starred for more than eight years as spokesman "Cliff from IHOP." He appeared in TV and radio commercials, traveled the country making personal appearances, and signed more than 70,000 "Cliff at IHOP" pictures for fans. Bemis was invited to appear and participate in various charitable fundraising events and restaurant openings. As spokesperson, he raised more than $2 million for charities, ranging from the Special Olympics to various police and fire organizations.

IHOP's philosophy is simple: Be yourself and come as you are. With so many menu items, everyone in the family will be happy. And perhaps most important: You can get breakfast anytime, day or night.

The mid-'80s introduced additional menu items for the entire day instead of just breakfast: fresh salads; taco salads; the "Super Stack," with ham, turkey, and Swiss cheese on a French roll; and the "Big Cheese," three cheeses on a cracked wheat roll topped with bacon and tomatoes.

One of the largest product launches was in 1984: the Rooty Tooty Fresh 'N Fruity, consisted of four thick buttermilk pancakes topped with your choice of glazed strawberries or peaches and whipped cream. All-you-can-eat pancake specials have been rolled out a number of times over the

A busy 1963 Sunday in Toluca Lake, with fans waiting for a table

years, offering two buttermilk pancakes, two eggs, hash browns, and your choice of protein, followed by as many pancakes in sets of two as you can eat. The pancake varieties that once topped out at forty-eight were pared down to sixteen in the 1970s. Not that they're going spartan: Today you can request your buttermilk, harvest grain, or chocolate pancakes with such toppings as New York cheesecake, blueberries, or cupcake batter. On the other hand, menu items under 600 calories are available for those not wishing or able to so indulge.

> **Sweet & Savory Crêpes**
> + Breakfast (scrambled eggs, cheese, bacon, and ham)
> + Chicken Florentine
> + Strawberries & Crème
> + Swedish (with lingonberries and lingonberry butter)

Al Lapin started diversifying his personal business portfolio with two dozen subsidiaries, including ice cream, clothing, advertising, marketing, home-improvement services, and secretarial training. Rapid expansion brought debt and other challenges, and when lenders called in loans in 1970, IHOP undertook substantial layoffs. Furthermore, some franchisees claimed they'd been forced to pay inflated prices for supplies and equipment, and in 1973, a federal judge in Kansas City ordered the company to pay back franchisees by reducing their royalties. Lapin sold his interest and left in 1973, and three years later, the company was reorganized by its creditors and renamed IHOP Corporation. Wienerwald Holding AG of Switzerland bought the chain in 1979 and expanded its non-breakfast menu, adding hamburgers, fries...and bratwurst. It also introduced the Swiss-style dirndl outfits for IHOP waitresses. The hamburgers and uniforms lasted for years; the bratwurst didn't.

After sixteen years on the New York Stock Exchange, the company returned to private own-

Pancakes today

Modern branding

ership in 1981. The chain was revitalized by introducing seventeen new "homey" dinner items, such as fried chicken and pot roast, to great success. In 1992, IHOP opened its 500th location; nine years later, the 1,000th IHOP opened, in Layton, Utah.

Fun fact: Placing a photo of an item on the menu can boost its sales four times over menu items without a photo. Therefore, IHOP can make a menu choice profitable by photographing higher-priced items, even if they're not the healthiest choices. (Hint: Fried chicken photographs much better than baked chicken.)

> **It Really Is International**
> You'll find IHOPs in Bahrain, Thailand, Ecuador, Qatar, Guatemala, India, Kuwait, Panama, and in a dozen or so other countries.

Alternative fun fact: IHOP celebrates National Pancake Day each year by raising money for charities in the communities it serves. The tenth anniversary of Annual Pancake Day in 2015 raised a record-breaking $3.5 million; the company has raised nearly $20 million since the "holiday" was launched.

IHOP is by far the most successful pancake chain in the world. The newer locations are without the blue A-frame buildings, but you can spot the logo and the bright blue sign from blocks away. Today, you still get a pot of coffee on your table and an array of syrups to choose from, just as Al Lapin envisioned on the day he opened his first restaurant in Toluca Lake.

The International House of Pancakes

Round Table Pizza

SLOGAN: "Pizza Royalty"
PREVIOUS SLOGAN: "The Last Honest Pizza"
ORIGINAL LOCATION: 1225 El Camino Real, Menlo Park

OPENED: December 1959
FOUNDER: William ("Bill") R. Larson
PARENT OWNER: Global Franchise Group
Original location is still in operation.

There are more than 400 locations in 8 US states and Mongolia.

roundtablepizza.com

AFTER MILITARY DUTY, while in his twenties and working as a driver delivering raw goods to restaurants, William ("Bill") Larson started thinking about pizza. Specifically, great pizza and the lack thereof. He decided he would open his own pizza parlor, but first he had to learn the business. He took a job at Hambones, a popular pizza joint in Santa Monica, followed by a management position at a pizza restaurant in San Mateo.

He then took his meager $1,800 in operating cash and chose his space in the old Menlo Park Waterworks building on busy El Camino Real. To save money, Bill worked with his father, Henry, to build the restaurant tables out of redwood. One of them was round and sat in the middle of the dining area, so he dubbed it the Round Table. Naturally, the restaurant became Round Table Pizza Parlor and Pub.

Bill spent many hours developing recipes for the pizza crust and sauces, most of which are still used today. Just as on the first day, each location hand-rolls the dough and makes the sauces from scratch. All of the vegetables are sliced by hand; they do not come in pre-sliced. When the restaurant opened in 1959, the most expensive item on the menu was also the largest: Bill's Special Combination pizza for $3.17.

His vision was to create a place where families could go to relax, feel at home, and share an excellent pizza. A few years after opening, Bill incorporated drawings of King Arthur (of Round Table fame) enjoying pizza with his court. For years the three coats of arms in print and media ads spelled out "FUN."

Left: Founder Bill Larson

Over the years, the company has made many advances in pizza production, such as updating the ovens from stone to conveyer and offering delivery services, beginning in 1994. In 1962, Bill started franchising to independent owners. In 1978, he sold a majority ownership of Round Table to a corporation; twenty years later, employees bought Round Table through a stock-ownership plan. It became the top pizza chain in California in the 1980s, thanks in part to the award-winning "The Last Honest Pizza" ad campaign.

In the mid-1980s Bill retired from the family business, and a few years later, two of his children, Bob and Linda, purchased the original Menlo Park location; they then added two nearby locations to their portfolio. Bob continued his father's tradition of giving back to the community ("You do right by somebody, they do right by you" was Bill's motto) by holding fundraisers for schools and donating to nonprofit organizations like Habitat for Humanity and Make a Wish Foundation. "Pizza and community go hand in hand," Bob said.

Innovative Pizzas
- Bill's Special Combination
- Combination (everything but shrimp and anchovies)
- Gourmet Veggie
- Imported Anchovy
- Italian Black Olives (with or without pits)
- White Mushroom (cooked in butter)
- Linguica
- Louisiana Shrimp
- Maui Zaui (pineapple, bacon, cheese, ham, and peppers)
- Right Hander Special (mushroom, shrimp, and olives)

Bob was born into the pizza business—he started clearing tables and serving customers at the age of twelve—and as of today, he still owns the original location and two others. Most of Bill's nine children have also been in and out of the pizza business over the years.

In 1994, as American franchises were spreading around the world, Round Table Pizza opened in the United Arab Emirates, offering the same menu as in the United States, except pork products were replaced with beef and poultry. Today, the only remaining international location is in Mongolia (it opened in 2013).

The original Menlo Park restaurant

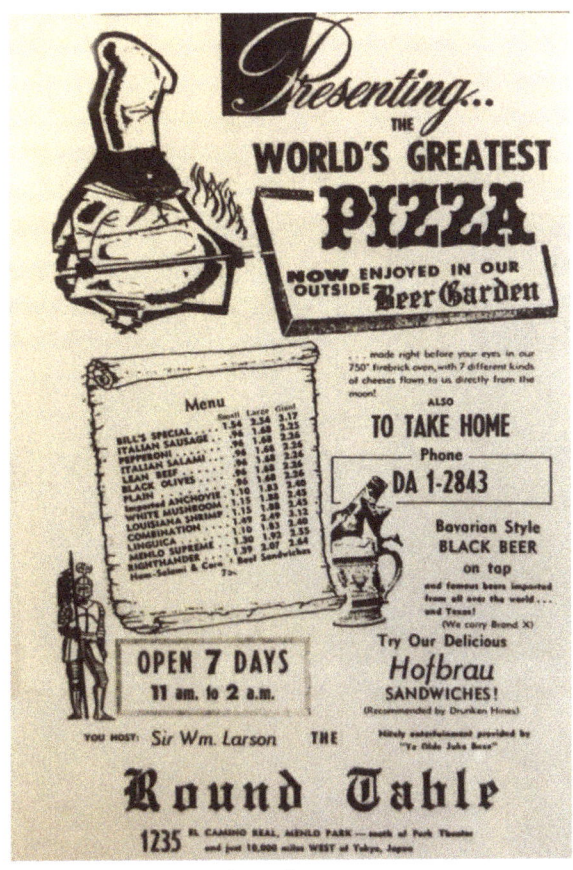

An early menu

On November 15, 2006, Bill Larson passed away, leaving nine children, twenty-five grandchildren, and three great-grandchildren.

In the intervening years, Round Table has tried new concepts. The Round Table Clubhouse, introduced in 2016, brought a full bar with microbrews and a menu that went beyond pizza to include things like Harris Ranch burgers and beer-battered fries. It also added new experiences, including an arcade area for the kids and live sporting events on big-screen TVs. Round Table Pizza, Wings, and Brew locations have a smaller footprint, with limited seating, and are most commonly seen in hotels, airports, and downtown locations. Round Table also has an Innovation Center that creates and taste-tests new dishes.

In the fall of 2017, Global Franchise Group took over Round Table Pizza, which led to a new look and a new logo, incorporating the original font from 1961. The year before its sixtieth anniversary in 2019, *Nation's Restaurant News* named Round Table one of the top pizza chains in the nation. For its anniversary, Round Table also launched a new motto: "Pizza Royalty." The motto suggests King Arthur and his Round Table—and also Bill Larson.

The modern iteration of Round Table

D/W
Der Wienerschnitzel

Hamburger lovers are going to the dogs.
Der Wienerschnitzel
18¢

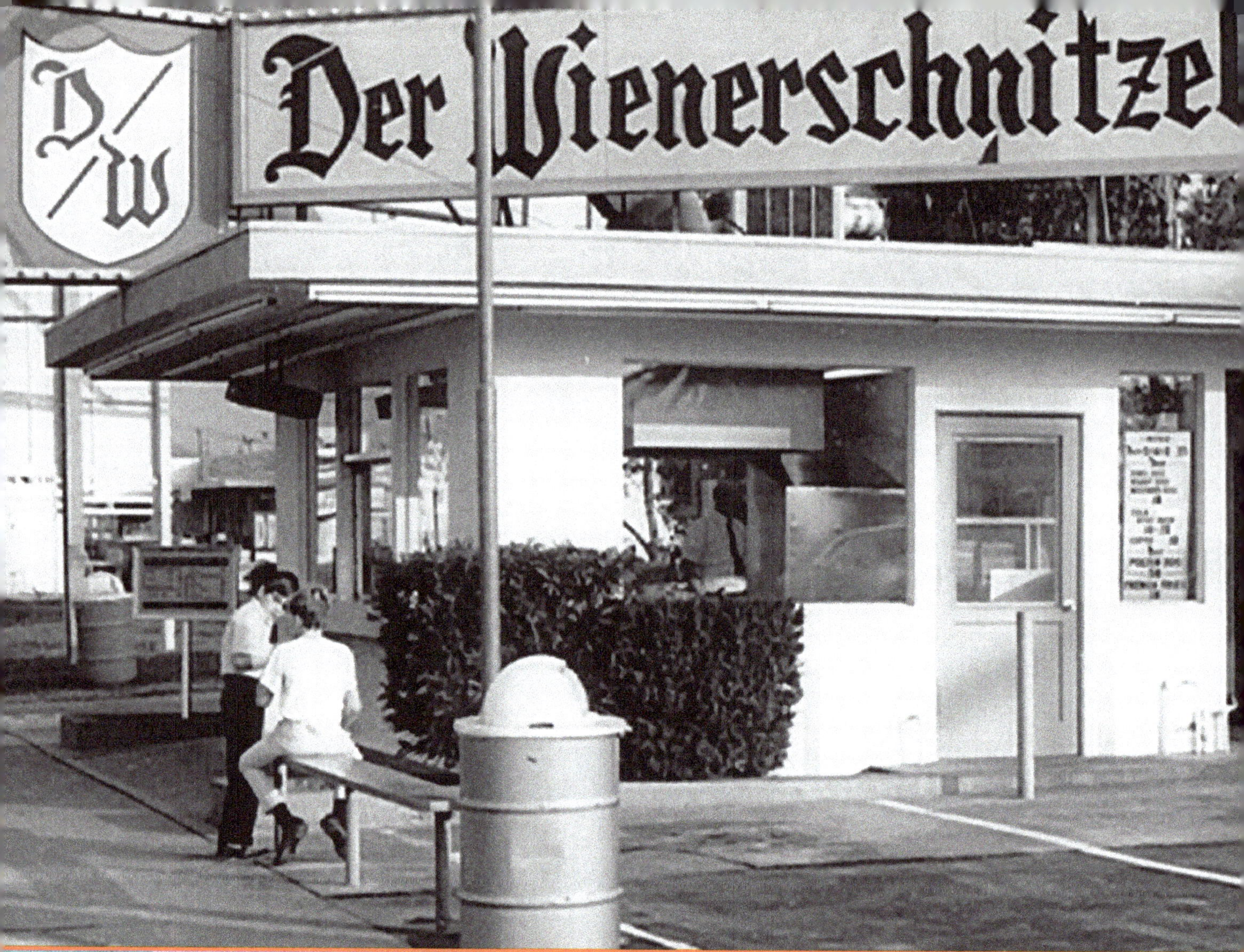

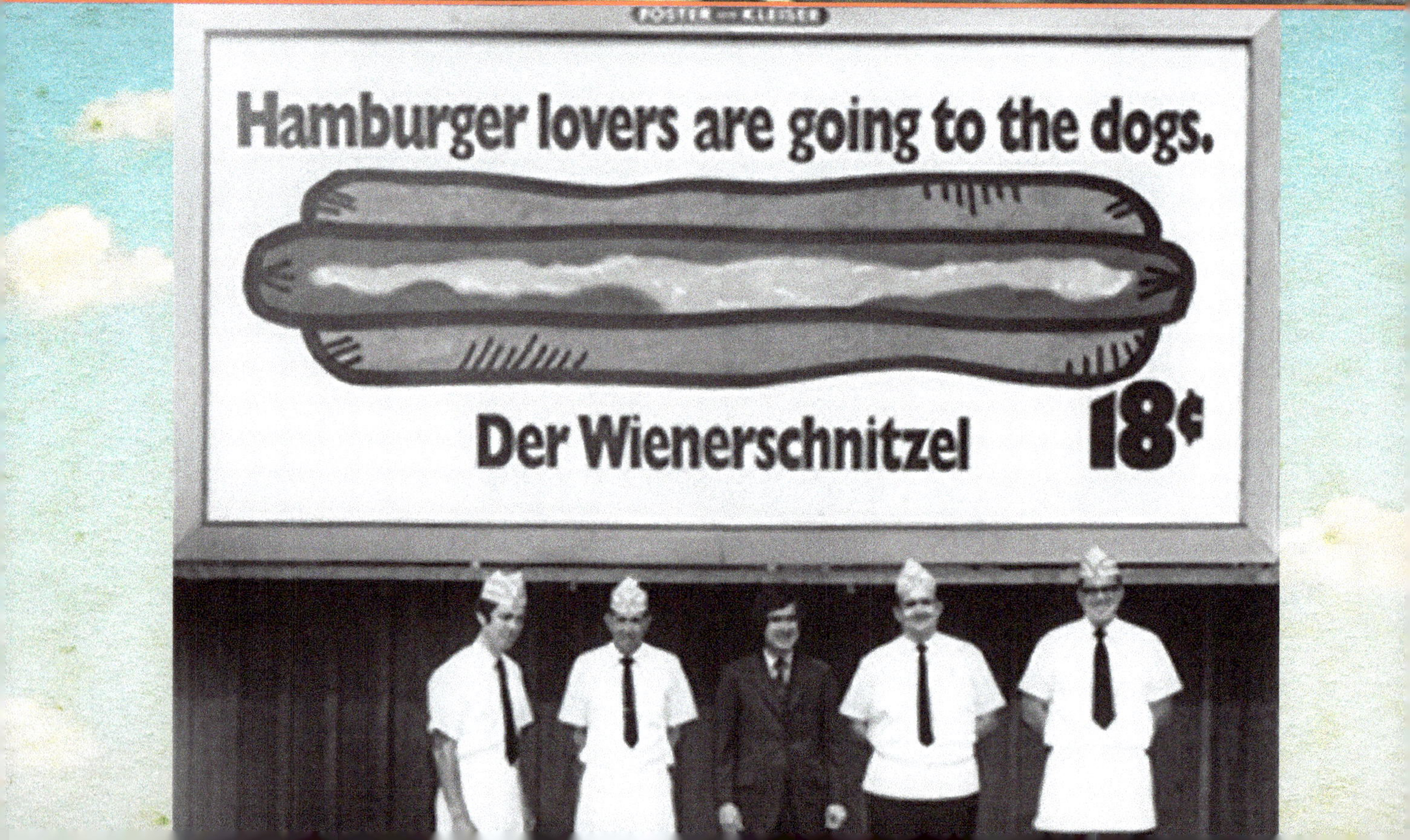

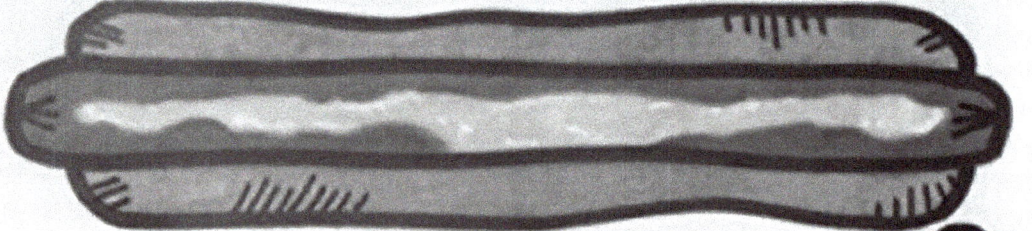

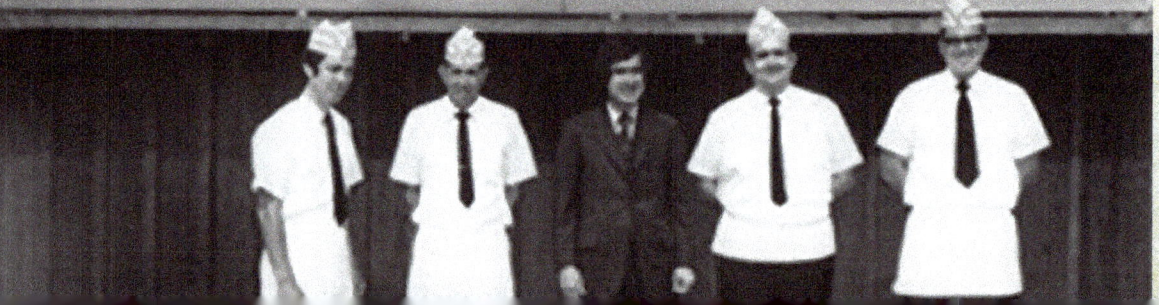

Der Wienerschnitzel

NAME TODAY: Wienerschnitzel
SLOGAN: "The World's Largest Hot Dog Chain"
ORIGINAL LOCATION: 900 West Pacific Coast Highway (at Gulf Avenue), Wilmington

OPENED: July 1961
FOUNDER: John Galardi
CURRENT OWNER: Galardi Group Inc.
CURRENTLY AT THE FIRST LOCATION: Still Wienerschnitzel

Wienerschnitzel currently has more than 300 locations in 10 states and Guam.

wienerschnitzel.com

John Galardi

YOU COULD SAY that food and entrepreneurship started at a young age for John Galardi. In the late 1950s, he was looking for work. While walking down Colorado Boulevard in Pasadena, he came across a woman hosing down the driveway of Taco Tia (page 229). He chatted with her and later found out that she was the wife of owner Glen Bell, and she put the young Galardi to work doing any job that needed to be done. Taco Tia was growing in the Riverside and Pasadena areas, so Bell decided to open up a central commissary and picked Galardi to run it (with a substantial pay increase). Within a year, Bell promoted Galardi to manage the newly opened Long Beach Taco Tia.

Taco Tia's rapid growth led Bell to get in over his head financially. He needed capital to open his many new locations. Bell knew that Galardi was saving every cent he made, so he asked him for a $6,000 loan to be paid back within three months. Three months came and went with no payment. Still strapped for funds, Bell offered the Long Beach location to Galardi for an unheard-of $12,000—minus the $6,000 Bell still owed him—handing him one of the great real estate deals of the day.

Bell owned a piece of land about five miles away in Wilmington that he was saving for his father-in-law. Seeing how successful the Long Beach Taco Tia location had become, Bell offered to lease it to Galardi with a handshake deal, as long as he didn't sell Mexican food. Bell also introduced Galardi to Macy Coffin, one of the premier fast-food restaurant architects at the time. Coffin financed the cost for the first location build-out in exchange for 6 percent of the gross profits.

Galardi began dreaming of the types of foods that he could sell. The McDonald brothers, Burger

Top: The first stand • Bottom: An early billboard

King, and the Snyders had focused on hamburgers; Colonel Sanders had the market on chicken; tacos and burritos were Bell's domain. The last hot fast food left was hot dogs. Hot dogs were inexpensive, didn't require utensils to eat, were easy to prepare, and could be dressed in countless ways. Galardi knew he needed something to set himself apart from other fast foods: a "special sauce" for his dogs. Back at the Taco Tia commissary, Bell helped him adapt his Taco Tia chili recipe to create a thick, no-bean chili to top the hot dogs. Galardi decided to sell chili, mustard, and sauerkraut dogs, along with soft drinks. He made up the name Der Wienerschnitzel to sound German, although the word refers to a completely unrelated Austrian specialty (ah, marketing!).

Top Dogs
Chili Cheese Dog
Corn Dog
Mustard Dog

Galardi was always on the lookout for exclusive products to try. While talking with real estate man Bill Trujillo about up-and-coming areas of Wilmington for future locations, Trujillo's friend Bill Linder mentioned that he'd recently had a delicious Polish sandwich in Santa Ana, about forty-five minutes away. They jumped in the car so Galardi could try it: a grilled Polish sausage sliced lengthwise and opened flat, served on rye bread with Swiss cheese, dill pickle, and mustard. This inspired his Polish Dog, a premium menu item at 30¢, while the other dogs were only 15¢. Yet it became an instant success.

He asked customers what foods they wanted, and baked beans and french fries were requested over and over. He added a cup of baked beans as a side dish and invested in a deep fryer to try out the fries. On the first day fries appeared on the menu, they out-sold the beans ten to one. The beans were scrapped.

Architect's drawing of the new A-frame design

An A-frame in action

Shortly after Der Wienerschnitzel opened, car clubs started using it as their meeting spot for weekend get-togethers. Soon, upward of one hundred kids were drinking in his parking lot while accounting for only 5 percent of his business, and likely driving away other customers. Galardi rethought his building design and remodeled it with a drive-thru. Customers drove their cars directly through the building, so the kids couldn't get out of their cars and would have to leave with their hot dogs. Galardi was environmentally conscious before his time—orders were written on the back of the bags that, eventually, the hot dogs and fries would be placed into. Unlike the McDonald brothers in San Bernardino, who had pre-prepared wrapped food, Galardi felt that it didn't take too much time to place a cooked dog into a pre-warmed bun and dress it in sauerkraut, chili, or other condiments.

After opening a second location that Bill Trujillo helped him secure, Galardi knew that he wanted to create a brand that was instantly recognizable, just like the Golden Arches. Through his builder, Macy Coffin, Galardi met Bob McKay, who had just designed the hacienda buildings for Bell's latest concept, Taco Bell (page 229). McKay came up with the idea of an eye-catching A-frame, Alpine-style building with a bright "ketchup red" roof. The new building style debuted at his third location, in 1962 in Compton, with the drive-thru building, a walk-up window, and a few outdoor seats. In 1965, only four years after opening the first Wilmington location, Galardi had twenty locations and had started franchising his concept. Hot dogs with a condiment were only 18¢. To add chili, the price shot up to 22¢.

Der Wienerschnitzel

John also rolled out his first motto: "Hamburger lovers are going to the dogs" (reminiscent of the recent billboard campaign for a Southern chicken company, with cows saying "Eat More Chicken"). In 1974, he jettisoned the A-frame design in order to create a dining room and outdoor area with a drive around the entire building. The former drive-thru, which divided the kitchen from the stockroom, created problems for employees, who had to wait until a car was out of the drive-thru to get to the other side of the building.

In 1973, Galardi noticed that the sales figures for the Fresno franchise were skyrocketing. He learned that they were offering a "Buy a Coke, Keep the Glass" deal. Since customers didn't just want one glass but an entire collection, the promotion created multiple repeat visits. It was so successful that the company sold 15 million Cokes as part of the campaign. The fast-food giveaway was born.

The 1970s brought a few more changes, including dropping "Der" in the name (but try telling that to Californians who grew up with the Der and won't let it go). The logo was changed to a big yellow *W* with the name Wienerschnitzel in red below—ketchup and mustard colors. In 1998, TDO, or The Delicious One, became the new mascot (an upright hot dog with legs and arms and the bun as his clothing), replacing the caped, masked Der Wiener Dog that had been the mascot for two decades.

You cannot go to a baseball game, America's pastime, without eating a hot dog. In 1999, Wienerschnitzel became the official hot dog of Anaheim Stadium, home of the Angels. Five years later, it became the official hot dog of Petco Park, home of the Padres, in their new stadium in downtown San Diego. Galardi was now supplying the hot dogs for the two baseball stadiums that were closest to his corporate offices.

In 2001, to be relevant during the new food-truck craze, Weinerschnitzel outfitted a forty-foot catering wagon that could roll up to any park, party, or event at a moment's notice. The Wiener Wagon still makes appearances around the L.A. area today.

In 2003, the Galardi Group acquired Tastee-Freez, a soft-serve ice cream and shake company. Using just a little space and at minimal cost, franchisers started outfitting their locations with the dessert treats. This concept became an instant success, since Weinerschnitzel didn't serve milkshakes or desserts. In 2004, marketing started revving up with localized hot dog names such as the New York, the Chicago, and the Midwestern.

Galardi died on April 14, 2013; his second wife, Cynthia Galardi-Culpepper, took over as CEO, and his son, J.R. Galardi, became COO and president. Karen Galardi, his daughter, is director of corporate giving. In September 2014, when the original Wilmington location was designated Los Angeles's 1,046th historical landmark, the entire family was on hand. Galardi's children said that the company had just begun and expects to keep expanding eastward.

Weiner Slogans of Yore
"Der fixin's are derlightful/there's fun in every bite-ful" (1960s)
"Wiener dude attitude!" (early '90s)
"Everyone loves a wiener!" (late '90s)
"Pushing the Boundaries of Taste" (mid-2000s)

The Delicious One pops a wheelie

Pioneer Take Out

NAME TODAY: Pioneer Chicken
ORIGINAL LOCATION: 1321 Echo Park Boulevard (at Sunset), Los Angeles
OPENED: December 1961
FOUNDER: H.R. ("Rick") Kaufman
CURRENTLY AT THE FIRST LOCATION: A new building that contains Little Caesars Pizza

In 1987, there were 270 locations: 220 franchises and 50 company owned. Today, only 2 locations remain, both independently operated.

WHEN H.R. ("RICK") KAUFMAN was in his early twenties, he worked at the famed Hollywood Ranch Market on Vine Street at Fountain. While working (he called it his apprenticeship) at the market, he was in charge of the barbecued chicken. It was a small but busy area of the market. He learned the ins and outs of how to work the chicken counter while being paid 95¢ per hour. He was fired after only six months, accused of giving free food away, supposedly to his father. But Kaufman knew the chicken wasn't very good, and he never would have subjected his father to the substandard poultry. While he worked, he thought about how he'd make the chicken better. He told himself that one day he'd be back, across the street from the Ranch Market, with his own chicken place.

Kaufman met with fast-food professionals to learn all he could. He told them he didn't want to serve hamburgers, tacos, or hot dogs, and they all thought he was crazy. But in 1961, Kaufman opened his first Pioneer Take Out, next door to Pioneer Market, a local chain, on the corner of Sunset and Echo Park Boulevard in the Echo Park area of Los Angeles. He never did open a location across from the Ranch Market, but in time that market closed.

Pioneer's chicken was dipped in a wet batter and deep-fried until crisp. It emerged orange, with a thin, tempura-like coating, and it was very greasy. When you bit into a piece of Pioneer chicken, you'd hear the crunch, and the coating would shatter and fall all over the place. People loved it. Warren Zevon even immortalized it in his song "Carmelita."

With a popular product and a successful franchise system, Kaufman was soon opening store after store around the Southland, later expanding to Arizona, Nevada, Northern California, and Hawaii.

In the mid-1970s, Kaufman created the Pioneer Man of the Year award. He honored the recipient at a black-tie dinner held at the Beverly Hills Hotel. Recipients included California lieutenant governor Mervyn Dymally and boxer Sugar Ray Robinson, in recognition of his youth foundation.

Kaufman knew that Pioneer's biggest competitor was Kentucky Fried Chicken (KFC), whose

The Pioneer chuckwagon sign

crispy chicken, coated with a dry mixture before frying, contrasted with Pioneer's wet-batter technique. KFC had only takeout locations at the time. Noting that McDonald's had started adding dining rooms, Kaufman decided that following suit would set Pioneer apart from KFC. So did its longer menu, which included fish and chips, fried shrimp, and sandwiches.

In 1977, Pioneer competed in the California State Fair and won medals, including one for Orange Bang, a new orange drink that Pioneer created. An entirely new company was formed to distribute it: the Orange Whip Corp.

Seeing how popular Ronald McDonald was with the kids at McDonald's, Pioneer introduced the character Pioneer Pete, a chef holding a whole cooked chicken while sitting in the driver's seat of a stagecoach wagon. The signage had Pioneer Pete spinning above each location. For a short time, Pete even had his own comic book, just like Bob's Big Boy (page 59).

By the end of the '70s, Pioneer had dozens of locations in the Hawaiian Islands. These became the highest-volume locations for the company year after year.

As the money rolled in for Kaufman, he purchased the entire town of Blue Jay in the mountains near Lake Arrowhead, where he planned to build a convention center, condominium complex, and seven-phase shopping center. The plans for the development proved quite controversial, making residents of the quiet mountain retreat very unhappy. This venture into the recreation business was short-lived. Meanwhile, his investments in other businesses and his lack of focus on the chicken business led to problems. Pioneer's sales dropped for the first time in 1985. Scaling down operations in the Fresno area and closing twenty-eight locations was just the beginning. Kaufman then pared down the number of company-owned stores to thirty-four from ninety-five, from Hawaii to Phoenix. On paper, Pioneer returned to profitability after selling some of the closed locations.

Chicken dinner at Pioneer

In 1986, California Fried Chicken opened in Jakarta, Indonesia, as an offshoot of Pioneer. The logo didn't have Pioneer Pete, just the wagon in red and white. It became one of the fastest-growing food companies in Indonesia. Today, that country has 269 locations, which no longer have anything to do with Pioneer.

In the summer of 1987, county marshals arrived at the company-owned locations close to the end of the day and emptied the cash registers. A court judgment said that the Cummings Inc. sign company was owed for nonpayment of invoices. A few weeks later, the IRS took legal steps to collect overdue taxes directly from the franchisees. In turn, the California Department of Corporations ordered Pioneer to stop selling franchises until it could prove it was solvent.

Forty-four of Pioneer's 225 franchisees sued the company, maintaining that they'd bought their franchises on the basis of misleading and fraudulent information supplied by Pioneer. Their suit also alleged that Pioneer funds were inappropriately loaned to Kaufman's other enterprises. Kaufman searched for a buyer for the company, but the lawsuit and the discord within the company, not to mention the drop in sales and in Pioneer's value, made it difficult to find one. The franchisees stopped paying the fees on their accounts.

The Last Two Standing
904 South Soto Street, Boyle Heights
6323 East Florence Avenue, Bell Gardens

Pioneer lagged behind in product launches as other companies competed for the chicken market. In 1981, McDonald's launched Chicken McNuggets and chicken sandwiches. New fresh-cooked chicken restaurants, such as El Pollo Loco, sprouted up, and the Southern chain Popeye's started opening in the west, further hurting Pioneer's sales. In 1993, the parent company for Popeye's bought the ailing Pioneer company in an auction, converting most of the remaining Pioneers into Popeye's.

But if you walk into one of the two remaining Pioneer Take Outs, you'll feel like you stepped back into 1970. The colors of the interior: dark red, mustard yellow, and sunburst orange. All the fixtures are original; the trash can is held together with duct tape. They even serve Orange Bang, and Pioneer Pete still twirls overhead, lighting the evening sky.

One of the last of two L.A. locations

Taco Bell

EARLIER ITERATIONS: Taco Tia; El Taco; Bell's Burgers
ORIGINAL LOCATION: 7112 Firestone Boulevard, Downey
OPENED: March 1962
FOUNDER: Glen Bell
CURRENT OWNER: Yum! Brands (Yum China within China)
CURRENTLY AT THE FIRST LOCATION: A new Taco Bell building; the original building was moved to the corporate headquarters in Irvine

There are more than 7,400 locations—7 percent company owned and 93 percent franchises—in 31 countries.

tacobell.com

GLEN BELL, a food entrepreneur, started his first restaurant, Bell's Drive-In, close to the McDonald brothers' business in San Bernardino. His menu was hot dogs and hamburgers. Many burger restaurants dotted the Southland after the success of the "Speedee Service" of the McDonald brothers. Across the street from his drive-in, customers formed lines out the door of the Mitla Café. Bell wanted to generate lines like *that*. Mitla was serving a folded, heated tortilla filled with meat and cheese: a taco. Bell was intrigued: How long did it take to cook the shell? How long to fill the order? How could he do it faster and better?

A few years later, Bell opened Taco Tia, selling tacos for 19¢ each. If the lines didn't go around the block, the stands were successful enough that he opened two more in the San Bernardino area. He then sold Taco Tia and opened a noncompeting taco stand in Long Beach called El Taco's.

Bell hired a Sherman Oaks architect named Robert McKay to create a distinctive new look for a California fast-food business. The buildings had to be practical, small, and easy to build. Bell had only a handful of menu items that he was working with, so the kitchen didn't have to be huge. McKay came up with a twenty-by-twen-

Top: The costumed staff at Taco Tia • Bottom: The first El Taco

Founder Glen Bell at window

Opening Menu
Bell Beefer (seasoned beef burger)
Burritos
Frijoles (pinto beans and cheese)
Tacos
Tostadas

Taco Bell 229

The first Taco Bell

ty-foot concept with an arched and tiled California Mission motif. A rooftop bell would soon become the company's signature image. (McKay would go on to close his architecture business and become president of Taco Bell once the franchises started selling.)

The first Taco Bell opened on Firestone Boulevard in Downey, serving tacos, burritos, "Bell Beefer" burgers, and tostadas with just one protein: ground beef. Other items included pinto beans and cheese (frijoles) and Royal Crown Cola. All menu items were 25¢ each. The original Taco Bells featured walk-up windows only, with no indoor seating or drive-thru service. In later years, Bell installed a firepit and some seating in the front of the buildings.

Bell opened fifteen locations around the Los Angeles area before selling his first franchise in 1965 to retired Los Angeles police officer Kermit Bekke. Bekke's location was the first to be completely self-sufficient; Bell's locations were dependent on an off-site central commissary. On Memorial Day weekend, the new Torrance location celebrated with family-oriented grand-opening festivities featuring clowns, balloons, and mariachis. Bekke sold his location after only eighteen months of operation, and the location no longer exists.

The oldest continuously operating location is at 1822 Santa Fe Avenue in Long Beach (the second location built after Downey). Arizona was the first state outside of California to have a Taco Bell; it opened in Scottsdale in 1966, taking some heat from its Mexican neighbors for its inauthentic "Mexican" food. (Today there are multiple Taco Bells in Scottsdale alone, and nearly 200 in Arizona.)

Taco Bell has been known over the years to create food names and products that are not in the Spanish or English dictionary. Franchisee Dan Jones, for example, created the "Enchirito," a cross between a burrito and an enchilada. It was made with seasoned ground beef, beans, diced onions, and cheese, wrapped in a flour tortilla, topped with a red sauce and three olives in a row, and placed in a foil dish that could be reheated at home. It was tested in five Albuquerque locations and then placed on the menu after being patented in 1970.

By 1978, Bell had opened or franchised 868 Taco Bell units. He then sold his company to PepsiCo (Taco Bell's Royal Crown Cola products were quickly replaced with Pepsi versions). Seven years later, PepsiCo purchased the Pup 'n' Taco chain (page 241) and converted one hundred locations to Taco Bells. These were prime spots on or near major intersections.

Over the decades, Taco Bell has introduced dozens of creative menu items, price deals, and cross-promotions with films and

Glen Bell's Former Companies

1948–1952	Bell's Drive In (all closed)
1952–1956	Taco Tia (Redlands)
1956–1962	El Taco (San Pedro & Anaheim)
1962–present	Taco Bell
1965	Taco Bell's first franchise

Taco Bell's Owners

1962–1978	Glen Bell
1978–1997	PepsiCo
1997–2002	Tricon Global Restaurants
2002–present	Yum! Brands

Taco Bell today

Discontinued Menu Items
- Beefy Crunch Burrito
- Beefy Melt Burrito
- Beefy Mini Quesadilla
- Blackjack Taco
- BLT Taco
- Cheesarito
- Chicken Caesar Grilled Stuft Burrito
- Chicken Fiesta Burrito
- Chiliburger (Bell Burger, Bell Beefer)
- Chilito
- Chipotle Chicken Loaded Griller
- Chips and Salsa
- Cinnamon Crispas
- Cool Ranch Locos Tacos
- Double Decker Taco
- Enchirito
- Fiery Doritos Locos Tacos Double Tostada
- Fully Loaded Nachos
- Grilled Stuft Nacho
- Meximelt
- Nacho Crunch Grilled Stuft Burrito
- Potatorito
- Power Menu Burrito
- Seafood Salad
- Spicy Chicken Crunchwrap Supreme
- Taco Grande
- Taco Lite
- Volcano Taco
- XXL Grilled Stuft Burrito

with other brands. In the 1980s, it offered an up-sized taco, the BellGrande; if that wasn't grande enough, Taco Bell boosted it to Supreme. Today's menu features Nachos BellGrande, but the largest and most successful new product launch was the Nacho French Fries: nacho-flavored fries served with nacho cheese sauce. Fifty-three million orders were sold in the first three months of 2018; the item was unavailable as of this writing.

The popular Run for the Border initiative consisted of single menu items priced at 59¢, 69¢, and 79¢. This brought hungry eaters in the door, many adding on items they had not tried before, attracted by the low price. "Dollar Deals" offered a range of items for under a buck. In one of the first film-food promotions, for the 1989 *Batman* starring Michael Keaton, Taco Bell featured new collectible plastic Batman cups with scenes from the movie, and became one of the first fast-food outlets to offer free refills.

In 1991, Taco Bell Express locations opened in truck stops, airports, and shopping malls; besides having a smaller footprint, these units offered most food items for less than a dollar. Taco Bell Cantinas, which serve alcohol, have opened in major cities around the country; the Las Vegas location is open twenty-four hours and in 2017 started conducting weddings. PepsiCo co-branded pairs of its fast-food companies in order to create locations with options: Taco Bell with Kentucky Fried Chicken (KFC), and Pizza Hut with Long John Silvers, which are still operating today.

Founder and mentor Glen Bell died in 2010. In 2015, at the urging of preservationists, the original Robert McKay–designed Taco Bell building in Downey was saved from the wrecking ball. Late at night, the building was put onto a truck bed and moved to Irvine. You can see the original building for a brief moment in Quentin Tarantino's 2019 film, *Once Upon a Time in Hollywood*. Or, as Glen Bell might have thought of it, Once Upon a Time in Downey.

The Coffee Bean & Tea Leaf

ORIGINAL LOCATION: The Brentwood Country Mart, 13020-D San Vicente Boulevard, Los Angeles

OPENED: 1963
FOUNDERS: Herbert & Mona Hyman
CURRENT OWNER: Jollibee Foods Inc.
CURRENTLY AT THE FIRST LOCATION: Velvet by Graham & Spencer Clothing Store

There are currently more than 1,200 locations in 16 states and 30 countries.

coffeebean.com

Herb & Mona Hyman

IN 1963, during his undergraduate years at UCLA and before coffee was a gleam in his eye, Herbert Hyman created a successful vending-machine business, selling soft drinks, snacks, and cigarettes. Selling suited him. When he sold that business, he started an office coffee service, a fortuitous move: He met his bride-to-be, Mona, at one of the accounting offices he serviced.

After their marriage in 1965, Herb and Mona made several trips to her native Sweden, where Herb fell in love with the richness of European coffees, something that was lacking in the United States, where canned coffee was considered all that. The couple decided it was time to educate Americans about the many varieties and roasting styles of coffee.

The Hymans started their premium-coffee business in a small store in the Brentwood Country Mart, an upscale westside L.A. shopping center. Herb built the beautiful oak cabinetry himself. The wood paneling on the walls showcased the origins of the coffee beans. The location launched what was to become the oldest and largest privately held specialty coffee and tea retailer in the nation.

Their store had its own roaster, and the Hymans sold bags of freshly roasted beans by the pound. They also had a "sample bar" where you could taste the different attributes of each of the coffees. Herb offered lessons in how to properly brew the coffee. He even invented equipment, including the Classic 100, a special drip coffee maker, and a thermos made of double-walled plastic with an expandable rubber gasket. By 1977, according to a *Los Angeles Times* article on the company, The Coffee Bean & Tea Leaf boasted twenty varieties of coffee beans, including Colombian Supremo, and a full line of coffee paraphernalia at its main store. It wasn't until the late 1970s that Herb started selling drinks made from his beans. Full cups of coffee, espresso drinks, and more were introduced for sale. In the beginning, the drinks made up only 10 percent of daily sales, while coffee beans constituted 90 percent. But with

The cozy, cluttered first location

The first shop, at the Brentwood Country Mart

the coffee revolution that started in the 1990s, those numbers soon reversed. Coffee connoisseurs began going out for coffee instead of making it at home.

Thanks to the Brentwood store's elite location, celebrities passed by regularly on their way to the studios in Hollywood or the San Fernando Valley. Many became fans, including Johnny Carson, Dinah Shore, Lee Marvin, Ronald and Nancy Reagan, and Jacques Cousteau. Marvin loved to get behind the counter, packaging beans and helping customers. In 1968, when Mona was pregnant and her water broke, Marvin was in the store and looked over at Herb. "Herbie, are you going to take her to the hospital or am I?" You could say that daughter Anne ("Annie") Hyman was born into the coffee business. Of her four siblings, Annie was the only one who worked for The Coffee Bean. Over the years she worked in many of the stores and later served as CEO.

In 1979, with the roaster in Brentwood servicing more than ten stores around the Southland, Herb sought out a new location to expand production. Camarillo, a small beach town between L.A. and Santa Barbara, fit the bill. RAD (Roasting and Distribution) was born. The 35,000-square-foot facility started as part roasting plant, part mail-order processor, and part offices. Little by little, the roasting plant pushed out the others, and currently the corporate offices are on Wilshire Boulevard in L.A.'s Miracle Mile. The RAD facility roasts and packages more than 7 million pounds of coffee annually, along with more than 1 million pounds of tea from eight countries.

Herb was hands-on with his company. He personally traveled to visit coffee farmers in more than twenty-four countries, from whom he sourced green coffee beans and tea leaves for his blends. He promoted the idea of paying good prices to coffee farmers and was passionate about helping people and giving back. He would purchase only the top percentage of the beans grown in the world for his stores, even though some regions were embroiled in conflict and civil wars. He traveled often to Central and South America, including Guatemala, Costa Rica, El Salvador, Nicaragua, and Brazil. Herb traveled without Mona, as he felt it was too dangerous for her in some of the unstable communities that he visited. Instead, she was running all of the stores. He didn't travel to Africa or Southeast Asia, as governments there required that buyers go through special brokers who purchased very large lots from the government. The governments of Kenya and Ethiopia were still controlling coffee exports when Annie was the CEO and coffee buyer in the 1990s. Today, Jay Isais, Coffee Bean's director of coffee, selects the top 1 percent of Arabica beans from the world's best coffee-growing regions in East Africa, Latin America, and the Pacific.

Diane Martell, who started as a barista in the Westwood Coffee Bean & Tea Leaf and became the manager there, helped revolutionize the operations and the menu. She opened the store a few hours earlier and brought in poetry readings and other moneymaking ideas. Herb noticed how much sales at the Westwood location had gone up, and he wondered what this twenty-one-year-old knew that others didn't. When Martell was trying to lose a few pounds, she brought in her own blender to create a lunch out of powdered meal supplement, ice, and a cold coffee extract. It was too bitter, so she added some of the chocolate powder that Herb had created for the hot drinks. After a few weeks, Diane omitted the meal-replacement powder and just used the ice, coffee, and chocolate powder. The shop was small, and the UCLA students who were regulars saw her drinking a cold beverage and asked about it. Thinking quickly, she added 50¢ to the price of a hot mocha, making the iced version the highest-priced drink, at $2.25. Her store's sales grew to double those at all the other branches.

A few years later, Coffee Bean opened a branch on the newly renovated Third Street Promenade in Santa Monica, as did a competing Starbucks, which had just come to town. Martell walked the Promenade with samples of the ice-blended drinks. Before long, cold coffee drinks were on the menus at Starbucks and other coffeehouses. It took about three years for the drinks to be integrated into all of the Coffee Beans, because of the challenges of installing blenders and ice machines. The blenders were so loud that they had to house them in wooden boxes for soundproofing. Over twenty years and through different ownerships, Martell worked on many continents for The Coffee Bean & Tea Leaf, eventually leaving to become a landscape designer and consultant.

Seasonal Drink Flavors
Candy Cane
Cookie Butter Latte
Eggnog
Peppermint Mocha
Pumpkin Spice Chai
Red Velvet Cake

In 1998, Hyman sold the International Coffee and Tea Corporation Inc. to the Sassoon family. When Herb sold the company, he had thirty stores in Singapore and Malaysia and forty stores in America; Sunny Sassoon became the "Coffee King" of Singapore by bringing the coffee there. That also was the year that chai tea latte drinks were launched, a first in the industry.

In September 2013, Advent International, CDIB Capital, and Mirae Asset Private Equity acquired a significant equity position in the company. In 2015, after serving as CEO of Johnny Rocket's, John Fuller became the CEO and president of The Coffee Bean & Tea Leaf. He's led a large expansion effort, including more domestic and international franchises and new store designs. Thinking outside the coffee can, The Coffee Bean & Tea Leaf of Las Vegas started a mobile truck business that houses a full coffee bar. Traditional street-side locations and shopping malls represent the majority of the cafés worldwide, but there are also more than forty airport locations, as well as branches on university campuses and military bases.

On April 28, 2014, the "grandfather of specialty coffee" died in his home, not far from the roasting plant in Camarillo, California. Herb Hyman was eighty-two. Since serving as CEO of the company, daughter Annie Hyman now runs her own consulting business.

In the summer of 2018, Coffee Bean opened its 184th store in California, in the city of Placentia. The new concept is a stand-alone building with interior and exterior seating areas as well as a drive-thru. A year later, Jollibee Foods, known for its signature mix of fried chicken and sweet spaghetti, bought Coffee Bean, which is helping the company grow in the expanding Asian markets.

The company that brought the world's coffee to the United States now brings its coffees and Iced Blendeds to the rest of the world.

Casa Del Taco

NAME TODAY: Del Taco
ORIGINAL LOCATION: 38434 Yermo Road, Yermo

OPENED: September 1964
FOUNDER: Ed Hackbarth
COFOUNDERS: David Jameson & Dick Naugle
CURRENT OWNER: Del Taco Holdings Inc.
CURRENTLY AT THE FIRST LOCATION: Burger Den

There are nearly 600 locations in 15 states and Guam.

deltaco.com

WHEN ED HACKBARTH got out of the Air Force in 1954, his next job was much more down to earth: managing Bell's Hot Dog Stand on Route 66 in San Bernardino. Bell's was co-owned by Glen Bell, who later went on to create Taco Bell (page 229). Hackbarth invested $12,000 to build his first Casa Del Taco location in the one-street desert town of Yermo in 1964 with help from his brother, Tony. The menu was limited: 19¢ tacos and tostadas and 24¢ cheeseburgers. The motto was "Getting good food served very fast." On his first day, he made $169 in sales, the equivalent of 900 tacos.

In 1966, Hackbarth brought in David Jameson to help him open two other locations, in Barstow and Needles. In 1967, they opened a third, a mile from Jameson's home in Corona. This was the first location with a drive-thru—a smart move, as it was only a block from the Interstate. This was ten years before McDonald's started switching to drive-thru. Hackbarth and Jameson also introduced red and green burritos, and the same recipes are still used today. To build the brand, they felt the name needed to change, so in 1973, they dropped "Casa" and called it just Del Taco, with the idea that "Del" stood for Delicious.

Hackbarth and Jameson recognized the potential of Del Taco. They restructured the company under the name Red-E-Food Systems; added a third partner, Dick Naugle of Naugles fame; and headquartered the business in Corona, with Jameson as president. By 1976, Hackbarth and Jameson realized they had accomplished what they'd set out to do and sold their chain of fifty restaurants to a group of investors. They then sold the rights to use and develop the Del Taco brand outside of California to W.R. Grace & Co., which in turn formed Del Taco Restaurants Inc.

Many founders who have sold their companies to investors fade out of the spotlight they created. Not Hackbarth. He kept hold of a number of locations, and his family still owns and manages them. He

Milestones
Year	Locations
1964:	1 location
1967:	3 locations
1977:	50 locations
1978:	100 locations
1981:	352 locations
1998:	325 locations
2006:	500 locations
2021:	596 locations

Top: The first Del Taco, in Yermo • Bottom: The same location today

Ed Hackbarth

even attends grand openings—smart parent companies know that founders provide good publicity.

Del Taco flourished during the 1970s. Two years after the purchase by investors, the number of Del Taco locations doubled. The menu also grew, expanding to include items like the bun taco, quesadilla, and ice cream sundaes. In 1988, Anwar Soliman purchased Del Taco and merged it with the Naugles chain, thereby greatly increasing the number of locations and the geographic reach. Del Taco also began to stay open all night as demand increased for twenty-four-hour fast food.

In the '90s, Del Taco focused on aggressive growth, customer service, and branding. By 2006, the chain had nearly doubled in size, opening its 500th restaurant in Burbank. It launched a dessert, Caramel Cheesecake Bites, which continues to be a big hit, and had fun creating the Del Taco Super Special Show. By introducing the "Del" taco, the Buck & Under menu, and more fresh ingredients like hand-sliced avocado, Del Taco continued to be a leader in serving appealing food at value prices. Management takes pride in chopping, grilling, and shredding on-site every day, and employees are known for

Secret Menu Items
- Bun Taco: Everything in the classic taco tossed onto a burger bun instead of a tortilla
- Going Bold: fries and secret sauce rolled into whatever you order

their work ethic. And as demand for healthier food grew, Del Taco updated its menu in 2013 with lighter fare.

Fifty years after the first Casa Del Taco opened, Del Taco was still going strong—and so was Hackbarth. In 2014, the anniversary year, the company named its new training center after the founder and presented him with a plaque honoring his vision and legacy. Hackbarth, at eighty-five, helped with the reopening of the east Corona location, which had to be moved by 600 feet for the widening of the 91 Freeway.

In 2018, Del Taco became the first major fast-food chain to offer vegan-friendly Beyond Meat plant-based dishes, ahead of the trend that is now sweeping the industry. This has helped set the stage for continued growth into the 2020s, as diners increasingly try to marry their love for fast Mexican food with a desire to be more environmentally—and healthfully—aware.

Ad for the grand opening in Anaheim

A whole new look today

Pup 'n' Taco

ORIGINAL LOCATION: 333 South Rosemead Boulevard, Pasadena

OPENED: 1965
FOUNDER: Russell C. Wendell
CURRENTLY AT THE FIRST LOCATION: Taco Bell

Pup 'n' Taco sold 95 locations to Taco Bell in 1984; 3 locations stayed private and changed their names to Pop 'n' Taco.

RUSSELL C. WENDELL was a doughnut-machine salesman who built and founded the Big Do-Nut shops (page 179). After selling ten of them, he looked into opening a drive-thru restaurant that served hot dogs, tacos, and pastrami sandwiches. The first officially branded Pup 'n' Taco opened on the corner of Rosemead (California Highway 19) and Thorndale Road in 1965.

The buildings were created for Wendell, and unlike the Big Do-Nut chain, they were plain, with nothing on the roof like a giant hot dog or taco. Instead, they were small versions of the A-frame buildings like those that housed International House of Pancakes and Der Wienerschnitzel.

The buildings had just a drive-thru and a walk-up window, with a few tables and chairs lining the side of the building. The A-frame roofline was a bright red; it had two white stripes down the center, and the sides of the building were a dark brown.

The menu offered a mix of hot dogs, tacos, hamburgers, pastrami, and Royal Crown (RC) Cola. If a guest asked for a Pepsi or a Coke, the employee would have to correct them with, "That is an RC Cola, correct?" Pup 'n' Taco was also one of the first fast-food establishments to serve a diet-cola product, Diet Rite, a new lower-calorie drink that had just come on the market. Pup 'n' Taco was also the first chain to have frozen or "slushy" drinks on the menu, grape and cherry. This wasn't entirely a taste-based decision: The slushy had a higher profit margin than a milkshake, and the milkshake mixture had an expiration date, while the slushy was just flavored sugar water.

By early 1972, just seven years after the first location opened in Pasadena, Wendell had fifty locations around the Los Angeles area. They were primarily on the corners of major intersections or just one lot away, so it was easy to see the rotating sign. When print ads in the Sunday newspaper would come out with coupons, the locations were known only by the intersection and not the physical address. Wendell knew that if you could see the sign, there was no need for a street

1973 Prices
Beef Burrito: 69¢
Chili Dog: 29¢
French Fries: 29¢
Pastrami: 99¢
Refried Beans: 29¢
Taco: 29¢
Taco on a Bun: 59¢

Russell C. Wendell

The first Pup, in Rosemead • Opposite top: Happy employees • Opposite bottom: An A-frame location

number. The greatest growth occurred in 1973, with a new Pup 'n' Taco opening every month.

PepsiCo had been watching the Pup 'n' Taco brand, noticing Wendell's strategic and successful placement of his restaurants. Since PepsiCo was planning to build its Taco Bell brand quickly, purchasing the Pup 'n' Tacos would fit into the Taco Bell portfolio perfectly. With ninety-two Southern California locations and three out of state, none of the locations overlapped with the existing Taco Bells. At first, the Pup 'n' Tacos were a step backward from the newer look of Taco Bell, as Pup 'n' Tacos had no dining rooms. Evaluating the equipment and menu of Pup 'n' Taco versus Taco Bell, it was apparent that half of the equipment, such as fryers and grills that were once necessary for french fries and burgers, was no longer needed, freeing up kitchen space to add small dining rooms. It took PepsiCo only eight months to convert all of the locations. RC Cola, as well as slushies, fries, hot dogs, and hamburgers, were taken off the menu.

Three locations in Albuquerque, New Mexico, owned by a member of the Wendell family were not part of the PepsiCo deal. These locations had to have a name change as part of the sale, so they were renamed Pop 'n' Taco, which required just a slight signage change. These have since closed, and the properties were sold off by 2014.

There are no longer any Pup 'n' Tacos in existence—but next time you see a Taco Bell on the corner of a major intersection, look closely: There may be the ghost of a Pup 'n' Taco lurking inside.

Milestones
1965: 1 location
1972: 50 locations
1985: 98 locations
1986: 0 locations

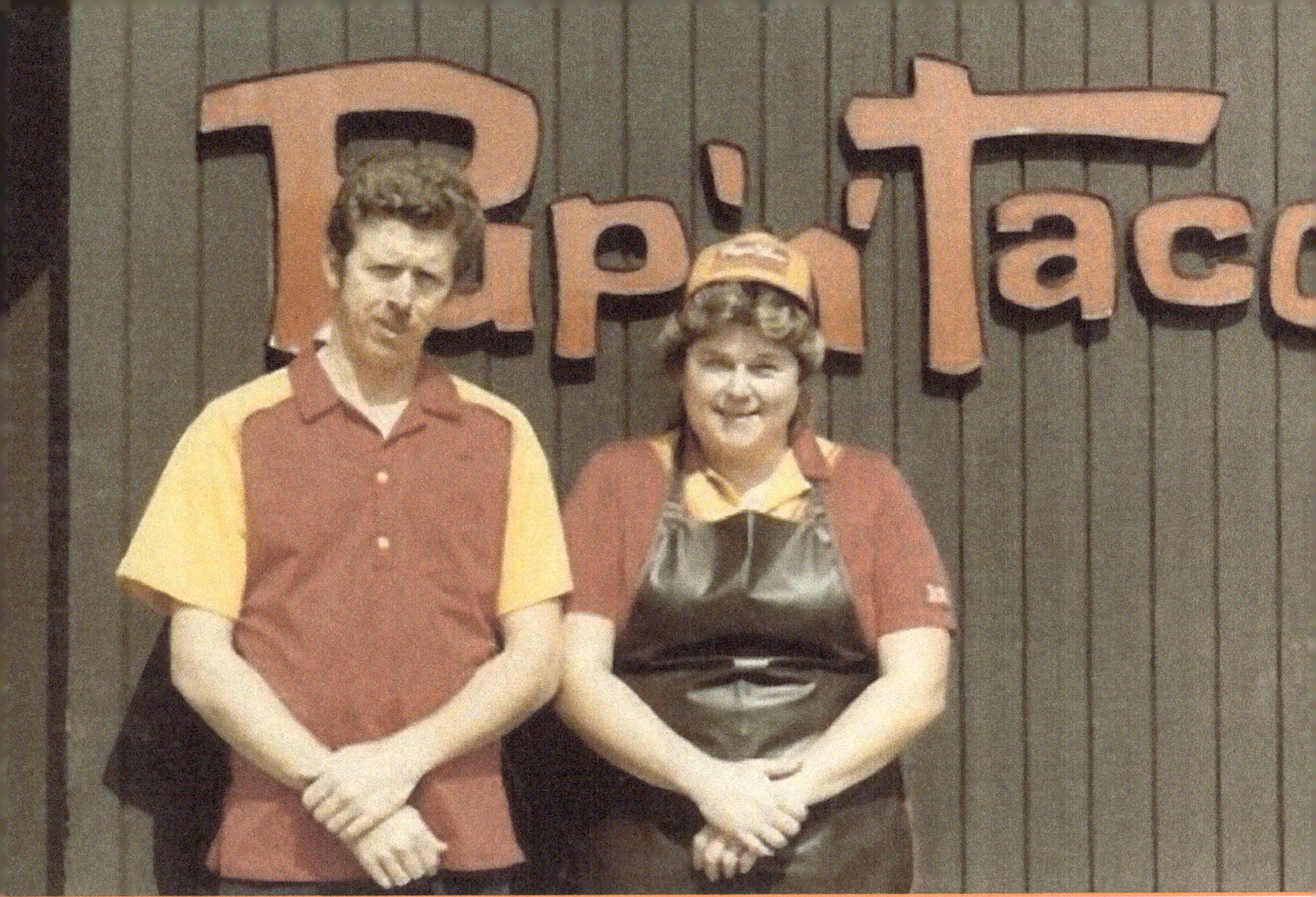
Pup'n'Taco

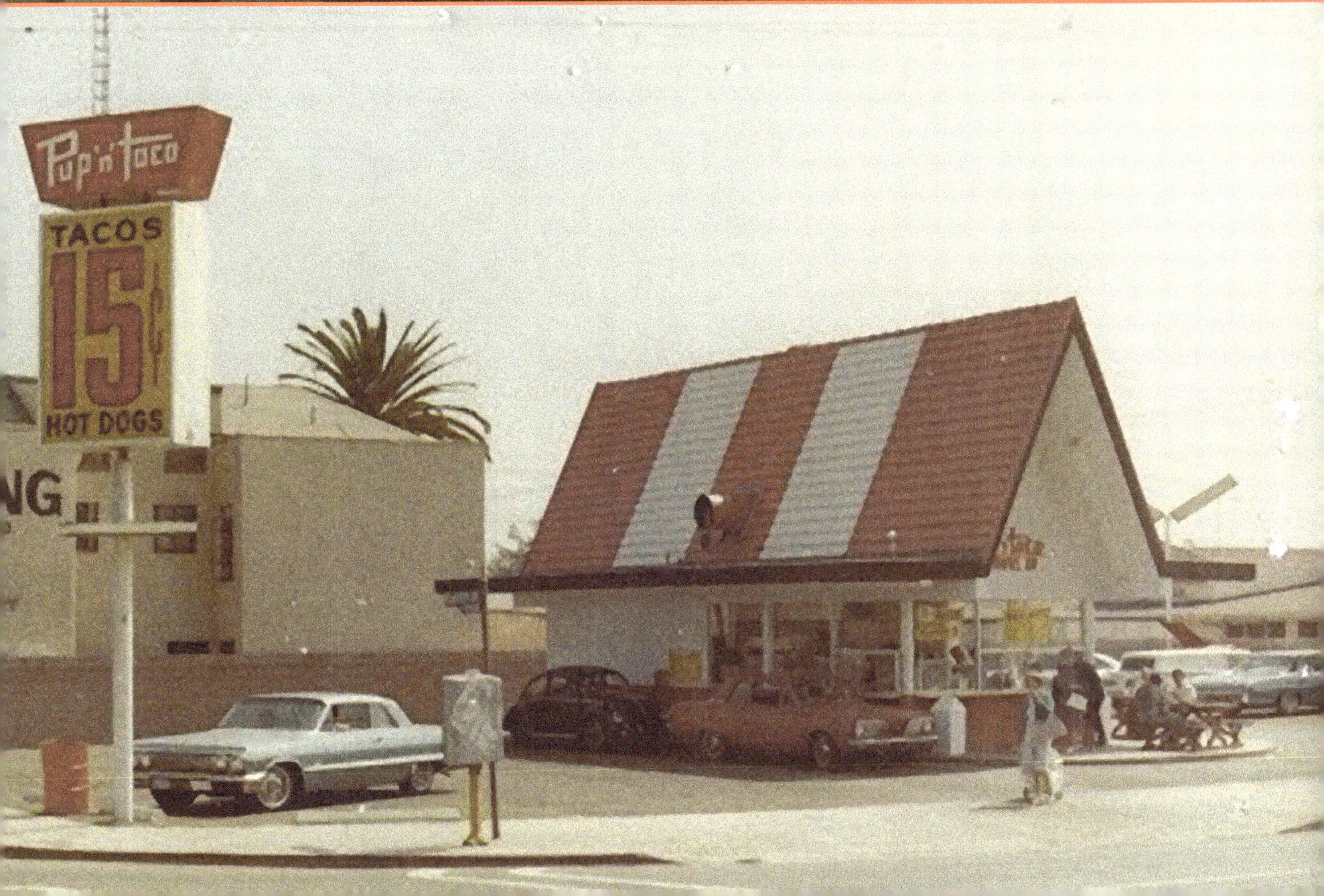
Pup'n'taco
TACOS
15
HOT DOGS

House of Pies

ORIGINAL LOCATION: 7303 Reseda Boulevard, Reseda

OPENED: November 1966
FOUNDER: Al Lapin Jr.
CURRENTLY AT THE FIRST LOCATION: Reseda Discount Fountains and Pottery

There were 32 locations until 1973; today, 4 remain in California and Texas, and all are independently owned.

houseofpiesla.com

"Dial-a-Pie" spinner from the kid's menu

AL LAPIN JR. was known as the man behind many major California restaurants and fast-food brands. From International House of Pancakes (page 209) to Orange Julius (page 45) to Copper Penny Family Restaurants (page 201), Lapin defined food in Southern California and beyond.

House of Pies opened during a three-day celebration the week before Thanksgiving in 1966. For the gala, Lapin offered a free slice of pie to everyone in attendance. The locations also had lunch and dinner favorites, such as club sandwiches, soups, and salads and dinner meals of chicken-fried steak and meatloaf, but a place called House of Pies had better be known for its pies. So each location baked its own pies in an open kitchen for all to see.

Lapin created a building using Howard Johnson's colorful chalet-style restaurant architecture as a model to catch the eye. Appropriately, House of Pies restaurants were "cottages" painted white with pink trim. The signage featured a house with the pi symbol inside, and featured the slogan "A unique coffee shop."

When setbacks caused the delay of two House of Pies openings in Glendale and Panorama City in October 1967, the company used humor—and a delicious deal—to deflect criticism. Newspaper ads featured pictures of pastry chefs being "pied" with a pie. "We deserve it… we got meringue on our face!" the ads read. "Our two House of Pies have been delayed… so, to make amends, we are extending the

L.A.'s last remaining location, in Los Feliz

First 6 Locations
1043 Westwood Boulevard, Westwood
411 North Brand Boulevard, Glendale
1032 Hollywood Way, Burbank
501 Wilshire Boulevard, Santa Monica
8608 Van Nuys Boulevard, Panorama City
1869 North Vermont Avenue, Los Angeles

hours of two other locations and we'll put ice cream on your slice of fruit pie at no charge."

Lapin also used newspaper ads to promote citywide franchising, which gave a franchisee the rights to own many locations in one city. Unfortunately, three years later several franchisees filed a class action lawsuit claiming antitrust violations involving price-fixing and restrictions on ordering supplies. The parent company denied this claim but reached a settlement that cost more than expected. In 1971, there were thirty-two locations in Southern California alone, but by the end of 1973, the parent company divested itself of the chain, and many branches closed.

Today, one lone House of Pies in its original cottage-style building is still in operation, at the corner of Vermont and Franklin in L.A.'s Los Feliz neighborhood. It opened in 1968 and has been owned and operated since 2007 by Victor Watana. At this writing, Watana is planning to open

Left: Early logo
Bottom: The Houston locations have their own look

Pecan pies and fruit pies

two additional locations in the L.A. area, but don't look for the white and pink cottage. Instead, the buildings—one in Venice and one in Glendale—are ultra-modern and were created by Coscia Day Architecture & Design. There are four House of Pies in Houston; these franchises are independent of the L.A. stores.

Today, driving around Southern California, you can spot what once were House of Pies cottage buildings. Many have been transformed into Asian restaurants or used-car dealership offices; but if you walk in, you may be able to smell the aroma of days gone by.

Just Some of the Opening-Day Varieties

Banana Lemon Cake	Fresh Strawberry
Bavarian Chocolate	Georgia Peach
Bittersweet Chocolate Meringue	Grasshopper
Boysenberry	Italian Almond
Chocolate Banana	Northern Blueberry
Coconut Meringue	Pippin Apple
Country Rhubarb	Pumpkin Supreme
Dutch Apple	Pure Lemon Meringue
French Black Bottom	Raisin Walnut
French Butter Macaroon	Sherry Pecan
French Chocolate Cream	Sour Cream Apple

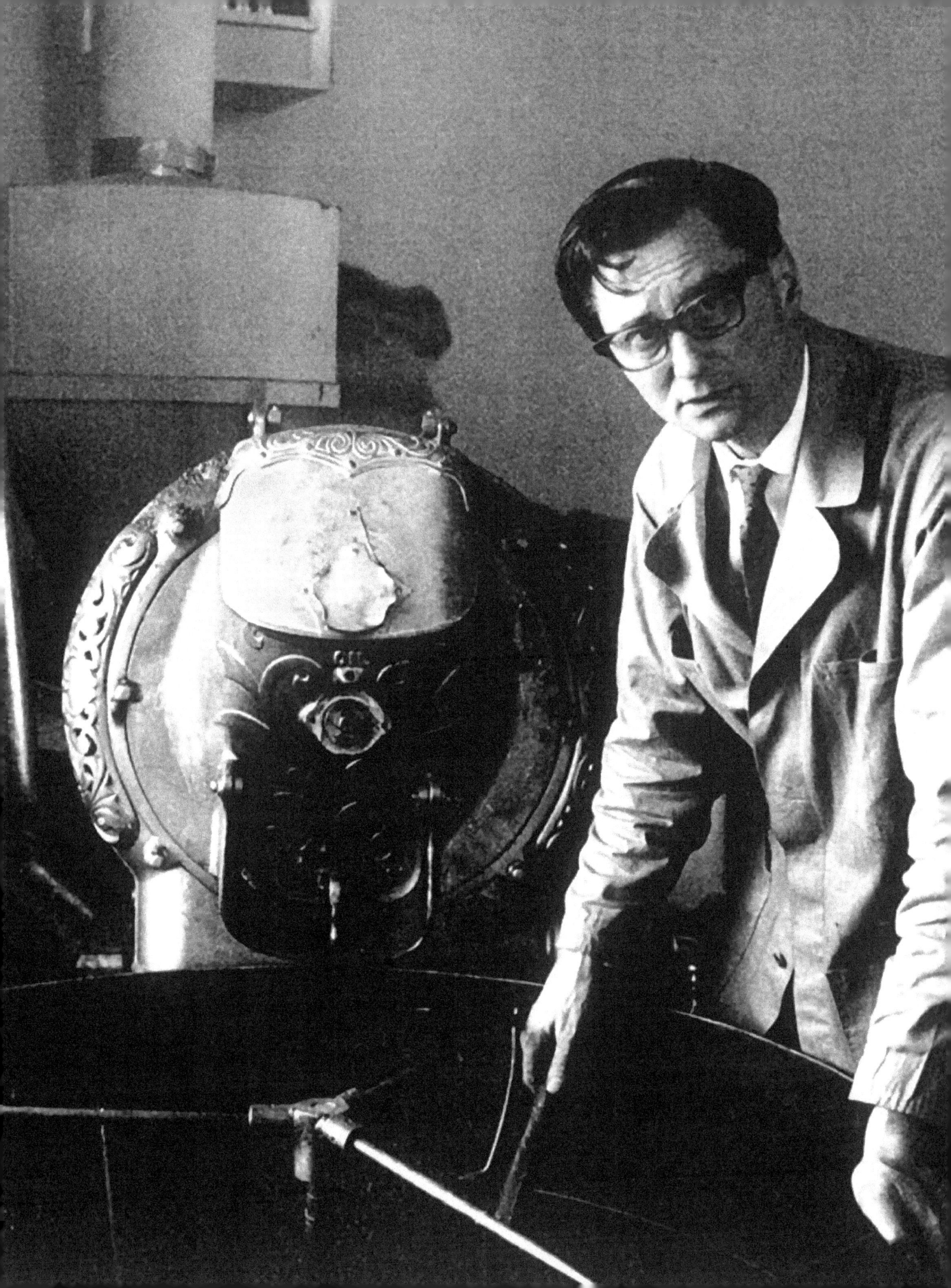

Peet's Coffee, Tea and Spices

NAME TODAY: PEET'S COFFEE
ORIGINAL LOCATION: Peet's Coffee Inc., 2124 Vine Street, Berkeley

OPENED: April 1966
FOUNDER: Alfred H. Peet
CURRENT OWNERS: JAB Holdings Company

There are 334 locations in 10 states, with 5 coffee bars in Shanghai, China.

peets.com

ON A VERY QUIET street corner, among apartments and houses, sits coffee history. Peet's Coffee is part of the quilt of the neighborhood and fabric of the world.

Born in 1920, Alfred Peet had coffee running through his veins. He grew up helping at the family's small coffee roastery in the Netherlands. As a teenager, he worked as an apprentice in a coffee and tea company, and in 1950, after World War II, he worked as a tea taster in Indonesia. Five years later, San Francisco Bay was next on his travel schedule, moving him from one side of the world to the other.

Upon arriving in the Bay Area, he tasted what the locals called coffee but what he considered to be watered-down brown liquid. It reminded Peet of dishwater. "I came to the richest country in the world, so why are you drinking the lousiest coffee?" he wondered. He was going to do something about it. Since everyone was drinking coffee from the supermarket that came ground up in a can, he assumed that Americans wouldn't know coffee was a bean until it was possible to buy a pound of roasted beans and a grinder.

Peet found a storefront at the corner of Walnut and Vine streets, a block from Berkeley's main thoroughfare. In later years, the few blocks surrounding Peet's became an enclave of gourmet stores, restaurants, and other types of food establishments—hence the area's nickname, Gourmet Ghetto. Followers of Peet's Coffee began calling themselves Peetniks. Today, this is the name of its customer-loyalty program.

Along with Herbert Hyman of Coffee Bean and Tea Leaf (page 233), Peet helped usher in the high-end coffee revolution in America. The evolution of any major coffee roaster today can be traced to Peet's first store. He taught many the art of roasting and the proper way to make a cup of coffee. Originally, he sold only roasted beans and coffee-making equipment; Peet was one of the first to sell high-grade beans and to roast them longer, resulting in a more rounded, rich taste than ordinary coffee of that era. Drip coffee was first introduced in 1966. Espresso didn't come along until 1985.

Alfred H. Peet at the roaster

The original location, in Berkeley

In 1979, Peet sold his company to. Sal Bonavita, an international importer of whole-bean gourmet coffee, specialty tea, espresso-making equipment, and accessories. Peet remained on the payroll as the company coffee bean buyer and consultant until 1983. During his five years of ownership of Peet's Coffee, Bonavita started its expansion by opening additional retail stores as well as developing mail and wholesale operations.

But the expansion was slower than one would expect. It took five years to open a second location, in Menlo Park, and another nine years for a second Berkeley location. The year 1997 brought store openings outside of Northern California, in Pasadena and La Jolla. Recently, Peet's launched stores in New York and other major cities with Capital One Bank as a licensing partner.

The company's focus was not on opening a coffee location on every corner of every city but on building the business through grocery stores. You can now buy a bag of Peet's coffee (whole beans or ground) in more than 15,000 retail locations nationwide. The plant date-stamps each bag of beans, and distributors are required to buy back any bags close to ninety days from the date of roasting. (Coffee brewed in the cafés is discarded every half hour to maintain freshness.)

With other coffee companies introducing blended beverages, Peet's created the Freddo in 1996 and the Javiva in 2015: a blended drink made with coffee brewed double strength, ice, 2 percent milk, and a proprietary blend of vanilla powder, sugar, monk fruit extract, and flavorings. Other competitors use instant coffee powder, coffee syrups, and extracts rather than pots of double-brewed coffee, as Pete's does. Costs are higher, but the quality and taste profiles make up for it.

Former Roasting Plant Locations (in Order)
Vine and Walnut, Berkeley
Hubbard Street, Emeryville
65th and Hollis, Oakland
1400 Park, Emeryville
Current plant: Alameda Harbor Bay Business Park, Alameda

Inside the first location, 1960s

In 2015, Peet's launched a cold-brew coffee in all of its retail locations.

In 2017, Peet's made its debut in China with its first International Coffee Bar in Shanghai, marking the formation of Peet's Coffee China, an independently run joint venture formed by Peet's Coffee and Hillhouse Capital. This remarkable coffee bar is 3,900 square feet and includes an in-house roastery and a Discovery Bar, which offers a coffee education through tasting flights and courses led by roasters and baristas. All coffees are sold or served within twenty-eight days of roasting.

As befits a company founded in Berkeley, Peet's has a strong corporate sense of responsibility and sustainability. Its two biggest roasters capture and reuse some of the heat (up to 550F degrees for roasting and 1,650F degrees for burning off gases created in the roasting process) that's typically wasted during the roasting process, cutting the company's use of natural gas by 40 percent. The company's new roasting plant is Gold LEED certified, the first roastery in the country to meet that standard. Landscape mulch is made by combining nearby Ghirardelli cocoa and Peet's coffee grounds.

The plant roasts about half a million pounds of beans a year, but as Alfred Peet did, they're roasted in small batches, staying true to the company's founding principles. Peet's has consistently invested in social-responsibility efforts, including People & Planet, an initiative featuring curated coffees from small-batch, environmentally aware farmer communities.

Even with the company's growth, Peet's espresso is still hand-pulled and not automated. If a machine needs cleaning or a shot is pulled too quickly, customers will taste the difference. And Peet's customers keep returning.

Peet's Coffee, Tea and Spices

Acknowledgments

THE MAXIM "It takes a village" is so true. Many people helped with my research and led me in the right direction to get me the information I needed for this project.

Thank you to my late father, who didn't know at the time he was taking me to the first Foster's Freeze when I was seven. I loved driving with him to see his clients, knowing that if we passed the Inglewood Foster's Freeze, I'd have a second chance at getting a dipped cone at the Hawthorne location only a few miles down the street.

Thank you to my family and friends. If everyone had such a supportive mom, the world would be such a great place. My mom goes to the ends of the earth to be at my appearances and watch my morning shows. I thank you from the center of my heart. Neil, my husband of thirty-nine years (okay, seven, as it was not legal before that), for agreeing to be dragged to food locations around the state. You always are ready for an adventure, and you tell me that it is never dull. We make life an adventure together. My two sisters for loving me. Jonathan, my assistant tour guide and great longtime friend. Diane St. John and Linda Thieben, for being my second set of eyes on the page.

A very special thank-you to publisher and friend Colleen Dunn Bates at Prospect Park Books for taking on this project, and to her, Julianne Johnson, Katelyn Keating, Susan Champlin, Leilah Bernstein, and Margery Schwartz for their persistent editing. My publicist, Trina, of the Trina Kaye Organization, for making this the eighth book we've launched together. Amy Inouye of Future Studio, for making this third book we've done together such a beautiful work of art. Keegan Dunn, for taking the additional photos that we needed for the locations.

I cannot recall everyone who helped me gather information over many years of research. I've tried to include everyone who worked in the research centers and libraries I contacted or visited. If you have been omitted, I am so sorry. Thank you in particular to the staff at Anaheim Central Library, Anaheim Heritage Center, Los Angeles Central Library, Riverside Public Library, Sherman Library & Gardens, and the Valley Relics Museum.

Many larger companies have their own research and historical departments, and some have only one person, while others use outside sources. I would like to thank the many people who worked hard to get me answers to my never-ending requests. I've also included the passionate family members who are still carrying the torch of generations before them. Thank you to: Sandra Acosta, Danielle Alvarado, Brian Ball, Debbie Pelonis Berry, Raven Bouie, Richard ("Dick") Campana, John A. Case Jr., Robert Castaneda, Rich Cope, Phyllis Cudworth, Cindy Culpepper, Autumn Drummond, Jeff Earle, Pat Egan, Eva Ein, Kate Fortune, Susan Frank, Tommy Gelinas, Emily Glickman, Jackie Gomez, Patricia Grimm, the Hundertmark family, Ashley Keehn, Mark Kelegian, Gary Landi, Austin Lewis, the Love family, David MacMahan, Karla Marin, Diane Martell, Whitney McChane, Ruth McCormick, Leslie Mendoza, Lisa Merrell, Maia Migliore, Sarah Mueller, Jane Newell, Chris Nichols, Michael Palmer, Julie Pantiskas, Sanjay Patel, Patti Swensen Pedroli, Dean Peters, Richard Pink, Annie Hyman Pratt, Elizabeth Ricardo, Ron Salisbury, Dawn Schlegel, Haley Silvers, Chad Stevens, Megan Stoner, Kathy Taggares, Baldeep Tahin, Bartsch Thomas, Karen Upson, Kelly Walsh,

Morgan Walsh, Erin Walter, Lincoln Watase, Roger Wendell, and Thayer Wiederhorn.

Lastly, I would like to thank the entire morning team at KFMB-TV (CBS affiliate), my home station, for the many hours we are on the air together. Tiffany Frowiss, you are one of the greatest producers in the business.

Photo Credits

Courtesy of the Anaheim Heritage Library Collection: 88, 89 (all), 91, 131, 132, 133, 134, 135
Courtesy of Apollo Global Management: 170, 172 (all), 173
Courtesy of Baker's Burgers Inc: 174 (top), 175, 176, 177 (all)
Courtesy of Debbie Pelonis Berry Family Collection: 150 (top & middle), 151, 152, 153
Courtesy of BR IP Holder, LLC: 92 (all), 94, 95, 96, 97 (all)
Courtesy of Capital Spring Investments: 159, 161
City of West Covina Archives: 57 (bottom)
Courtesy of Clifford Clinton Papers, UCLA: 54, 56 (bottom)
Courtesy of Del Taco Holdings: 236 (top), 238, 239 (bottom)
Courtesy of Denny's Corporation: 182, 183 (all), 184
Courtesy of Dine Brands Global: 208, 210, 211, 212, 213
Courtesy of Du-par's Corporation: 64, 65, 66, 67 (all)
Courtesy of Jeff Earle Collection: 162 (all), 164 (bottom), 165 (all)
Courtesy of FAT Brands: 114 (all), 116, 117
Courtesy of Foster's Freeze, Inc.: 98, 100 (all), 101 (bottom)
Courtesy of Galardi Group, Inc.: 218 (all), 219, 220, 221, 223
From the collection of George Geary: 11, 12, 14, 17 (bottom), 18 (all), 19, 30 (top), 38, 40, 51 (top), 53, 63 (right), 73 (top), 86, 126 (bottom), 128 (all), 130 (all), 139 (top), 142, 144 (bottom), 149, 150 (bottom), 158, 160, 164 (top), 171, 174 (bottom), 202, 216, 224, 226, 227, 236 (bottom), 244, 246 (bottom), 247
The Glendale Historical Society Collection: 59, 61
Courtesy of Global Franchise: 106 (all), 108, 109, 214, 215, 217
Courtesy of a Great American Brand LLC.: 20, 22, 23 (top)
From the Hundertmark's Family Collection: 23 (bottom)
From the Hyman Family Collection: 232, 233, 234
Courtesy of In-N-Out Burgers: 120, 121, 122, 124
Courtesy of International Dairy Queen, Inc.: 44, 45, 46, 47
Courtesy of JAB Holdings Co.: 248, 250, 251 (all)
Courtesy of The Jacmar Companies: 190, 192, 193 (all)
From the Kelegian Family Collection: 13, 178, 180, 181 (all)
Courtesy of Lawry's Restaurants, Inc.: 16, 17 (top), 68, 69 (all), 70, 71, 72, 73 (bottom)
Courtesy of the Lewis's Hamlet Hamburger Collection: 166, 168, 169
Los Angeles Times Archive: 50 (top)
Courtesy of Love's Barbecue Inc.: 129
Courtesy of McConnell's Fine Ice Cream's: 154, 156 (all), 157 (all)
Courtesy of McDonald's Museum of San Bernardino: 80 (all), 81 (bottom), 82, 84
From the collection of Chris Nichols: 63 (left), 81 (top), 83, 101 (top), 195, 198 (top), 245, 246 (top)
From the Patti Swensen Pedroli Family: 140, 141, 144 (top), 145 (all)
From the Richard Pink Collection: 74, 75, 76 (all), 77, 78, 79
Courtesy of QN Foods: 146, 147, 148

Riverside Enterprise News: 202 (top), 239 (top)
Courtesy of Riverside Public Library Archives: 200 (all)
Courtesy of Ron Salisbury Collection: 32, 33, 35, 36, 37 (all)
Courtesy of See's Candies: 24, 26 (all), 27 (all), 28, 29, 30 (bottom), 31 (all)
Courtesy of Sherman Library and Gardens, California Collection: 136 (top), 138
Courtesy of Sizzler USA Restaurants Inc: 204 (all), 206, 207 (all)
Courtesy of Chad Stevens: 194, 196, 197, 198 (bottom), 199
Courtesy of Tomdan Enterprises, Inc.: 102 (all), 103, 105
Valley Relics Collection: 126 (top)
Courtesy of Trader Vic's Corporation: 42, 55 (all), 56
Courtesy of Marc Wanamaker, Bison Archives: 41, 42, 43
Courtesy of Welch Family Private Collection: 110, 112 (all), 113 (all)
Courtesy of Rodger Wendell: 240, 242, 243
Courtesy of Eric Wrobbel (www.ericwrobbel.com/collections): 58
Courtesy of Xperience, XRG Restaurant: 186 (all), 188 (all)
Courtesy of Yum Brands Inc: 228, 229, 230, 231

Photos by Keegan Dunn:
Pages 63, 65, 74, 97 (bottom), 98, 118, 133 (all), 136 (bottom right), 178, 193 (bottom), 244, 251 (bottom)

About the Author

GEORGE GEARY is the author of many hit books, including *L.A.'s Legendary Restaurants* and *The Cheesecake Bible*. He is a cooking teacher, pastry chef, culinary travel guide, television personality, and in-demand public speaker. A California native, he lives in the Los Angeles area.

Learn more at www.georgegeary.com.